# NOMONHAN

## JOHN COLVIN

Quartet Books

First published by Quartet Books in 1999
A member of the Namara Group
27 Goodge Street
London W1P 2LD

A catalogue reference for this book is available from the British Library

ISBN 0 7043 7112 X

Phototypeset by Intype London Ltd
Printed and bound in Great Britain by CPD (Wales) Ltd

For Prudence and Colin

# Contents

# Acknowledgements

The premise of this book as outlined in the Foreword, although first suggested to me by the late Professor Owen Lattimore and, later, confirmed by Professor John Erickson of Edinburgh University, could not have been expanded by the author without the source material afforded by Alvin Coox's *Nomonhan* (Stanford University Press, 1985). My most particular homage is due to Coox's huge, brilliant and magisterial account of this hideous and tumultuous battle, the only one available in English. Without that work, *this* book could not have been written. Although confined to the battle itself and preceding skirmishes, Coox's *Nomonhan* is the extraordinary account of one of history's decisive battles, whose dread consequences no one then living could have foreseen.

I thank also Professor John Erickson, Professor Michael Branch (Director of the School of Slavonic and East European Studies, London University), Professor John Chapman (Sussex University), Professor Charles Bawden and Dr Alan Sanders (lately, London University, School of Oriental and African Studies), the Japanese and Russian Embassies at London, the Libraries of the Public Record Office, the Imperial War Museum, SSEES, SOAS, (both London University), LSE, the Foreign and Commonwealth Office, the Ministry of Defence, the Japan Society, the British Museum; Ian Buruma, Field Marshal Lord Inge, Cameron La Clair, Sir Sidney Giffard. Warm thanks are, of course, also due to the publisher, Naim Attallah, his editor Jeremy Beale and, once more, to Gaye Briscoe who typed the manuscript.

# Foreword

Some Japanese still really believe that their country was created by the Gods, specifically by the Sun Goddess, ancestress of the first Emperor. From the twelfth to the nineteenth century the country was governed by warrior families, the Shogun, appointed by the Emperor; in the thirteenth century they defeated Mongol invasions and, in the sixteenth, unified Japan under the Tokugawa Shogunate. Tokugawa Ieyasu pursued national isolation, 'the closed country', until two visits by US Commodore Perry's squadron led to the 'open door' and the acceptance of modern technology. In 1868, the Tokugawa were overthrown and nominal powers restored to the Emperor Meiji, eventually with a parliament (diet) supervising an industrial society. However, the dominant force in political life lay with the armed forces, for some of whose number the diet was to become too much.

Military victories over Korea, China and, in 1905, over Tsarist Russia provided legitimacy to the regime, expanded the territories of Imperial Japan and restored domestic unity. But immense industrial advance based on European and Asian markets was damaged by a severe lack of territory and of raw materials. (Japan's population, incidentally, more than doubled between 1890 and 1950.) Emigration, furthermore, from the Home islands was almost entirely prohibited by legislation in most countries, while exports were impeded by trade barriers and hindered by insecure access to foreign natural resources.

To secure these aims – exports, territory and raw material – and to create a client state of Russia or, at least of North Manchuria, and of Siberia between Vladivostok and Lake Baikal, and to integrate the Siberian economy with that of Japan was the undeclared objective of the seventy-thousand-strong Japanese contingent in the Allied intervention of 1918 against the nascent Bolshevik revolutionary regime. The force, unlike the British, French, Italian, American and Canadian units, remained in Russia until April 1922, continuing until 1925 to occupy North Sakhalin with its oil, coal, timber and fisheries. But even then, Big Business and the Samurai remembered: 'In the first war it will be enough to reach Baikal. In the second war we shall plant our flag in the Urals and water our horses on the Volga'. The day would come . . .

The worldwide depression of the 1920s and 1930s led to virulent nationalism, riots, attempted armed coups, assassinations of statesman and political leaders. The Army and Navy, in collaboration with the *zaibatsu* (major industrialists) took over Government in an unbreakable centralised bureaucracy.

Thus, economically frustrated, in 1931 the Japanese Kwantung Army staged the Mukden Incident, after which Manchuria became Manchukuo, Japan's virtual colony and economic and military base on the mainland of Asia. To acquire yet richer prizes, the fortuitous and temporary disappearance of a private soldier at the Marco Polo Bridge near Peking in July 1937 was contrived to lead to the massive invasion of China and war against Chiang Kai Shek's Kuomintang armies and, later, those of Mao. This, in turn, ran on uselessly until 1945, absorbing Imperial Japanese troops who could have been deployed elsewhere more effectively.

Outer Mongolia, as opposed to Inner Mongolia in China, had moved in the turbulent days of 1921 from a flimsy independence under her own god-kings to the status of first satellite of the USSR. In that capacity, her value to the Soviet Union lay chiefly in her meat and milk production and her position as a buffer state against the Japanese in Manchuria. It is true that, because Japanese Manchukuo was encircled in 1938 by Soviet and Mongol territory containing forces twice as large as her own, Japan had plans for an autonomous Greater Mongolia under her influence. Nothing came of it; had it done so the Soviet Far Eastern defences would have been torn open.

So stood Japan in 1939, overblown with conceit,

resentful at the West – in particular Britain – for patronising, even abandoning a great nation. Ambitious for glory and riches but prevented by racism from acquiring either peacefully, Japan was determined thus on the conquest of her despised Russian neighbours whose lands should form her own deserved reward and fortune. Japan was about to strike North.

Khalkin Gol of Halha river was claimed by the Ching Dynasty in the eighteenth century to demarcate, although somewhat imprecisely, the 'borders' between Mongolia and Manchuria. In 1932 Japan, accepted the arrangement and created the puppet state of Manchukuo out of the vastness of Manchuria. The USSR, however, extended the territory of its Mongol ally several miles eastward, all the while accusing the Japanese of pursuing 'geographical warfare' in a *westerly* direction. No documentary evidence was conclusive in resolving the conflicting claims. Khalkh in Mongol means shield, border or defence. It is also the designation of the dominant 'tribe' of Mongols comprising more than 80% of the total population of Outer Mongolia, once the Communist People's Republic, 'the First Satellite'. The Khalkh were descendants of the eastern Khanate of Khalka, defeated by Galdan the Oirat in the eighteenth century, acceding to the Manchu Empire under K'ang Hsi at that time.

The landscape on either side of the river is low and flat, although usually higher on the west or Mongolian bank. The Khalkh's waters provide some green pasture, even in winter; snow does not lie heavy there or often. But the region is a freezing, barren place from autumn onwards, even cold in summer after the sun has gone down, while fiercely hot in the unpolluted day, a trackless land ocean, thin grasses, dunes and desert sands, stark, empty wastes.

The battle of Nomonhan, or Khalkin Gol, although commemorated in English only by Coox's masterpiece, '*Nomonhan*', and by a few footnotes elsewhere, helped lead to the destruction of the four European empires in Asia, to the defeat of Nazi Germany, and to the rise of the superpowers, the USA and the USSR, a decisive 'Battle of the World', yet one hitherto unremarked.

This book relates the story of the struggle and its consequences, comparable in its strategy to the encirclement at Cannae, fought and supplied over unimaginable distances: 'Old, unhappy, far-off things and battles long ago.'

# NOMONHAN

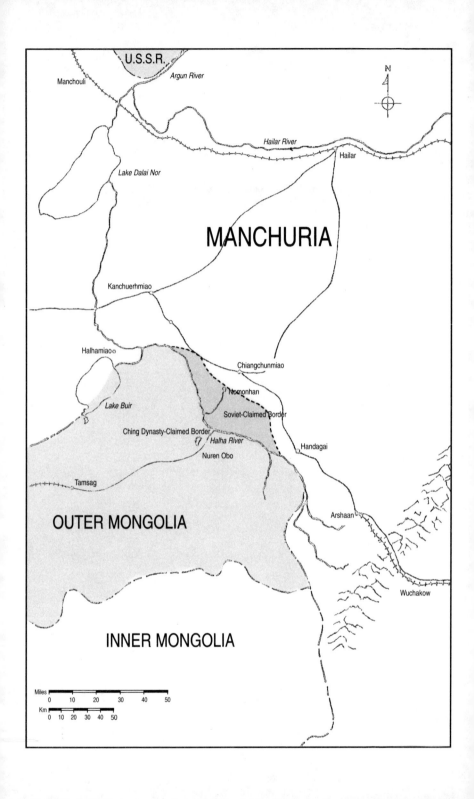

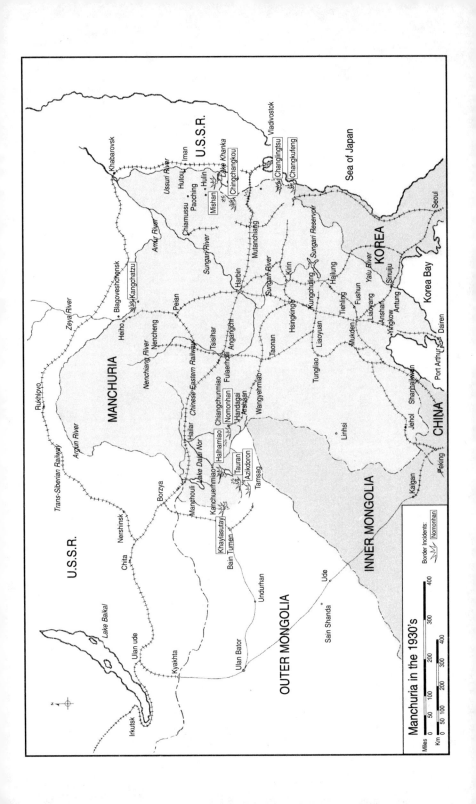

Manchuria in the 1930's

# 1
# The Russian Disaster of 1904 - 1905

The consequences of Japan's defeat of Russia in the war of 1904–5 had been, in their own way, no less substantial than those of the battle at Nomonhan in 1939. Although the Trans-Siberian railway and Russian railways within Manchuria itself remained, along with her alliance with China, Russia was forced to disgorge her lease of the Kwantung (Liaotung) Peninsula including Port Arthur, to cease her military occupation of Manchuria, to return that part of Sakhalin seized in 1875, and to recognise Japanese primacy in Korea. In southern Manchuria, the Japanese secured the base from which, in the following century, her attack on China would be launched.

More importantly, Russia's military defeat in 1905 at the hands of an Asian country for the very first time caused other Asians to question the omnipotence of European colonists and even produced the first hairline crack in the self-confidence of those Europeans. In Russia, furious resentment combined with humiliation among the Tsar's subjects, culminating in the revolution of 1905, obliged Nicholas II to devise the October Manifesto with its programme of constitutional reform, a step which made its own contribution to the final explosion of 1917.

Russian pre-eminence in Siberia dated from the seventeenth century, and had extended into Manchuria by the mid-nineteenth century along the banks of the Amur and Ussuri rivers. China was no better able to defend its territory in those regions than against the Japanese, to whom, after the war of 1894, she had to give up Formosa, the Pescadores and the Kwantung Peninsula, as well as pay a substantial indemnity in the Treaty of Shimonoseki in 1895.

These territories were, however, returned to China shortly thereafter as a result of forceful diplomacy by powers other than Britain. A Russo-Chinese alliance and a loan were agreed, and it was then that Russia's railway system, guarded by her own troops, first penetrated Manchuria. In 1898, Russia leased Port Arthur from Peking. This action, and French, German and British demands, led to the Boxer Rebellion, and thence to a massive influx of Russian ground forces (a hundred thousand men) into North Manchuria where they remained, despite the departure of the other international contingents, and even detached troops to southern Manchuria in 1902.

Meanwhile, after years of preparation, Japan had by 1904 constructed an army, including reserves, of almost half a million men, equipped and trained by German and French experts, and a respectable navy, in whose creation England had played the leading rôle. *Bushidó*, embodying the offensive spirit to the point of suicide, was the chief characteristic of these services. (The Anglo-Japanese alliance of 1902, extended in 1905, although rooted in naval interests, had immense political provisos of benefit to both powers.) Facing these forces were some seventy-five thousand Russian servicemen in the Far East, while up to four million more were theoretically available in Siberia and in 'European' Russia as reinforcements, on an eventual scale of about thirty thousand men a month carried via the Trans-Siberian and branch lines to Harbin, Dairen and Mukden, each army corps requiring 267 trains on what was often a single track.

In February 1904, without warning or declaration of war, Admiral Togo attacked the Russian fleet in Port Arthur with torpedo boats and blockaded the harbour. It was not until April that Admiral Makarov managed to temporarily break the blockade. By May, the Japanese 1st Army under Kuroki, having landed at Inchon, crossed the Yalu river and defeated a numerically inferior Russian force under Sassulitch near Wiju. After these battles, any Japanese feeling of inferiority to the European disappeared, apparently for ever.

Russian transport now began to roll out of Moscow across the snow-covered plains, across wheat lands with their granaries and little isolated log houses, through forests of pine and birch, to the Urals and on into Asia. The trains, with bathrooms, sleeping cabins and dining cars where food was served not at mealtimes only, but all day, now crossed the rivers and treeless steppes of Siberia, to disembark their passengers at Irkutsk on the tenth day.

No railway round Baikal existed at that time. The lake had to be crossed by sledges or ice-breakers, the ice cracking loudly at their passage between the almost perpendicular sides of the mountains. On deck, huge Siberian riflemen in long grey greatcoats and fur or sheepskin hats mingled with Jewish and Greek traders bound for Harbin. From the eastern shore, four days by train were required to traverse Transbaikalia, over the Yannevoy mountains, then through fields carpeted with spring flowers, past stations whose sidings were crowded with troop trains, the men singing cheerfully to concertina or balalaika. Most of these soldiers were so ignorant of the world that they believed that the Japanese fought in medieval armour.

Harbin, at that time, was no more than a construction site of brick and corrugated iron, ill-lit, occupied by Russian ex-convicts and blonde whores and, in the only tolerable quarter, by the general staff, bankers, railway officials and the retinue of Admiral Alekseiev, Viceroy of the East. The Admiral himself was more salubriously placed in a train in Mukden, about two days distant across rolling downs and rich green fields of millet, homesteads roofed in tiles embellished with gargoyles and dragons, blue, scarlet and gold. He had lost command of the army to General Kuropatkin, previously War Minister, the Russian 'Bobs' or Lord Roberts, now at head-quarters in Liao-Yang. As Kuropatkin's forces were still inferior in number to the Japanese, the General had decided that until reinforcements from Russia built up, his policy had to be: 'No battle before we are in superior force.' The Japanese, waiting for the landings of the 2nd, 3rd and 4th Armies (Generals Oku, Nogi and Nodzu) from Kwantung, Korea and Man-churia, were for the time being in a similar mood. But *bushidō* determination to rid (Chinese) Manchuria of the Russians, plus the confidence afforded by the British alliance were sharp goads to their aggressive as opposed to the Russian passive attitude.

Oku, after landing north of Port Arthur, mounted a direct frontal attack in overwhelming numbers on the Russians, who were professionally dug in on Nanshan Hill. (General Nogi's son was killed in this battle.) After fierce and protracted fighting, sometimes hand-to-hand, the Russians retreated, having lost a great part of their artillery plus fifteen hundred out of three thousand men, against Japanese losses of four thousand out of thirty thousand. The Japanese armies, other than Nogi's 3rd Army now directed at Port Arthur, then moved north towards Kuropatkin's positions in the mountains before his garrisons at Liao-Yang and Mukden.

The Tsar now personally ordered the commander in chief to ensure the security of Port Arthur. Against his better judgement, Kuropatkin sent Stackelberg, a German in Russian service who commanded thirty-five thousand men, to attack Oku's 2nd Army, retake Nanshan and advance on Port Arthur. Stackelberg, who was accompanied by his wife, a maidservant and a cow, spent the battle in the saloon of a special train. His severe defeat and that of his Siberians by Oku at Wa-Fang-Ho was judged by some as at least in part attributable to those circumstances.

An immediate Japanese advance thereafter was held up by the sortie in June of the Russian fleet, now repaired, from Port Arthur and the appearance of the Vladivostok squadron in the Tsushima Straits. Togo had, in the meanwhile, lost two battleships to mines. But the Port Arthur vessels returned to skulk in harbour, and the Vladivostok units did not immediately reappear. An attempt by Kuropatkin to take the initiative against General Kuroki's 1st Army was not rapidly enforced and a Japanese counter-attack obliged the Russians to fall back on An Ping before withdrawing via prepared redoubts to Liao-Yang.

Marshal Marquis Oyama, a *grand seigneur* of the Satsuma clan, a poet and collector, at once calm and beloved by his men, yet harsh and imperturbable, was now supreme commander of all Japanese armies in Manchuria, including those converging on Liao-Yang. He lacked, however, the numbers to secure total victory; his men were disposed in a broken chain of seven divisions. But the Russian General Orlov broke, Zarubaieff in Liao-Yang pleaded only a handful of men in reserve, Stackelberg was much shaken, while the Japanese Kuroki, Oku, Nodzu and, especially, Brigade Commander Okagaki held and pressed forward. Against the superior artillery, the courage of the men of the Russian Empire, Siberians, Daghestanis, Caucasians, Mongols, even Poles, Finns and Jews, defending the pagodas of Liao-Yang, was not enough; the Russians lacked good officers, modern equipment and their own crack European regiments.

On 4 September 1904, with only three intact divisions, Kuropatkin retreated from Liao-Yang to Mukden where reinforcements were now arriving in quantity. Japan had won the battles so far, but, not the war and, indeed, had exceeded her resources. Her troops had died in their thousands under rifle fire at the wire and in the trenches, displaying a total indifference to death. This comportment contrasted with the behaviour of the Russian officers retreating in carriages and barouches, while their wretched men plunged knee-deep through the mud. But the fighting in Liao-Yang had been horrible for officers and men alike; many went raving mad in the Mukden hospital as they recalled the horrors of the inner positions and the inferno of the trenches.

On 11 October, Stackelberg and Zarubaieff led the 1st and 4th Siberian Army Corps in extended order, with Generals Bilderling and Kondratovic in support, over hilly country and across millet fields, over short brown grass and up rugged precipitous slopes. The 1st and 3rd Army Corps under Rennenkampf and Daniloff attacked the passes to the east. The results were deplorable. The Japanese pierced the Russian centre, broke, beat and drove it back towards the Sha-ho river, although without permanently dividing the western and eastern armies. The Russians were in full retreat. One regiment, originally two thousand strong, emerged from the carnage with only one officer and forty men. But by the end, Stackelberg's Eastern Army and the 1st, 2nd and 3rd Siberian Army Corps still held the heights above the west bank of the Sha-ho, with the Japanese guns captured at Lone Tree Hill the one Russian success of this battle.

Over one thousand Russian officers had been killed among total casualties of perhaps seventy-five thousand men. The Russians began at last to understand that they were inferior to their opponents. They lacked the intelligence, leadership and, above all, maps. Their guns were superior in range, but not mobility; the Japanese used their inferior weapons to better effect. The Japanese infantry was superb in its remorseless use of the bayonet, of the 'group' as opposed to the extended line approach tactics, and of entrenching tools. Their hygiene, support services, catering, morale and discipline were infinitely higher than their opponents, with *bushidó* the guiding principle, 'the way of the warrior'. The Russians' use of cavalry was rare, sporadic and unsystematic. They seemed, in general, to lack method and forethought, and had probably been saved on the Sha-ho only by the exhaustion of their Asian opponents.

On 17 October at Putilov Sopka, Maurice Baring for the *Morning Post* reported on the horrifying spectacle, bandages covering the road, the corpses lying there 'in the cold dawn with their white faces and staring eyes, like hateful waxwork figures'. In July, in the company of a Cossack unit, he saw a Russian and Japanese locked in hand-to-hand struggle. The Japanese was taken prisoner, while the Russian was severely wounded. The Russian refused to be taken to the ambulance unless the Japanese was taken with him; the Russian said he was *his* Japanese. They were put together onto the same hospital train and the Russian refused to be separated from the Japanese, spending his time looking after him, fanning his head, repeating to all his visitors that this was *his* Japanese.

Meanwhile at Port Arthur, Nogi, who had taken the town in a day during the Russo-Japanese War in July, this time only managed to break through. Now he was checked by General Stössel's defence works, trenches and redoubts, backed by a garrison originally of some forty thousand. Japanese bombardment, supported by an infantry assault which had taken two forts to the northeast, began on 19 August but Russian resistance forced the 3rd Army to adopt siege tactics, employing *inter alia* hand grenades and mortars. Although by November Nogi, his early brilliance diluted by excessive drinking, had lost an additional thirteen thousand men, the Japanese launched yet another assault on 26 November, which caused a further twelve thousand casualties. This assault was doubtless prompted by Kuropatkin's apparent renaissance further north and, certainly, by the news of the departure for the East of the Russian Baltic Fleet under Admiral Rozhestvenski. A final assault, although costing the Japanese another ten thousand men, against the strongpoint of 203 Metre Hill, led Stössel to surrender on 2 January 1905, an action considered by some treasonable, involving an alleged bribery of $65,000 from the Japanese, although sufficient reason may be thought to have lain in the thirty thousand Russian casualties suffered in the eight months of the siege. The Japanese lost nearly twice as many.

At sea, the Port Arthur squadron had been defeated in August and either scattered or destroyed by Admiral Togo. Four days later, Admiral Kamimura found and defeated the Russian squadron based on Vladivostok under Jessen. The Baltic Fleet, after nearly causing a war with Britain by firing at British trawlers – thought to be Japanese torpedo boats – on the Dogger Bank, reached Madagascar, from there proceeding with reinforcements from the Baltic to Camranh Bay, which was to become a main base for the US Navy during the Vietnam War of the 1960s and after that for the Soviet Navy. Togo with his newer, faster, more manoeuvrable ships, now met this great, ancient Russian fleet steaming line ahead in close cruising formation off Tsushima in the straits. The ensuing battle was fought in late May, on a scale equalling Trafalgar and just as magnificent a naval triumph; it resulted in the capture or sinking, by armoured cruisers, destroyers and torpedoes, of almost the entire Tsarist force, leaving only one effective cruiser and five destroyers out of eight battleships, eight cruisers and nine destroyers. Speed, seamanship and gunnery had won the day; the Russians lost ten thousand men, the Japanese one thousand.

On land, the battle of Sandepu in January 1905, fought mainly in a snowstorm, had brought twenty thousand casualties and another major Russian reverse, this time involving the resignation of the 2nd Army commander, General Grippenberg, inexplicably unsupported by his colleagues Linievich and Kaulars. Morale, hitherto improved by reorganisation and fresh troops, fell markedly again, and dissension was evident in the higher ranks of the army.

The last encounter of the war, fought under this shadow, included some three-quarters of a million men, evenly allocated between the two sides. The battle of Mukden began on 23 February and lasted for two weeks; the Japanese, under Marshal Oyama, comprised Oku, the brilliant Kuroki, Nogi, Nodzu, Kawamura (5th Army) and three hundred thousand men, facing Kuropatkin. The Russian forces were of a similar size, although much reduced in the fighting. Kuropatkin, caught in a vice by his attackers, could only avoid encirclement of his immensely strong positions by withdrawing in the hideous cold from Mukden towards the north, where frostbite added to the Russian toll. On 10 March 1905, the Japanese Army entered the capital of Manchuria, having lost over ninety thousand men in the whole campaign, perhaps thirty thousand in the single battle of Mukden. General Kodama and Admiral Yamamoto told Tokio that Japanese resources would not permit the continuation of the war.

Linievich succeeded Kuropatkin, who returned home. Japan, exhausted and with her exchequer almost empty, proposed peace negotiations through Theodore Roosevelt, then President of the United States, which were agreed by the Russian Government. These negotiations, conducted at Portsmouth, New Hampshire, in August and September 1905, resulted, as has been noted, in the surrender by Russia of its lease of the Kwantung Peninsula and Port Arthur, the evacuation of Manchuria, the cession of half Sakhalin and of the Harbin-to-Port Arthur branch of the Chinese Eastern Railway from Changchun to the Sea of Japan, and recognition of Japan's permanent position in Korea. Riots involving over a thousand casualties took place in Tokio against what was regarded as the inadequate exploitation of victory. Admiral Togo's flagship exploded in dock, possibly through sabotage.

General Sir Ian Hamilton, official observer on the Japanese side of the 1904–5 war, and, in the Great War, the unsuccessful commander at Gallipoli, once observed that he thought that 'the value of human life had sometimes been rather exaggerated'. Perhaps he acquired this philosophy in the Russo-Japanese conflict in Manchuria. He had said at that time, on 203 Metre Hill: 'Here the bodies do not so much appear to be escaping from the ground as to be the ground itself. Everywhere there are bodies, or portions of bodies, flattened out and stamped into the surface of the earth as if they formed part of it . . .' The losses there and in Port Arthur, in a succession of 'Charges of the Light Brigade' by the Japanese, haunted General Nogi, who had become reclusive, depressive, even suicidal, until the day he died. In these actions, 'boiling oil was used and electrified wire; planks with nails hammered through them to spear the feet' in the dark, hot, rainy nights. 'The yellow races turned green in death . . .'

# 2
# The Bolsheviks Take Siberia

The Russians had retained the Chinese Eastern Railway (CER) via Manchouli to Vladivostok and began to build another line, the Amur Railway, to Vladivostok from Chita via Khabarovsk, to take the strain should the CER be lost to Japan in wartime. The Japanese, for their part, had acquired under the Treaty of Portsmouth the rights to the Russian railway from Changchun (Hsinking) to Port Arthur, which became the South Manchurian Railway Joint Stock Company (SMR or South Manchurian Railway).

The SMR trains chugged along with their wood-fired boilers at twenty miles an hour, clouded in steam, sparks shooting out of the funnel, along seven hundred miles of track, doubled from Mukden to Dairen and converted to standard gauge from the Russian broad gauge. The first chiefs of the SMR were generals of the Imperial Japanese Army, initially Kodama, Chief of Staff during the late war, succeeded by Terauchi, Minister of War. It was plain from the beginning that the SMR's real purposes were as a control for South Manchuria and a contingency planning base for Japanese strategy against the Russian Army in North Manchuria, which was not due to depart under the treaty until 1907.

Mutual distrust and dislike between Russia and Japan was accentuated by the 1904–5 war. In the years leading to the First World War, moreover, the power of the Russian Far Eastern Army was seen as a principal obstacle to Japanese military subjugation of the Asian mainland in their relentless search for raw materials, iron, lead, zinc, nickel, oil, rubber, wool and cotton.

Japanese troops were responsible to the Kwantung Military Government, originally two divisions plus garrisons at Port Arthur, Dairen, Mukden and so forth, together with railway guards as defence against rebels and *hunhutzes*

(Manchurian bandits). The first civilian Governor-General, an office, like head of the SMR and commander in chief of the Kwantung Army hitherto occupied only by military men, was not appointed until 1919. At that date the strength of the army in Manchuria stood at one division and six battalions of railway guards. Elsewhere, Japan had been greatly admired for her soldiers' unusual decency in China during the Boxer Rebellion in 1900. Since she had been accepted by the British in 1902 as the UK's main Eastern ally, her assistance in the First World War, whether in the seizure of Germany's Shantung Leased Territory with the port of Tsingtao, today still noted for its excellent beer, her seizure of the German islands of the Pacific, or in her purely naval contribution on the high seas, the Mediterranean and the Pacific, was welcomed by the Allies. Even successful Western diplomatic opposition to the importunate Japanese Twenty-one Demands on China did not rule out improvements to Japan's position in Manchuria, extending the railway lease and that of the Kwantung Peninsula itself. Such improvements and a freer hand in China were the objectives of the Japanese contribution to the war effort in the first place, aimed indirectly at blocking Russian access to the Pacific. Trade, furthermore, with all sides, placed the Japanese economy in an enviable position.

In 1918, after the Russian Revolution, pro-Soviet rebels against Tsarism in Harbin tried to substitute a 'Soviet of Workers and Peasants' for the Russian board of the Chinese Eastern Railway. The Japanese saw the Revolution and Russian chaotic weakness as the moment to take over North Manchuria completely and, notionally with China who had already sent troops to the threatened railway, to move against Siberia and Russia. Japan's real objectives, indeed, were not those of her Allies, but were the creation of a buffer state between Vladivostok and Lake Baikal and the integration of the Siberian economy with Japan's: *nothing that follows is comprehensible unless that is understood*.

Marshal Foch, Supreme Allied Commander on the Western Front, as early as November in the previous year had proposed to the Allies that they should invade Siberia. Although the idea was initially rejected by Lloyd George and President Wilson, Japanese and British warships shortly thereafter anchored in the great harbour at Vladivostok, ostensibly to protect military supplies stored there from the Bolsheviks.

The Czech Legion, former Habsburg troops captured by or deserting to the Russians in order to fight their former leaders, were now trying to escape from Russia in isolated troop trains over six thousand difficult miles against the murderous violence of Trotsky's Red Army. Their plight in the summer of 1918 excused Allied landings at Vladivostok and the invasion of Siberia. The Allies consisted of seventy thousand Japanese, seven hundred American infantry, the 'Hernia Battalion' of the Middlesex Regiment, aged and unfit, a thousand French colonial troops, an Italian unit, and a Canadian troop who stayed a few weeks only. They joined the Czechs who were fighting alongside White Russians and the Cossacks of Ataman Krasitnikov, under the overall command of Admiral Kolchak, the Supreme Ruler of Russia, in the valley of the Volga river. The campaign to reverse damage by Bolshevism to the Allied cause had begun. At least Knox and Janin, the British and French commanders, were authorities on Russia, if not notable soldiers.

Some months after *all* the Allied landings had taken place in Archangel, Far Eastern Russia, the Black Sea and the Caucasus, only the central part of European Russia, corresponding to the medieval Grand Duchy of Moscow, was firmly in the hands of the Bolshevik Government. The British, notably with a rather natty military band playing Gilbert and Sullivan in dusty or snow-bound Siberian townships, penetrated west of Irkutsk, while the Whites, Czechs, Austrians, Germans and Cossacks took Samara, Kazan and Sibirsk. Whites and Cossacks reached and temporarily held Kharkov, Perm, Voronezh, Orel, parts of the Ukraine, the Baltic States, Tsaritsyn, later Stalingrad. Even St Petersburg and Moscow only just managed to hold off the separate attacks of Kolchak,

Yudenich from Estonia, and Denikin. General Wrangel was successful in his operations in and from the Crimea.

By September 1918 the Amur area and the Primorski Krai (the Maritime Provinces) in the Far East were in Japanese hands, and a detachment commanded by General Fuji under the orders of the Kwantung Army was some three hundred miles on the road to Chita before the snows fell. Nearly all of Siberia east of Lake Baikal was thus under Japanese control.

The armistice of 1918 led, however, to the withdrawal of German and Austro-Hungarian soldiers from Siberia. The Czech Legion also began to leave Russia. Trotsky's 'Eastern Front', or 'Army Corps', with the former aristocrat Tukhachevski, aged twenty-five, (later to be shot by Stalin for collaboration with Nazi Germany) drove the Whites across the Volga. But, in 1919, White commanders under Denikin were still victorious in the south, Kolchak in the Urals, Yudenich had moved on St Petersburg, and the Poles were advancing on Vilna and Minsk. The Red Army was split between old soldiers and young Communist officers. It was now that the Donets basin, Tsaritsyn, Kharkov and the Ukraine fell.

Then the 1st Red Cavalry Army under Budenny of the huge moustaches, the great Zhukov of Nomonhan and the 1944 German Front, Timoshenko, jokes about whose 'Irish' ancestry (Tim O'Shenko) were common on the BBC and the Beachcomber column in the Second World War, turned the tide. Yudenich retreated into the Baltic States, Denikin was defeated and fled to the Black Sea and the Caucasus, the Ukraine was recaptured, Kolchak driven eastwards by Tukhachevski. The young Joseph Stalin in May 1920 became political commissar to the new Commander, Yegorov, of the South-Western Front, Voroshilov having occupied this role with Budenny in the 1st Cavalry Army. A general offensive began against the exhausted, desperate and weakened White armies, abandoned by their American, French and British supporters once these realised that the need for a united resistance against Germany had disappeared at that nation's surrender. Russian corruption grew, morale collapsed, panic and anarchy spread. Other ranks murdered their officers, the Supreme Ruler was powerless to rule. In the Crimea, whence Wrangel had mounted an offensive to help the Poles and later organised seaborne landings on the Sea of Azov, coherent White resistance was destroyed by Frunze, Budenny and Marshal Blyükher in November 1920, followed by seaborne evacuation by the Royal and other navies of White soldiers and their families to find refuge in Western Europe and the United States.

The Red Army was not immediately strong enough to attack the one hundred thousand Japanese and motley Chinese, Mongol, Serb and Cossack allies under Ataman Semënov, the Russian Mongol leader, in the Primorski Krai. The Soviets accordingly established a Russian Far Eastern Republic without apparent formal Soviet attachments, as a buffer state between Russia and Japan. Tokio, simply in order to control it, recognised the Republic in July 1920. In the meanwhile, brutal reprisals were being conducted against Soviet partisans under their leader Lazo, which did nothing for Tokio's reputation in the Maritimes. Lazo, for example, after capture with two colleagues was 'handed over to White Guards under Japanese officers. A man of peak physical strength, he resisted the attempt to throw him alive into the furnace of a locomotive . . . but was struck down by a guard and hurled in, after which his two companions were also burnt alive.' Such actions, however, were comparable to those of the Red Baltic Fleet sailors who murdered their officers by stuffing them alive under the ice.

By February 1922, the army of the Far Eastern Republic under Blyükher was nevertheless at Spassk *en route* for Vladivostok and, by October, now commanded by an ex-Imperial officer named Uborevich, in contact with Japanese troops. As a consequence of the military situation, of US support for the Far Eastern Republic at the Washington Conference in April 1922 and of Allied resistance to Japanese demands there, the Imperial Japanese Army at last withdrew to their homeland and Manchuria from all areas of Russia except Sakhalin. Before this could happen, in the days immediately preceding their evacuation, despite earlier abuse by Japan, the Mayors of Vladivostok and Nikolsk joined a deputation to implore the continued occupation of Siberia by Japanese troops 'in order to prevent disorder and lawlessness'. The Vladivostok Assembly fruitlessly petitioned the powers for the continued presence of the hated occupier to whom, however, territorial and economic victory in Russia had become unattainable.

The Far Eastern Republic almost instantly, in November 1922, demonstrated its 'independence', and illuminated the first of innumerable US misjudgements in the American century, by then 'voting' for incorporation in the USSR.

The troop trains returning the Imperial Japanese Army to Manchuria took thirty-six slow and jolting hours to reach Harbin, each compartment lit only by a single guttering candle, the electric light bulbs all broken. The White Russian guards, dirty and unkempt, resembled sansculottes in the French Revolution. At the Manchurian frontier, inspections were conducted alternately by Japanese, Chinese and Russian officials, then, on entering Manchuria, by Chinese replacements for the Russian railway guards. In Manchuria, Chinese and, occasionally, Japanese troops, at attention with fixed bayonets, guarded the railway stations. Chinese drill and equipment were uniformly less than adequate, sloppy and ill-maintained. Around Harbin, some forts were held by Chinese, others by Japanese. The Red Army was forbidden access to Manchuria and the CER, the latter owned by the Russo-Asiatic Bank, but under initial Chinese 'control'.

The city, referred to by Kolchak as 'that gutter Harbin' was divided into zones, White Russian under Ataman Semënov, Japanese and Chinese, each with its own restaurants, tea houses and dance halls, three different countries at the same time. Orthodox Russian services continued with all their pomp and exuberance while, in the lanes, addicts could get a shot of morphine in the arm by passing a coin or two through a hole in the wall. Further south, at Mukden, an obelisk commemorating the victory over the Russians in 1905 marked a square which, during the 1904–5 war, had been an empty plain. In the night-clubs, the tradition of Russian prostitution for Asian customers began its voluptuous and lucrative trade. But there was a British club, tennis, golf, bowls, skating, riding and shooting for the old China Hands, including fur merchants; and St Barnabas' church boasted a Japanese Anglican vicar.

Meanwhile, in Outer Mongolia, an insane White officer formerly with Semënov, the paranoiac Count Ungern Sternberg, sought to recreate the Empire of Chingghis Khan, by massacring, torturing and plundering amongst the Russian, Mongol and Chinese inhabitants of Urga (now Ulan Bator). But his overthrow of the Chinese regime there and the restoration of a king (revered as the Living Buddha) ended in May 1921 with defeat and execution by the Soviet Army and Sukhe Bator's Mongol forces. The consequent Soviet satellite state lasted until the Mongols rebelled in 1990 and threw the rascals out.

Japan's project of 1919 for an 'autonomous' Greater Mongolia under Japanese influence was instigated by Semënov. Nothing came of it, then, and it never subsumed Outer Mongolia, although armed action to compel Urga's incorporation was contemplated. The defection of Outer Mongolia to Japan would, indeed, have torn the Soviet Far Eastern defences open, but only Inner Mongolia, Bargut territory and certain Buriat lands were ever seriously affected.

# 3
# The Soviet Army Between 1918 and 1937

In the West, external threat, plain error and signals confusion ruled. A huge, three-army, Soviet formation under General Yegorov, known as the Southwestern Front, ex-Sergeant-Major Budenny's brilliant Cossack 1st Cavalry Army under command, young Stalin the political commissar, was menaced from Romania and by the 'Black Baron' Wrangel. For these, and for 'communications' reasons (a commissar, for instance, failed to countersign an order from the commander in chief), the Front did not directly support Tukhachevski's attack in August 1920 northwest against Warsaw itself. Indeed, Yegorov's 13th Army was savagely weakened by White leader Wrangel. Dazzling Polish counter-attacks by Piłsudski and Sikorski then resulted in the destruction or withdrawal of the Russian 3rd, 4th and 15th Armies and of the 3rd Cavalry Corps, and in the headlong retreat east of Lvov and the Dniester of the 1st Cavalry and 12th and 14th Armies. In the Zamosc Ring, twenty thousand horsemen, black tassels and silver bridles, clashed in Europe's last cavalry battle, the garland to the tattered Polish pennants. . . At the Treaty of Riga in the spring of 1921, after racing through Byelorussia in a bitter, murderous drive, the victorious Poles retook the empire of 1792 and all the territories seized during the advance.

But the most momentous effect was the defeat of Soviet plans to export Bolshevism through Poland to Western Europe. 'The Miracle on the Vistula' had saved the West from a catastrophic occupation, as Charles Martel at Tours in 732 had rescued it from Islam, in battles as full of bloody slaughter as those between Frank and Arab when 'the men of the north stood as motionless as a wall: they were like a block of ice frozen together. . .' Another dreadful consequence for the USSR, because of Tukhachevski's criticisms of the South-western Front and, implicitly, Stalin's mistakes, was Stalin's purge seventeen years later of that officer himself and thirty thousand others, whose qualifications might at least have minimised Russian losses in 1941 at the frontier. When the German wolf came down at last on the fold, Timoshenko, Voroshilov, even Zhukov and Budenny, were not yet adequate substitutes for the murdered Tukhachevski, Yegorov, Blyükher and other colleagues outside the charmed 1st Cavalry.

The Red Army of the civil war contained guerillas, Marxist ideologues, bandits, former Tsarist generals and field officers, young Red commanders or cadets, deserters, political commissars of fanatical violence, disaffected warrant officers, former 'workers and peasants'. And all their backs were 'supported' by the bayonets of the Cheka under the evil Felix Dzerzhinski, himself by birth a *Polish* nobleman . . .

On one occasion, the Kronstadt Naval Mutiny of 1921, a motley crew of anarchist revolutionaries in the fleet on the one hand, rigid Bolsheviks on the other, met in mutual and deadly assault across the Finnish ice. All the fighting of those years, as later in Finland, was conscienceless and elemental, a silent, animal ferocity, mirrored later in the Gulag, impossible even now to contemplate without terror. Troops in temperatures of minus forty-five degrees died of cold where they stood or, destroyed by *francs-tireurs*, lay under a white shroud of snow until the hot sun came again. Poverty, the elements and history, too, in those frightful latitudes, precluded decency or any attribute other than brute, mindless survival.

The Ukrainian Jew, Leon Bernstein, a.k.a. Trotsky, became the first Soviet commissar for War. Appointed in 1918, his army then consisted of little more than a division of Baltic snipers and, outside the army, the Red Guards. (Most of the peasants had abandoned the armies to enforce land claims after killing the proprietors.) Trotsky organised forcible conscription through the trade unions, netting over a million men, including one hundred and fifty thousand Tsarist officers and NCOs. Trotsky's 'military specialists'. This latter measure was, although balanced by Communist cells and by political commissars, vigorously opposed by the extremists, among whom were numbered, to Trotsky's ultimate nemesis, Voroshilov and Stalin. But Trotsky, from his well-appointed train at Kazan, 'his gaze clear and direct, a smile unexpected and celebrated: a voice of bronze', had almost won the civil war by 1920. Nor could he be blamed for the failure against Poland; although Tukhachevski was certainly a protégé, Trotsky had opposed the campaign as premature in relation to the feeble resources then available for the ultimate, overwhelming aim of conquering Western Europe.

To win the civil war, he had recreated a regular army with a traditional divisional structure. Thereafter, he planned an army based on territorial class militia in the industrial centres of Russia. This concept, considered appropriate for the defensive strategy he now supported, was opposed by M. V. Frunze, a former civil war commander, as quite unsuitable for 'the primacy of the offensive' which, after the initial defence of the borders, was his philosophy. Frunze pressed also for higher technical standards, better training, and the 'principle of manoeuvre' based on mobile civil war action; he sought, too, recognition of the 'political principle'. Trotsky responded with arrogance and vicious ridicule, but the Frunze group and the Stalin–Kamenev–Zinoviev triumvirate, the latter two, incidentally, also Jews, used Lenin's terminal illness to insert Budenny and other 1st Cavalry officers into the Revolutionary Military Council. By 1925, to Trotsky's stupefaction, they had overthrown him and secured his dismissal as commissar. 'It was,' he complained, 'a real conspiracy, comprising all the Politburo but me . . .'

Frunze continued the system of military districts, Moscow, Leningrad and so forth, which gradually absorbed as well the armies of Central Asia and the Caucasus in their struggle against the Muslim Emirates and other minorities. He appointed an able general staff, cut the central administration, instituted the commissariat and inspectorates, decentralised within the armed forces, revived the academies. He reduced the regular or cadre army to seventy-seven divisions, that is forty-six territorial militia and thirty-one cadre, with the territorial militia forming about fifty per cent of the Red infantry. He organised the cavalry, Budenny, Timoshenko, Zhukov, into eleven divisions and two corps, and the riflemen into seventeen corps.

When he died, or was murdered during surgery by Stalin's doctors in 1925, he was succeeded by the political soldier, Voroshilov, whom Trotsky considered incapable of handling any formation larger than a regiment. By this transfer, however, Stalin realised his necessary ambition, control of the army. For that institution, Frunze had laid the foundations of a fairly disciplined force, diminished somewhat the role of political commissar, placed authority with the Red commanders, emphasised cavalry mobility and an offensive strategy in defence of the motherland. He had rationalised the air force, and started to deal with the old sweats of the navy and their worn and ancient vessels. Voroshilov had to cope, however, with an inadequate inventory – from tanks to boots – shocking roads, not enough trucks or cars, incompetent communications, uneducated soldiers, negligent administration, and poor small-arms results. He found, furthermore, tensions between the 'military specialists' and the Party men, relationships even less happy because of Cheka intrusion into barrack room and company office.

In Germany, contemporaneously, General Hans von Seeckt, Commander and creator of the post-war Reichswehr and, from 1934 to 1935, adviser to Chiang Kai Shek, founded in 1921 a group within his ministry to evade the restrictions of Versailles and to insure against Poland, by clandestine military co-operation with the Soviets. Karl Radek, a Soviet 'journalist' purged by Stalin in 1937, who had originally visited Berlin to investigate the possibilities for Red Revolution in Germany, returned to Russia in 1921, convinced on the contrary that his country's future lay in German–Soviet military–industrial collaboration. Thereafter negotiations approved by Trotsky between Moscow and Berlin led to participation in Russian territory by Krupp, Junkers, Rheinmetall and others, in aircraft, artillery, submarines, small arms, poison gas and tank ('large tractors') production. Joint training in the application of these arms followed, including massive exercises on the frontier, also observed by German officers, involving Zhukov, Rokossovski and Malinovski. These exercises, which involved the use of mobile groups – infantry, artillery, armour and air – to break through the enemy's weak points, encircle and destroy, were the inspiration of Marshal Tukhachevski, but there is still no evidence of treacherous contacts between the latter and the Reichswehr. In 1932, Hitler, advocating extreme anti-Communism, became Reichskanzler, so that by 1933 most German-Soviet joint projects were ended, the German staff and equipment withdrawn. In his last talk with the German Reichswehr representative, Tukhachevski declared, in French: 'Do not forget, my friend, that it is politics, your politics only, which separate us, not our feelings, our most friendly feelings for the Reichswehr.'

The Russians by 1935 had built or acquired seven thousand light, heavy or amphibious tanks, including sixty from Britain, and had motorised a high proportion of their artillery of which, incidentally, they had themselves made three thousand guns by 1932, when they also had at their disposal one hundred and fifty thousand lorries and two hundred and fifty thousand rifles. In 1935, the Red Army mustered nearly one and a half million men in four cavalry corps, sixteen divisions each of three cavalry regiments and six independent brigades, ninety infantry–rifle divisions in twenty-three rifle corps, each division numbering one artillery and three infantry regiments. The artillery that year, as a body, comprised one hundred and thirty regiments. Armour was organised by mechanised brigades of one tank, one light tank and one machine-gun battalion each, and by tank brigades of three or four tank battalions.

By 1934, there were also indoctrinated Communist commanders with the 'correct' class background to reduce yet further the influence of the political commissars who, because of the high ratio of industrial workers to disaffected peasants,

21

had become less essential anyway. The territorial system was abolished too in favour of a regular conscripted army, the territorials reduced, disbanded or merged with the cadres. In 1935, officers' ranks and benefits were restored.

The air force was divided into a tactical and a bomber force, the latter designed and built in the USSR by the great Ilyushin and Tupolev: three thousand five hundred aircraft of all types by 1935, a higher quality to follow with time. The navy with over a hundred submarines was also moving to an ocean going surface force. By 1934, the armed forces budget had risen from 1.6 billion rubles to 5 billion which, with improved staff and technical colleges, permitted Soviet officers to concentrate on the execution of 'new' tactical and strategic doctrines.

These doctrines, plainly expounded in the Red Army Field Service Regulations of 1936, demanded rapidity in action and detailed co-operation between arms. The autumn manoeuvres of that year demonstrated that these aims had not yet become completely attainable, chiefly due to the inadequate training of junior officers and the neglect or mishandling of radio communications. The objectives were, as we saw earlier, admirable, especially the stress laid on the offensive *in real depth* by combined arms. Mobile assault groups comprising artillery, tanks, motorised and armoured infantry, tactical air support of ground troops, were intended to secure breakthroughs at sensitive hinges, and follow them to encircle and utterly destroy the enemy with massed infantry. The latter would be aided, according to the circumstances, by parachute battalions, the whole theory approved by knowledgeable commentators from European armies.

If, at that time, there was a difference between theory and practice, that is still not reason to suppose that further experience or training in a settled atmosphere of organisational continuity and command would not have produced a Red Army capable of defending its frontiers and annihilating the invader. That task, however, when it finally materialised, took nearly four years to accomplish, in large part because of Stalin's

paranoiac decision in 1937–1938 to destroy the putative archi-
tects of victory. In 1939, some of the same reasons had led to
the inability of 1.2 million Soviet troops to defeat in less than
*three months* (with sixty-eight thousand dead), the small Finnish
nation of only 3.7 million people. As a result of the great
purge, insufficiently trained young replacement commanders
had failed to comprehend the uses of air or ground-based
firepower, and had not adequately planned supply, transport,
wireless, training or even winter clothing.

Frunze's reforms of 1924, 'Make way for the Red
Commanders', have been interpreted as a relatively mild and
'faintly concealed purge motivated by political considerations
and . . . ambitions'. In the same year also, seven hundred and
fifty naval officers were replaced by less aristocratic, better
trained and more Communist officers. There were some anti-
rightist removals from the army in 1929 while, in 1934, Kirov's
murder led to the Yagoda NKVD terror at Leningrad in 1935.
This was followed by the more politically significant sentences
of death against Kamenev, Zinoviev and their adherents in
1936, together with rumours about the future fate of Bukharin,
who might indeed have been capable of overthrowing Stalin,
and of Rykov. Their prosecution was allegedly opposed by
many, including senior Red Army commanders, in the central
committee. The first three specifically Red Army dignitaries
to be arrested by the NKVD included Putna, a friend of
Tukhachevski and one-time military attaché in London. Stalin
replaced Yagoda, regarded as having botched the Kamenev–
Zinoviev trial as chief of the NKVD, by his own vile and
personal creature, Yezhov, who first established himself by
'purging the purgers'. Vishinsky then led the prosecution of
Radek, Putna, who 'inadvertently' blackened Tukhachevski's
name under interrogation, and Pyatakov. (When Bukharin,
Rykov and Yagoda came before the central committee in
1937, Yagoda had mocked Stalin by reminding him that he,
Yagoda, could have arrested the lot of them six months before.
Bukharin, for his part, wept and pleaded.)

Stalin, in his corrupt and diseased fantasies, saw rivals,

civilian or military, everywhere except within his own syco-
phantic group, Molotov, Voroshilov, Budenny. Of all sources of
treason, he most feared Bonapartism, identifying Tukhachevski
with that concept, the soldier who had so contemptuously
exposed his and his cronies' errors in the South-Western Front
before Warsaw. (There is, incidentally, a sad vignette of the
marshal on May Day 1937, walking alone, hands in pockets,
ignored by his fellow generals, 'out of the Red Square, out of
sight'.) In order to secure his enemies' conviction as well as to
persuade the military court of their guilt, Stalin exploited the
NKVD's association with the German Sicherheitsdienst under
Reinhard Heydrich, later 'Butcher of Bohemia', to provide
and circulate clandestinely forged documentary 'evidence' of
anti-Soviet traffic between the Russian accused and the
German High Command. (Some allege that no trials as such
even took place.)

The resulting 'conspiracy' was on a scale so gigantic
as to negate any chance of its reality. Those convicted included
Yegorov and Blyükher, thirteen of the fifteen army commanders, more than half the corps, divisional and brigade
commanders, the commanders in chief of the navy and air
force and the main commanders of both these services. The
artillery and air defence commanders, even six of the eight
officers of the military tribunal which tried Tukhachevski, all
disappeared into the Gulag or, more usually, were shot dead.
Army Commander Yakim went, proclaiming his loyalty, to
foul abuse from Stalin; Gamarnik, head of the Red Army
political administration 'committed suicide'; Uborevich, Kork,
Primakov, Shtern were all shot, in the end. In this grotesque
and bloody Punch and Judy show, the closest possible inspec-
tion of Wehrmacht and Soviet files has found no indication
that Nikita Khruschev's subsequent praise and declaration of
their innocence was less than the truth. Through the farrago
of suspicion and vendetta, they remain, as Khrushchev said,
'the praiseworthy men of our army'.

Between fifteen thousand and thirty thousand officers
had been purged to calm the dictator's nightmares. The mili-

tary consequences were the removal of the best leaders of the time, the cream off the milk, and the restoration of the commissar system, further limiting the Red Army's efficiency. *Esprit de corps*, initiative, loyalty and independence no longer existed, and would be hard to recover.

In the Far East, Stalin had despatched to Sun Yat Sen in 1923 a mission under Borodin, intended to transform the Kuo Min Tang (KMT) into a body capable of undermining the West, especially Britain, in China. Blyükher, as Borodin's 'military man', created the Whampoa Military Academy under Chiang Kai Shek, defeated Chiang's war-lord enemies, and built the National Revolutionary Army. But Moscow could not openly give complete support to Chiang and the KMT, while openly rejecting its naturally ally, the Chinese Communist Party, or 'socialism'. The objectives were incompatible and, in 1927, the Russians, for all their strength and help to China, had to abandon that country to counter-revolution.

The Soviets had come back to Manchuria in 1924 and had arranged joint Chinese and Soviet administration of the Chinese Eastern Railway with Manchuria's then ruler, Chang Tso-Lin, who was murdered by the Japanese in 1928. In November 1929, Blyükher led the Special Far Eastern Army against Manchurian raids by Chang Tso-Lin's son (Chang Hsueh Liang) at Fukdin across the Amur, incurring severe casualties, then moved against the Manchurians at Manchouli and, again, north of Vladivostok. It is not speculative to suggest that the Mukden Incident of 1931 and the creation of the Japanese puppet state of Manchukuo under the former Manchu Emperor, Henry Pu Yi, were in part reactions by Tokio to a perceived Soviet threat to Japanese interests in the region. After 1931 and the Japanese occupation of Manchuria, the Russians transferred the railway to Japan, a deal politically and economically advantageous to the USSR, but condemned as appeasement by the Red Army.

Reinforcements for Soviet formations in the Trans-Baikal and Far Eastern Armies followed the Japanese inauguration of Manchukuo, as did improved relations between

25

Moscow and the Republic of China. In 1933, the Soviet Foreign Minister, Maxim Litvinov, referred to Japanese policy as 'the darkest cloud on the international horizon'. Increased Soviet military and air establishments were developed in the defence of Mongolia, Eastern Siberia and the Maritimes (Primorski Krai). In February 1937, Blyükher is said to have commanded twenty rifle and three cavalry divisions, no less than a third of a million men, thirteen hundred armoured fighting vehicles (AFVs) and a thousand aircraft, split between the Trans-Baikal and the Far Eastern Armies under the Far Eastern Red Banner Front. Bombers from the Primorski Krai had the capacity to strike Tokio itself and submarines threatened the sea lanes of the Sea of Japan. General Hayashi Senjuro, while asserting Japanese moral superiority over the Red Army, admitted his country's technical inferiority. The double tracking of the Trans-Siberian railway had been per-fected, and fixed fortifications erected at likely invasion and other points on the Soviet side of the border. The Russians claimed that they had enough stores and weapons to fight for two years against the Kwantung Army in Manchukuo: 'Two soldiers for every Japanese'.

In May 1937, China signed a non-aggression treaty with the USSR. A Soviet loan of one hundred million Chinese dollars was agreed to enable Chiang Kai Shek to purchase enough Soviet equipment, aircraft, fuel, armour and lorries for twenty-four divisions. Between two and four hundred Soviet aircraft were said to have been delivered to China in that year, only a small proportion of the numbers supplied by Germany and Italy, supplies always subject to the inadequate Russian transport system and to the weakness of Soviet heavy industry. The 'China Incident' had meanwhile grown into the major Sino-Japanese War which was to endure until 1945 while, in Manchuria, Japan tightened its military and political hegemony.

At the same time, railway officials in Eastern Siberia were being convicted and shot on charges of collaboration with Japan and, later that year, officers on the staffs of the

Far Eastern Red Banner Front and the Trans-Baikal Military District, Marshal Blyükher's rear support area, were also seized by the NKVD in a continuing purge. Corps commander Rokossowski, later reinstated to command the 16th Army on the Western Front, was beaten up and imprisoned. Sixteen 'old' NKVD officers were liquidated. The main purge of Blyükher's staff and command was accelerated in raids and night arrests, with losses of 80% in the front itself, 70% at corps and division, and 40% up to regiment. The Red Banner Front, although Blyükher himself survived for a while, was broken up into three separate Far Eastern Armies.

In June, a senior Japanese officer published his view that the purges 'threatened the Red Army with disintegration; no longer could it be assumed that it was any longer a menace to Japan'. The Japanese General Staff was divided into 'the China school', and 'the Russian or Northern School', the aim of the latter being to produce a Japanese Army which could match and withstand the Soviets. The strategic objective, which predominated at that date in Tokio, was to exclude Russia from North China and Manchuria. Its corollary was to oppose further Japanese involvement in South China or South-East Asia in the period when the three to one superiority of the Soviets in the Soviet Far East over Japanese forces in Manchuria and Korea *seemed* to be slackening. 'The Soviet Army is down and out and can do nothing for some time,' said Tokio's Director of Military Intelligence, General Honma Masaharu in 1937, in a reference to the purges.

Honma was wrong. In China, Chiang Kai Shek was fighting Stalin's battle for him against Japan, drawing off the Imperial Army from the Soviet and Mongolian borders where the three to one superiority of the USSR held, surrounding the Kwantung Army in Manchuria. As significant, and as important as the USSR's naval, air and ground advantage, was Moscow's penetration, through the Sorge Spy Ring\*, of the inner secrets of the Imperial Ministries and Chiefs of Staff.

\* See chapter 11.

The USSR believed, unchallenged by Western or Japanese assessments, that it could fight a war in the East, as well as one in the West, a two-front war. It was, in fact, just as well that it never had to try.

In the Mongolian People's Republic (MPR), between 1929 and 1932, the nobility and the Yellow Faith Lamaist Church came for the first time under extreme leftist attacks. The New Turn Policy which followed, a sort of Mongolian version of the Soviet New Economic Policy (NEP), lasted until 1935 or 1936. This was succeeded by military and other purges as frightful as those conducted in the USSR. Since they were mounted by the NKVD through its parallel Mongol organs, they may be regarded as even more cynical. Their force fell once more against the Church, the *jas* (the church's capital fund of animals), and then, coincident with the fate of the Soviet marshals in the USSR, the army.

The USSR needed Mongolia as a base and buffer against the Japanese threat, whose menace to themselves did not seriously diminish or favour the Japanese Southern over the Russian and Northern school until *after* the battle which this book will describe. Since the MPR had fallen or succumbed to her giant northern neighbour as far back as 1921, there was never an alternative for that unfortunate and most lovable of countries.

But the purges, although 'covered' by detailed accusations of treacherous undertakings between Mongols and Japanese, were directed by Stalin and by his own interests from 1934, culminating in the show trials in 1937, as 'Japanese agents', of lamas and officers of the high command. Those murdered included former Prime Minister Gendun, Foreign and War Ministers Sambuu and Demid, the latter poisoned in a Russian buffet car on the Trans-Mongolian Express to Moscow, Generals Damba and Malji, the Chief of Staff, at least two corps and six divisional commanders, eleven provincial governors, four ministers. Hundreds of senior officials and middle-rank army officers were shot or imprisoned. Perhaps ten thousand people in all, including two thousand lamas, were arrested in circumstances of the vilest brutality. Questioned about a portrait of Lenin painted on the rocks above a blackened monastery, a Mongol official in 1974 replied sadly: 'He burned the lamasery down, why shouldn't he be there?' Of the seven or eight hundred monasteries operating, with their hundreds of thousands of lamas, fewer than ten were still functioning at the fall of the Communist regime in 1990.

The charges, at that time, of guilt by association in what was presented as a total, quite incredible penetration of the Mongolian state by Japanese clandestine services, were subsequently denied by President Tsedenbal immediately after Khrushchev's similar disclaimer at the Twentieth Party Congress: Japanese-inspired sabotage, mutiny and espionage were vigorously refuted.

It is possible that by 1938 the Mongolian Army comprised twenty or twenty-five thousand men in seven under-strength cavalry divisions, an air brigade, signals, security and other units. Soviet control was accepted, although not with approbation; training, morale and equipment were not first-class, perhaps comparable with those of the Manchurian levies. A Soviet defector to the Kwantung Army told the Japanese that the Russian military neither trusted nor respected their Mongol colleagues, attitudes reflected in reverse by the Mongols, in particular by Vice-Minister for War, General Damba, purged in 1937. Man-to-man relations between officers and men of the two armies were patronising on the one hand and rather resentful on the other.

# 4

# The Mukden and Marco Polo Bridge Incidents

Emperor Meiji's Imperial Rescript of 1882 to Soldiers and Sailors refers initially to the period before restoration in 1868 when political power rested with the military class, the Shoguns. That power which, anyway, had always been morally and nominally subordinate to the throne, had now returned to the Emperor, together with the fiefs of the feudal lords, the *daimyo*. The supreme command thus lay with the Emperor, the army his personal creature.

The rescript had five injunctions, the first being 'loyalty as the essential duty, duty weightier than a mountain, and death lighter than a feather', illustrated by the mass *seppuku (hara-kiri)* of the Forty-seven Ronin. The second refers to propriety: 'Inferiors should regard the order of their superior as issuing directly from us.' Soldiers might even defy the *law* if the end was to promote the Imperial interest. Valour was the third injunction, not violence 'when in the end the world would detest you and look upon you as a wild beast' as, alas, it did, after the rape of Nanking in 1937 and the other atrocities that preceded and followed it. Faithfulness, righteousness and simplicity were the subject of the fourth and fifth injunctions.

Brutality, surrender of the will, excessive adherence to the doctrine of ends and means, and unnecessary casualties suffered in mindless frontal attacks, were too often the eventual consequences of these counsels.

By the terms of the Washington Conference of 1922, and at the termination of the Anglo-Japanese Alliance, Japan not only had to yield most of the territory acquired during the Great War, but was 'abandoned' by Britain, its most significant ally, in favour of the United States connection. Recession caused the taking of serious economic measures in both army and navy. Chang Tso-Lin, as we have seen, challenged Japan's interest in Manchuria. Repeated Soviet military chastisement of his son, Chang Hsueh Liang, and the latter's defection to the Nationalists, led to a determination by elements of the army in Tokio to secure Manchurian markets and resources in order to maintain Japan's economic and, hence, military self-reliance. On 18 September 1931, north of Mukden, a lieutenant and a section in the Japanese Kwantung Army blew up a railway line without, however, damaging the target train, an action deliberately attributed to 'Chinese saboteurs'. This was the trigger for the destruction of Chang's forces in Central Manchuria, the infamous Mukden Incident, which preceded the creation of Manchukuo in March 1932.

In China, hatred of Japan grew. Rioting in Shanghai required the Japanese to send a battalion of marines to protect their citizens. This force was inadequate to break resistance from three Chinese divisions, including the 19th Route Army. Before an armistice could be concluded six weeks later, no fewer than three Japanese divisions and a marine brigade had to be despatched to overcome the despised Chinese infantrymen. The incident was followed by the adverse vote in the League of Nations at Geneva over the Manchukuo question; Japan resigned from the League.

The young officers in Tokio had planned for total war, plotting a series of coups d'état from March 1931 onwards, involving assassinations of senior officers and politicians culminating in the Grand Guignol murders of 26 February 1936. These brought about the death by army hit squads of the Lord Privy Seal, the finance minister, the Inspector-General of the army, and near misses against the grand chamberlain, the war and prime ministers, rebels even penetrating the gates of the Imperial Palace before isolation in the silent, snow-bound capital, trial and execution.

In August that year, the cabinet decided that the army's efforts should be directed to resisting Soviet armed strength in the Far East, with special emphasis on the improvement of Japanese Kwantung Army ability in Manchukuo and Korea to launch a major attack against Russia. (The navy's basic role

was to ensure naval supremacy in the Western Pacific against
the United States.) In July 1937, however, this programme was
interrupted near Peking at the Marco Polo Bridge, which
was decorated with stone lions. A private soldier (Shimura) of
the (Japanese) North China Garrison Army disappeared for
two hours, and war began. It eventually ran from Peking to
the horror of Nanking, one hundred and seventy miles up the
Yangtze, to Chungking, to the defeat of both Chiang Kai Shek
and Japan, and the seizure of power by the Chinese Red
Army, the Chinese Communist Party numbering four hundred
thousand even by 1940. Against the Nationalists under Chiang,
the two hundred thousand troops of the Japanese Imperialist
Army who had reached North China in October 1937 were
to endure forty thousand casualties by November. Their
replacement severely affected Japanese strength in Manchukuo
against combined Russian and Mongol neighbours. Later
losses against Mao depleted them further.

The Soviets in 1937 had undertaken a non-aggression
pact with the KMT, while concurrently reinforcing in Mongolia and the USSR. Japanese conscription which had reached
one hundred and seventy thousand in 1936, doubled each year
thereafter until 1941, providing twenty-four divisions in 1937
and fifty-one in 1941; in 1937, there were five Japanese divisions in Manchukuo (the Kwantung Army), one hundred and
fifty tanks and three hundred and forty aircraft. On 30 June,
however, there was only one under-strength Japanese division
in the precise area of the Amur River Incident, this 'clash' the
one hundred and eighty-fifth armed encounter between Japan
and Russia since 1931. (The Soviet Far Eastern Forces in
1937 numbered twenty-three divisions with three hundred and
seventy thousand men, fifteen hundred aircraft and about the
same number of tanks. Tukhachevski, incidentally, had at this
moment, just been shot.) On this occasion, a Soviet gunboat
was sunk by the Japanese and two Soviet divisions were put
on alert across the frontier. The Kwantung Army was then
ordered to stand down and both sides 'withdrew'. Japan, nevertheless, reoccupied without challenge the disputed territory,

confident in morale, in outflanking skill, in hand-to-hand fighting, in speed of response, especially in encirclement.

As a result, Tokio received the impression that the USSR would offer no significant opposition in either Manchukuo or North China where, a few days later at the Marco Polo Bridge, the long China Incident began. Whether the two events were connected – that the Kwantung Army on the Amur sought to give the green light to the North China Garrison Army at Peking – is unproven. This ferocious army, at all events, was frustrated at their restraining orders from Tokio.

But Japan, for a long time now, had rejected restraint. The Mukden Incident had achieved occupation of nearly all Manchuria: the province of Jehol, in North China, just north of Peking, rich in coal and of great natural and man-made beauty, mountains and palaces, was taken in 1933, Japanese troops with straw in their leggings marching forty miles a day at minus 40° in blizzards. Japan vetoed foreign loans to China in 1934 and had bought out the Russian Chinese Eastern Railway in 1935; the Chinese administration was driven out of Chahar in 1936, frequented once by Chingghis Khan; the war against Nationalist China was engineered in 1937. Academics and officials suggested that Manchukuo and North China had sufficient ethnic affinities for merged sovereignty, and that even the Mongolian People's Republic and Siberia should become part of the empire. But in 1936 a puppet Mongol force under Prince Te Wang, recruited by the Kwantung Army, had been defeated by Chiang's Nationalists in its attempt to annex Suiyuan, like Chahar a Mongol province of North China.

Moscow, which had already intervened in the Sino-Uighur–Moslem Chinese province of Sinkiang, regarded Japan's seizure of Chahar as ominous for Soviet interests in the Far East, Siberia and Central Asia, a portent of future threats to vulnerable Soviet possessions. Stalin, accordingly, lost no time in converting Sinkiang into a virtual satellite with Russian military contingents, a situation which endured until 1942 when his puppet Sheng-Shih-Tsai turned his coat for Chiang.

The islands of Japan, already home to an advanced industrial economy, were severely overcrowded. They almost wholly lacked raw materials, oil, rubber, wool and cotton, iron, nickel, zinc and lead. Their population growth in 1938 was the second highest in the world, resident in a mountainous country, terraced, but short of flat arable land. Her progress, furthermore, in the world's export markets was restricted by her trading partners' tariff, quota and other barriers. There were more people in the country than it could maintain. The armed forces sought Manchukuo as an economic base for Japan's landless, hungry, poor but disciplined and effective families, as well as a military blockhouse and springboard against Russia. The army, unlike the civilians, did not shrink – under cover of 'Asia for the Asians' of the Greater East Asian Co-Prosperity Sphere – from forcible expansion overseas, an objective which the requirement for only serving admirals and generals as navy and army ministers, made easy to impose.

The colonial powers and Thailand, as well as China, conscious of Japan's growing armed forces, were rearming throughout the region. Russia's hugely increased army, navy, air force and static defences along the whole frontier with Manchukuo were a direct response to the Japanese pressure which Sorge and the intelligence sources of the USSR reported almost daily to Moscow. The elimination of Russia as a Manchurian presence, and of the one-time Chinese 'buffer state' element, greatly enlarged the possibilities for military confrontation between the Red and the Imperial Japanese Armies. This liability had to be set against whatever contribution that Manchurian settlement made in improving the Japanese economy, through coal, steel, iron, wheat, timber, oil refineries, railways and livestock. But each yen of investment was matched by one expended militarily and, another debit, Japanese colonial rule was neither kind nor incorrupt, but harsh and unpopular.

Japanese Manchukuo was certainly encircled in 1938

by Soviet and Mongolian territory containing forces of all arms frequently twice as large as its own. Although they were able to fight on interior lines, the Japanese were unable, unlike the Russians, to strike the enemy's capital and main centres, ports and so forth, by sea and air. Even an island in the Amur river from which Khabarovsk could be shelled was in Soviet hands. Nevertheless, despite the blow delivered to Moscow with the signature of the Anti-Comintern Pact between Germany and Japan, tension did not much extend beyond the small border incidents, difficulties over the oil concession in Sakhalin, and the Soviet refusal to sign a fisheries agreement. Japan, for its part, rejected in 1932 the Soviet offer of a non-aggression treaty and demanded Red Army force reductions in Siberia.

No progress had been made by 1938 in seducing or bludgeoning the Mongolian People's Republic from her vassalage to the USSR. Mongolia, incurably light-minded in matters of finance, continued to subsist rather painfully and reluctantly from the Soviet economy, while accepting perforce accompanying incompetence and oppression.

In 1938, a Captain Bimba of the Mongolian People's Revolutionary Army (MPRA) defected to the Japanese in Manchukuo. According to him, when General Damba returned from a conference on frontier disputes in Manchouli with Manchukuo Mongols and a Japanese delegation, he spoke of his own involvement, as well as that of Generals Demid and Malji, in a conspiracy to exploit what they hoped would be a Japanese invasion of Outer Mongolia from Inner Mongolia. Another alleged Mongol defector, this time a colonel, caused the Japanese General Staff in 1939 to conclude that there really had been a genuine power struggle in Mongolia between the 'Soviet group' under Choibalsan, and a 'pro-Japanese' group seeking independence from Russia. But that is exactly what Choibalsan himself had put about in order to justify his Mongolian equivalent of the Stalinist purges; it is impossible to believe that misinformation, deception or, at the very best, poor assessment, did not play their confusing part.

There is, however, no doubt that the Japanese did mount propaganda campaigns, including leaflets, into Ulan Bator and equally no doubt that, as well as prisoner intelligence, they conducted *de visu* order of battle espionage against their target. In peace time, over thirty years later, a Mongolian minister congratulated a Japanese visitor on the excellence of his Mongol. But his accent, said the minister, was that of an *Inner* Mongolian 'tribe'. The Japanese did not deny the reproach, admitting also that he had been caught spying in 1939, disguised as a lama, by an MPRA patrol in the trackless wastes near Erh Lien. He had then taken the saddle from his horse, raised it high above his head in the Mongol gesture of surrender. The Mongol soldiers had not shot or arrested him, but had let him go, to die as they supposed . . . 'But,' said the visitor, 'they didn't know that I had a second horse, not so far away, behind sand dunes.' In his cups, as was his practice at that hour, he sniggered complacently.

'What!' cried the minister, unamused, '*you're* the man we've been searching for all these years . . . ?'

# 5
# Frontier Fighting, Mongolia and Manchuria

Open war, not border incidents, on the Manchukuo–Mongolian–Soviet frontiers in 1938, seemed improbable, if not impossible. Despite technical and numerical Russian superiority, few observers in the late 1930s anticipated a Soviet main attack on Manchukuo. Since Russia was largely self-sufficient in terms of resources, there appeared to be no pressing economic motive, nor did another Japanese military invasion of Siberia seem so imminent as to require a Soviet pre-emptive strike. The Anti-Comintern Pact, furthermore, between Japan and Germany, was seen in Moscow as likely to increase their risk of conflict with Berlin should the USSR engage in hostilities with Japan in a war which, anyway, contained no certainty of Soviet victory. It was also the case that although the Soviet military had the Japanese at a logistic disadvantage, Honma's comments about weakened Soviet leadership and command after the Great Purges were clearly, if tacitly, echoed in the Soviet High Command. The latter also had its own budgetary, training and re-equipment problems.

From the other side, Manchukuo's proximity to the Japanese home island might in itself seem to render more likely a Japanese assault on Russia. War Minister Araki Sadao, a leader of the 'Strike North' school against Russia, had said earlier that 'if the Soviets do not cease to annoy us, I shall have to purge Siberia as one cleans a room of flies'. It was also at about this time that Litvinov referred to Japan as 'the darkest thundercloud'. But since invasion had not been undertaken in the early 1930s before the completion of relatively successful Soviet Five Year Plans, when Russia was weak and virtually starving, the chances seemed correspondingly less in 1938. And, Honma notwithstanding, the Army General Staff and the Imperial

Japanese Army, other than the hotheads of the Kwantung Army, did not underestimate their Soviet opponents.

Japanese strategic planning changed over the years. The Army General Staff, when planning for war, allocated sixty out of ninety divisions against Russia and a similar proportion of aircraft and armour. A percentage of the IJA was already stationed in peacetime in Korea and Manchuria, the latter under the Kwantung Army responsible directly to the Emperor for the defence of Manchukuo. The original intention had been to strike eastward into the Maritime Province (Primorski Krai), the so-called Ussuri Front, and after destroying enemy ground, air and naval strength on Soviet soil, redeploy the IJA westward to the Hsingan mountains. Thence, after another Soviet defeat, the Japanese would drive on into Siberia, to Lake Baikal, Irkutsk and the wild blue yonder. Resource shortages and heavy military involvement in China had, by 1937, greatly reduced this concept. The seizure by Japan of Vladivostok and Voroshilov, indeed the whole Eastern strategy, was abandoned in favour of an ultimate major confrontation on a line between Rukhlovo in the USSR on the Trans-Siberian Railway and the Greater Khingan Mountains. The latter rose east of the plain of Hailar and ran through Manchuria from southwest Heilungkiang to southwest Jehol, northwest of Liaoyang and Mukden where the Russians broke in 1904, and northeast of Peking. The range is administratively not in Manchuria today but in Inner Mongolia and controlled from Huhehot.

The Russians allegedly offered troops to Chiang Kai Shek in 1931, ostensibly to 'maintain order on the Chinese Eastern Railway (CER)'. Some authorities in Tokio concluded that Moscow was seeking an excuse to confront the Kwantung Army; but no troops appeared. Border disputes connected with *de visu* intelligence collection and counter intelligence, spies and counter-spies, but also with opium and timber smuggling, began in 1932. (The first casualties between the Red and Kwantung Armies occurred in 1935.) Others followed, including an armed confrontation between fifty Soviet soldiers and forty Japanese. The Japanese were convinced that the incidents were part of a Soviet campaign to disturb, subvert and even incorporate Manchukuo citizens and territory. The Soviets attributed the trouble to Japanese (Manchukuo) provocation, referring to deaths among their frontier guards and to insecurity among the peasantry.

In January 1936, three Soviet officers grotesquely 'whipped three Manchukuoan defectors' into battle against their former masters from whom they had just mutinied. Later, on the Korean border, two deep-frozen Japanese corpses were ceremonially returned by the Russians after a skirmish there. There were many other incidents, armed raids, hand-to-hand fighting, violations of airspace, abduction of civilians. The border posts were frequently missing, always dilapidated, far apart along the circumference of the gigantic frontier, itself sometimes thickly forested and quite devoid of inhabitants. Proposals for delimitation and demarcation got nowhere, despite violent reactions by both armies to perceived infringements. The Soviets would not co-operate, without the non-aggression pact that the Japanese had refused, in establishing border commissions. For their part, the Kwantung Army saw no reason to give up territory through negotiation with an opponent who regarded those shifting sands and rivers as a 'fixed boundary'. Voroshilov told the Japanese Ambassador at Moscow that, if the Japanese really wanted peace – and 'Soviet policy meant peace' – they should control their irresponsible elements. In fact, both parties were playing their own Great Game, if at uncomfortably close quarters. Unlike the game in the Pamirs, Tien Shan and Hindu Kush, the Mongol nomads who formed much of the population were innocent about or quite indifferent to frontiers.

The most substantial border clashes were those in the Tauran region in 1936, and on the Amur river in 1937, to which reference has already been made. The Tauran Incident, of which there is no full Soviet record, occurred in miserably thin grass pasture and semi-gobi south-west of Hailar, inhabited by Mongol nomads, fishermen and canners on Lake Buir itself.

The boundary was, as usual, unclear, claimed by Japan as the Halha river, but by the Soviets as to the 'east of the stream': 'The Kwantung Army had moved it west in 1935,' carped Moscow.

The whole business of Outer Mongolia became prominent partly because the Russians were thought to be running supplies to Chiang Kai Shek through that country. The Japanese were, anyway, anxious to incorporate Outer Mongolia into their own sphere, or to create a Pan-Mongolian entity as a means of neutralising the Soviet Union and weakening China simultaneously. The first clash, with Japanese and Manchukuoan casualties, occurred in January 1935 at Khalkhin Sume, resolved by a three-company Japanese force using artillery, machine-guns and 'tankettes', which remained on the spot in temperatures of minus forty degrees centigrade for three weeks. A not dissimilar incident occurred at Khaylasutai, after which border talks took place at Manchouli; these, unfortunately, collapsed during the year. More fighting broke out at Adag Dulan-Bulan Ders in December and January, Mongolian units of up to one hundred men each employing armour and aerial bombing for the first time, although without success. Their gunners and mechanised cavalry, however, seem to have fought unexpectedly well. The Japanese motorised task force, forbidden to cross the MPR frontier, took casualties against a Mongol detachment of one hundred and forty horsemen before returning to Hailar. In late March 1936, a more powerful detachment from the Kwantung Army engaged the enemy, now including three hundred horsemen, motorised infantry, and artillery which, together with armoured cars, destroyed most of the Japanese tankettes (designed for scouting rather than battle). Mongolian biplanes, bombing at a maximum speed of eighty m.p.h. in the dive, were less fortunate, probably losing six out of eight aircraft to Japanese machine-gun fire. The gunners claimed to have seen the blue eyes of at least *some* Soviet pilots; there *were* Mongol pilots also, one of them encountered by the author in 1974, aged between sixty and seventy, with a face like blackened teak.

The Japanese captured one armoured car, which was then shelled by their own artillery, but were forced to retreat, leaving ten dead and much equipment *inside* the Mongolian People's Republic, supposedly *chasse gardée*. No Mongol corpses were available for repatriation, although Japanese pilots in subsequent sorties described the snow around the enemy as 'bright red with blood'. The outnumbered Mongols claimed to have fought for four hours, and the Japanese commander who, when night had fallen, mounted no counter-attack, was placed on the retired list. The Mongols did, nevertheless, admit more than two hundred Mongolian service deaths in the winter of 1935–6. There would have been more, or so they obligingly said, had it not been for Soviet aid.

There is some evidence that Japanese diplomats in Moscow might have sought to make their hosts' flesh creep by presenting the incident as a forerunner to a prolonged and serious attack against an enfeebled USSR. It has been suggested, on the other hand, that the Tauran engagement was part of a Soviet campaign to exploit the IJA mutiny and massacres in Tokio of February 1936. At all events, both sides, the Kwantung Army more subtly yet with greater violence, were perpetually fomenting plots and subversion on the Soviet, Mongolian and Manchukuoan borders. Spies were everywhere, triggering irritated responses by nervous sentries.

General Tojo Hideki, later to occupy the posts of war, home, foreign and prime minister, and to be sentenced to death for war crimes, was in 1937 Chief of Staff of the Kwantung Army, known contemptuously to General Ishiwara as 'Corporal Tojo'. (He was described in *The New Yorker* as being 'as close as a Japanese can to looking important'.) A ruthless field commander in Inner Mongolia and Chahar, he was strategically misguided in believing that the China War would end in early Japanese triumph, and saw no cause for action to protect the IJA's rear against a Soviet Red Army apparently weakened by purges and only capable of border reaction. In the sense only that the Red Army did not follow up the Amur river incidents of June 1937, he was right. This 'Strike South' proponent then advocated a non-aggression pact with the USSR and immediate action against China.

Channels and islands on both the Amur and Ussuri rivers in eastern Manchuria had been in dispute for years. In 1937, the Soviets renounced a navigational accord of 1934 and began to increase local military and naval activities in an apparent claim, based on old Sino-Russian treaties, on two islands, Bolshoi and Kanchatzu, which they then rapidly occupied (19 June), arresting or throwing out the local inhabitants, including Manchurian alluvial gold 'miners'. The Soviet Consulate at Harbin, when apprised, did nothing. Because the main local Soviet armed force was deployed elsewhere, and because Marshal Tukhachevski's execution had taken place only one week before, the 49th Regiment of the 1st Japanese Division, plus mountain artillery and five air squadrons of bombers and fighters, had been brought to attack readiness by the night of 28 or 29 June. On 23 June, however, Russian warships were sighted on the river near Bolshoi; local Soviet divisions on manoeuvres were reported returning to the Amur; three other divisions may have been mobilising in the neighbourhood; fifty Russian tanks were said to be on the move southwards from Blagoveshchensk and, most significantly, a message from War Minister Voroshilov had been intercepted, instructing the Soviets 'not to fight'. The Army General Staff in Tokio accordingly ordered a policy of 'non-expansion' and of diplomatic negotiation. The Kwantung Army was forced to 'postpone' the attack. One company landed on Kanchatzu, but after taking formal sips of water in the rite performed before battle, withdrew next morning without firing.

The Japanese explained the fighting that followed as originating in an attack by Soviet gunboats on the Manchukuo land positions to which the Japanese had withdrawn. The Russians, of course, claimed that the Kwantung Army had 'begun it' by sinking one of their gunboats with high explosive from horse-drawn 37 mm guns. The crew, swimming for dear life naked in the water, were shot up by machine-gun fire, after which another largish Soviet flotilla was driven off by

Japanese artillery. As a result of negotiations in Moscow between Foreign Minister Litvinov and Ambassador Shigemitsu, the Soviets withdrew, leaving the frontier question for later discussion. Salvage of the sunken gunboat and personnel/ *matériel* exchanges followed.

Although the Amur incident aroused fear of war, prompting one local Japanese official to contemplate the murder of his entire family rather than confirm such fears by evacuating them to Japan, the Kwantung Army assessed the Soviet performance as feeble, conciliatory and hysterically confused. Unless regarded as deception, not to be excluded with Russia, there were too many messages despatched *en clair* or in easily decrypted code for the Soviet Military Command to be considered competent.

The Japanese drew the incorrect conclusion that the Soviet Armed Forces were 'paper tigers'. Some Chinese Nationalists and Western collaborators suspected that this assessment provided the IJA with the incentive to mount the Marco Polo Incident, certain of Russian non-intervention. (One *internal* consequence was the widening rift between the Army General Staff and the Kwantung Army after the AGS's 'postponement' of the 1st Division operation. This dissension was artfully exploited by paranoiac Colonel Tsuji Masanobu, an anti-Russian 'Strike North' hawk in Manchukuo during 1938 and 1939, later to surface on the Bataan Death March, in Singapore, and in Burma before the annihilation of the Japanese Armies there.) Nevertheless, the diversion of large numbers of Japanese troops to China, the Soviet ring of steel around Manchukuo, in the Maritimes, in the MPR and in Siberia with a three-to-one Soviet preponderance in manpower, as well as air and naval superiority, began by 1938 to induce caution in the Japanese AGS and War Ministry. The defection in June to the Japanese, however, of Soviet General Lyushkov from Siberia caused one influential staff officer on the AGS to speculate on Soviet weakness, even to propose a reconnaissance probe, if not the full Strike North.

Much of Japanese military thinking was being regularly

revealed to the Kremlin by Richard Sorge, the Soviet master-spy, whose cover was that of Nazi press correspondent and of consultant to General Ott, German Ambassador at Tokio and representative of Japan's major ally, with access to soldiers and politicians at all levels. Stalin knew, for instance, that Tokio accepted Moscow's claim of a 'two-front war' capability and, insofar as he read or absorbed intelligence at all, knew everything that was knowable about IJA Order of Battle and intentions. Among those desiderata was the knowledge that Tokio was not yet determined on a major war with the USSR.

# 6
# The Battle of Lake Khasan or Changkufeng

Late 1937 and early 1938 were filled with rumours of large Japanese troop reinforcements through Harbin, the construction of new airfields in Manchukuo generally, more fighting (Islands 227 and 279) on the Amur, temporary reservation of Dairen port for military use, 250,000 Japanese and 180,000 Manchurian bayonets in Manchukuo, increased Soviet movements through Siberia, every siding crowded with troop trains.

In May 1938, General Tojo left Manchukuo for Tokio on appointment as Vice-Minister of War. In June, Litvinov warned against aggressors who sought their prey in 'flabby' territories, and reminded them that every inch of Soviet soil was protected.

On 6 July, the Kwantung Army claimed to have decoded a Soviet signal recommending occupation of a hillock in Manchuria just across the Tumen river in wild and beautiful country west of little Lake Khasan, on the borders of Manchukuo, Korea and the Maritimes. The hillock, Changkufeng, dominated the Korean railway and Possiet Bay, but not the Rashin port; authority was requested for one Russian company to dig in there. The (Japanese) Korea Army, in whose command this locality lay, recommended vigilance but, because of the area's unimportance compared with the Japanese effort in China, no action. By 14 July, unfortunately, Soviet defence construction had started and some forty Russian soldiers were on the hill, together with wire and a red flag. General Suetaka Kamezo, commanding 19 Division of the (Japanese) Korea Army, wished to concentrate his men in the locality.

Imperial General HQ may have wanted to use the occasion to demonstrate, by a 'fishing expedition', that a probe would not activate Soviet reflex interference in China, and that the frontier would remain quiet, if not a zone of peace.

'There was nothing to fear from Russia,' which had made no preparations for combat or reinforcement, and to fight on two fronts, (China *and* USSR) briefly, would enhance Japan's prestige abroad. On the other hand, the Vice-Chief of General Staff wanted to 'enlarge' the Changkufeng Incident precisely to persuade his colleagues to 'break off the fighting against China'.

The operation was to be conducted by Imperial General Headquarters in Tokio through the Korea Army and 19 Division. There was to be no air force participation, nor would armour be involved. (The Kwantung Army, black with rage, would not participate, other than logistically: 'If only this case were left to us, it would be over in a flash. Just one wallop, and the Russians would be gone. The Korea Army is too obedient to Papa.') On 15 July, a Japanese corporal was killed on patrol; protests were exchanged. Suetaka alerted an infantry regiment, elements of artillery regiments, signals and the usual tail. Three thousand men were in position by 19 July.

Then, because the elderly Prince Kan'in, Chief of Staff, War Minister Itagaki and Foreign Minister Ugaki had not properly briefed themselves, the Emperor forbade further action. 'The army's methods have been outrageous,' he said. Hirohito had apparently understood from the bungling Itagaki that the army were about to go to war with Russia. 'There must be nothing resembling the Manchurian and China incidents. Not even one man may be moved without our order.' The wretched Kan'in left the Imperial Presence in disgrace after only ten minutes, and all three functionaries were so ashamed that they considered resignation. Like the frustrated 1st Division in 1937, 19th Division stood down, and had mostly returned to quarters by 26 July, although one unit was clandestinely posted on a hill near Changkufeng.

On 29 July, Suetaka, choosing to exclude from the Imperial Prescription 'new' incidents and those plainly breaching the frontier, sent at least two platoons against a Soviet patrol of ten frontier guards under a Lieutenant Tereshkin near Bezimmeniya, the English translation of which is 'Nameless'.

His instructions to evict the enemy were written on a visiting card addressed to 75 Regiment Commander, Sato, much later commanding 31 Division at Kohima: 'You are to mete out a firm and thorough attack . . .' The attack went in at 'Nameless' and Changkufeng at dawn on 31 July in thick fog and rain, routing seventeen tanks and some six hundred Russian soldiers, and advancing to a depth of four kilometres. The Emperor, when the attack had been represented to him as 'in self-defence', raised no objection, but IGHQ ordered prudence and no provocation thereafter. About fifty Japanese were killed and three hundred wounded in these actions.

Marshal Tukhachevski had been executed without trial on 12 June 1937 after demotion to the command of the Pri Volga Military District, *en route* to which post he was arrested by the NKVD. Blyükher, his staff in ruins from the gnawing of the NKVD, still nominally commanded the Far Eastern Red Banner *Front* until his execution in November 1938. Corps Commander G. M. Shtern, a Jew with service in Spain, commanded the 1st Independent Red Banner *Army* and, from the middle of this battle, the 39th Rifle Corps, which directed it. (Shtern himself was executed with other old Bolsheviks in the 1940s.) At least three and probably four Soviet Rifle Divisions were subordinate to the rifle corps, against an approximate Japanese strength of eighteen thousand regular troops. By 8 August, Soviet strength was twenty-seven infantry battalions, armoured units numbering some two hundred tanks, and about one hundred guns. The Japanese had no armour and only fifty guns, including AA, to support their troops; there were shortages, particularly of anti-tank shells. The Soviet Air Force now went into action, large formations of aircraft, including four-engined heavy bombers, against the high ground and some targets in the Korean rear. Up to two hundred aircraft in seven hundred sorties were employed for eight days together with artillery bombardments, directed at the Japanese in their tunnels at Changkufeng and Shachaofeng. The bombing was very inaccurate, but the Russian artillery's precision improved: 'The hill crests seemed one mass of flame which became all the more vivid as darkness fell.' Although the ground turned to liquid mud under the rain and the projectiles, the IJA held in their bunkers as they were to hold obstinately in Burma and the Pacific during the 1939–45 war. There was little else that they could do, other than run, since Tokio had forbidden Suetaka's proposal to mount an offensive. Air action remained under the original prohibition. Bergamini reports a curious episode during this phase when two Japanese officers, one Tanaka Takayoshi, the enormous lover of the famous courtesan and spy known as 'Eastern Jewel', 'encouraged the troops against Russian tanks' by removing their trousers and displaying themselves to their men.

From 6 August, in very bad weather and therefore without air cover, the Soviets mounted two-division attacks (32 and 40 Siberian), plus heavy artillery batteries in direct frontal confrontations. Many Russian tanks, trapped between Lake Khasan, the marshes on the Tumen, Shachaofeng and the southern redoubt, were destroyed by 19 Division's anti-tank guns and never reached the hills. Where they appeared at all, they came shuddering over the horizon against the sun, presenting delectable targets to the Japanese guns.

In the persistent assaults, the Russians may have incurred five thousand casualties, of whom fifteen hundred were killed. Ninety-six tanks and thirty guns were knocked out, as well as machine-guns and anti-tank guns. Ten Soviet aircraft were shot down or crash-landed. The Japanese admitted to some five hundred killed and a thousand wounded. Casualties, as was usual in the IJA were particularly heavy among officers: two battalion and seven company commanders were killed. Some companies were down to twenty men. Corporals commanded platoons, a lieutenant even led a battalion: one out of five soldiers was a casualty by 11 August.

There was, after hostilities had begun, no escalation in the air. The 19th Division gazed hopelessly skywards for days to catch a single glimpse of the roundels of the Rising Sun. But when a cease-fire for 11 August restoring the status quo was signed in Moscow between Litvinov and Shigemitsu, possibly not unaffected by severe Russian losses, the Kwantung Army was to be reinforced by two divisions from Harbin and Tsitsihar, with minor additions further north. Tokio had apparently not intended to expand operations outside Chang-kufeng, but these movements, and the mobilisation of a heavy bomber group, were known to the Soviets, exercising unde-niable pressure on their freedom of movement. Despite Sorge's intelligence, if the General had been even informed, Shtern could not have been completely certain that the 'wild dog' Kwantung Army would not have acted without orders, as they certainly wished to do, to strangle the Russian forces around the Tumen river. Soviet countermeasures indicated strong, defensive sensitivity.

The Japanese, while admitting military stalemate, had successfully assessed Soviet reaction to pressure and inhibited Soviet interference in China. The Soviets may have thought that they had tied down Imperial Armed Forces in an insig-nificant sector when these could have been deployed in that more important situation to the southwest. Perhaps, even, the original Soviet telegram which, intercepted, set off the whole train of events, was itself an ingenious deception . . . 'At all events,' said a relieved and confident staff officer in Tokio, 'now we can get on with Hankow.' Others took a contrary view. Russia's considerable build-up should have demonstrated that the USSR was not a practical opponent for Japan and, as a corollary, that the China incident should be brought to a rapid conclusion without much regard for face, if Manchukuo were to hold. But instead, after Changkufeng, Japanese reinforcements flowed even faster to the China battle fronts, a complete reversal of those intentions of General Tada, Vice-Chief of the General Staff, expressed above.

The view from Moscow was quite different. Shtern spoke about the battle on 4 April 1939 to the Eighteenth Party Congress, as reported by Colonel Firebrace, British Military Attaché Moscow, to his ambassador. The General, while admit-ting that Changkufeng was only an episode, claimed that it was a real operation of modern war for which the Japanese troops had undergone special training and the Imperial Staff had carried out detailed reconnaissance over many months. After a sudden Japanese attack on Zaosernaya, Bezimmeniya ('Nameless') and other heights defended by frontier guards, Shtern said that the heights were in Japanese hands, over-looking all Soviet movements. The Soviet attack on heights fortified by the Japanese and protected by wire was through two narrow corridors less than five hundred metres wide, running North–South between Lake Khasan and the Tumen–Ula river. Every yard was covered by artillery and machine-gun fire. The attack on 6 August, preceded by air and artillery bombardment, carried out by infantry and tanks had recaptured all ground seized by the Japanese. From 7 to 11 August (the date of the armistice) twenty Japanese attacks using fresh troops had been beaten off by the Soviet Army with heavy Japanese losses. It was not true that Zaosernayo had been evacuated by the (Japanese) Korea Army due to flooding: the IJA, had been militarily defeated, suffering losses three times greater than the Soviets. The flooding had only occurred on 14 August.

Shtern asserted that Changkufeng demonstrated that the Soviet Army had been cleansed of 'spies and wreckers', and was not only better equipped than the Japanese Army but had more competent commanders, from platoon commander upwards. The purges, in other words, had been salutary. The Japanese had, however, said the doomed Shtern, not drawn the correct conclusions. The 'Nippo-Manchurians', as the Soviets called them, in China, Manchukuo and Korea now numbered 1.4 million. Those in Manchukuo and Korea had grown from 95,000 in 1934 to 400,000 in 1938. Airfields in Manchukuo had increased from 180 in 1934 to 250 in 1938. Roads had multiplied to 11,000 m in 1938 from 6.5 m in 1934. Preparations were mounting for war in Inner Mongolia. General Tojo had said that Japan must prepare for a two-front war, against Russia *and* China; now Russia's forces were ready for all eventualities.

In Tokio, nevertheless, the army was heartened by

what appeared to them as a tactical victory. The Soviets, in their opinion, while brave enough, lacked drive, effort, co-ordination and leadership, characterised by inertia, successful only as artillery. In the air, although capable aeronauts, their bombing was grossly ineffective against well-dug-in troops. Tokio's instruction, in other words, to 19 Division when the battle began, that 'they were not to cede an inch of territory we hold, and not attempt to take an inch of anyone else's', was executed to the IJA's satisfaction and with exemplary discipline.

It has been suggested that the Russians, in what seems a most unfavourable logistic arena, were probing Japanese resolution in the light of Sorge's reporting, or that the Japanese were testing General Lyushkov's views on Soviet weakness with the ultimate intention of abandoning the China War in order to fight a major war with the USSR. These are extreme views but, at a time when Hankow was the next domino to fall, Moscow may have at least sought to divert Japanese attention from China, and simultaneously to impress the Kuomintang with its support for their cause. (The cease-fire gave no comfort to Chiang Kai Shek.) Lord Chilston, then Ambassador at Moscow, gave an alternative explanation to his Secretary of State, Lord Halifax, which presupposed that, after the defection of Lyushkov, the Soviets had heavily reinforced their border guards at the point where he had crossed the Manchukuo frontier. The Japanese frontier guards, ignorant of this reasoning and considering themselves to be on Japanese territory, had sought to drive them away, thus initiating the whole incident.

The Changkufeng settlement on 11 August may at least have shown that, even though the Japanese were still on the peaks in what the Russians claimed as Soviet territory, Moscow was not prepared to risk a major conflict. Perhaps, the Russians also recognised that their military performance had not been good enough to warrant a continuation of some fairly bloody combat. There had been faulty staff work in the

1st Far East Army; 'measures were taken' to improve security and battle readiness.

Another measure, on the Japanese side, transferred *formal* responsibility for the defence of the Hunchun area, including Changkufeng, from the Japanese Korea Army to the Kwantung Army, which was also given power to deal with Manchukuo–Soviet border disputes. But on 29 June 1939, six months after the Nomonhan incident had begun, the Kwantung Army was instructed by the Vice-Chief of the General Staff in Tokio that the Emperor had refused to permit any advance, however temporary, into Soviet or Mongol territory.

# 7
# Deadlock in China

In China, although Private Shimura had rapidly returned to his unit, the Japanese made demands unacceptable to the Chinese Nationalists. Chiang Kai Shek, deprived of China's resources, that is his five northern provinces of Hebei, Shanxi, Ninxia, Shaanxi and Shantung, taken or under deadly threat, decided to stand and fight. In December 1936, the attempt, at Sian, under duress from Chang Hsueh Liang and associated with the Communists, failed to induce the Generalissimo to agree a merger on the ground between the Kuomintang and Mao's Communist forces. The Nationalists, apart from some occasional tactical combinations, continued to fight both the Imperial Army and the Communists as opportunity offered; in September 1937, however, the Chinese Communist Party 'accepted' Chiang's terms for ending the Civil War and for the inauguration of an anti-Japanese united front.

General Tojo with the Kwantung Army in 1937, while regarding Russia as the main enemy, had recommended to Tokio that 'the first blow should be struck at the Nanking regime' to protect the Japanese rear. The Army General Staff and ministers, on the contrary, had ordered negotiations with Nanking. A temporary and local cease-fire was secured. But after July further armed clashes took place between the two sides and by August General Terauchi commanded sixteen divisions (two hundred thousand men) in the North China area. Before Private Shimura's historic micturation, the Japanese strength had consisted of only one brigade.

General Ishiwara and others, who sought a Japan unencumbered by unnecessary commitments and ready for 'total war', warned despairingly that intervention in China would lead to the quagmire which it eventually became. Overconfidence, contempt for the Chinese military, the belief that war-lords, Communists and so forth would fatally divide China were, nevertheless, the decisive factors in the delusion that the war could be short and manageable.

The IJA had taken Peking by the beginning of August 1937. Nankow fell. Under Tojo himself, Kalgan and Tatung were occupied. On 21 November, the Federation of Mongolia and the Border Territories, which included Inner Mongolia, was proclaimed at Kalgan, signed in Uighur, Japanese and Chinese, 'in the 732nd Year of Chinggis Khan'.

Chiang moved his troops southwards from northern China. The Japanese, primarily to protect their thirty thousand citizens in Shanghai, took that city, albeit with forty thousand IJA casualties, and were moving on to Chiang's capital at Nanking. The Generalissimo with Soong Mei Ling, his beautiful and intrusive wife, left the city on 8 December; Nanking, its entire periphery now a bright circle of burning buildings, an *auto da fé*, was penetrated on 10 December. Its commander, who had ordered the destruction of the perimeter, decamped the same day, while the city gates were piled three feet high with the corpses of fleeing soldiers and pack animals, caught in the flames among the incoming explosion of heavy artillery shells. The Japanese Rape, an uncontrolled orgy of murder, arson, rape, looting, destruction and mass killing of women, men and children, then began – 'the Carnival of Death', bell-like echoes of Timurlan and Chinggis Khan, skulls, blood and stench. From now on also started experiments on the living bodies of prisoners: the removal or knifing of organs, the injection of germs (anthrax, tetanus, plague, rabies), dehydration, the drilling of skulls, the tearing out of eyes, the simulation of frost-bite and malnutrition, the infliction by Unit 731 of hideous, intolerable pain on human beings, regarded by their torturers as no more than 'blocks of wood'.

After one heroic Chinese victory at Taierchwang, the Japanese moved on to Hankow, incidentally China's last surviving centre of manufacture, where Chiang's German-trained armies broke. Chiang, after blowing up the Changchow Yellow River dykes at von Falkenhausen's suggestion, and flooding

China as far as the Yangtse, escaped to his new capital of Chungking on the upper Yangtse. In October 1938, a brilliant Japanese seaborne operation ended in the seizure of Canton, with more rape and brutality.

Chungking, beyond the gorges, was inaccessible to Japanese ground troops and, after the fall of Hainan Island in February 1939, an immense, inflationary stalemate afflicted the military situation in China. There was no further Sino-Japanese main force action for the five years after that date, although Communist guerillas under Mao in the north increasingly weakened the forces of occupation. The Japanese puppet, Wang Ching-Wei, never succeeded in completely undermining the Kuomintang, and defence costs, plus growing United States and European sanctions, began to gnaw effectively into the Japanese civilian and military economies, the dreaded quagmire. China, though mutilated, remained unified; Japan could not understand.

# 8
# Mongolian - Manchurian Armed Encounters

In 1939, Japanese military policy towards Inner Asia was devoted to the subjugation of both China and Russia.

As for the Russians, George Kennan, then chargé d'affaires at Moscow, told Averell Harriman in 1945 that Soviet policy toward China in the recent past had been directed at the achievement of maximum power with minimum responsibility, namely domination of those Chinese provinces in Central Asia contiguous to the Soviet frontier. ('China', in the pre-war and wartime context, subsumed Manchukuo, Inner Mongolia and other regions under Japanese occupation.) Soviet policy was, in fact, two-fold, aimed at 'power', as well as 'security' which, in the case of Manchukuo, meant the defence of Soviet interests against the Kwantung Army. That defence did not exclude *offensive* subversion, force and economic influence to penetrate Japanese possessions in China. 'Power', of course, was served solely or chiefly by just such offensive, not defensive, means in Manchukuo and elsewhere.

Since Soviet intervention in those territories continued even after the Japanese had been removed from China at their surrender, Kennen was right in describing Moscow's policy as directed against China itself.

The eastern frontiers of Manchukuo were slightly better marked than those with Outer Mongolia. In the west, the Japanese claimed the Halha river as the boundary, on the basis of Chinese Imperial documents dating from 1784, Chinese maps from 1918 and various others, even including one devised in England. The frontier claimed by the MPR, in this flat, empty land of grass and sand dunes, was, however, several miles into Manchukuo *east* of the river. Here nomadic Mongol shepherds of the MPR would peacefully gossip in felt *gers* throughout the harsh winters, equably whispering with their compatriots from Manchukuo. As has been said, supported by a Japanese historian writing on the post-war Tokio trials, the Russians and their Mongol satellites alleged that the Japanese 'moved' the old Imperial frontier westward to the Halha river in 1935. There were few, if any, border posts to prove it either way, only *obos* (cairns of religious significance), dilapidated, and at unpredictable distances apart.

It was not, therefore, surprising, given these factors and the tendency of both countries' policies, that hundreds of border incidents should have been the subject of official reports between 1934 and 1939; the main confrontations are those outlined in Chapter 5: Khalkin Sume, Khaylasutai, Adag Dulan-Bulan Ders. There followed a series of encounters, smallish, but involving armour and aircraft, culminating in an attack by the Japanese Shibuya mechanised unit (4th tank regiment) in battalion strength, plus artillery, signals and ancillaries. It was here, in the Tauran incident of March 1936, that 'the snow around the Mongols was red with blood'. Elsewhere the first specifically Mongolian air action was the destruction of Japanese vehicles in convoy by a unit commanded by Lieutenant Shagdasuren and also involving Pilot Gunner Dory, in April that year.

Casualties and damage were inflicted on both sides, but that clash was, once again, no repetition for the Japanese of their victories in the 1904–5 contest. The IJA did not seem to have grasped their own tactical failure. Neither did they understand that their successes against slow and lumbering Soviet and Mongolian aircraft offered no real guide to the future, nor that their armour, the tankettes, was adequate only for reconnaissance, but not combat. In the end the Japanese had had to retreat and did not even recover prisoners captured on earlier occasions. The Japanese press attributed Tauran to a deliberate Russian attempt to test Kwantung Army border defences in the west, in order to exploit any confusion resulting from the Tokio Mutiny of February 1936. *Pravda* took the opposite view, describing the fighting as originating in an intention by Tokio to exploit and manipulate current Soviet weakness perceived by the Imperial Government. It was, in fact, probably an act of Japanese revenge for an earlier incursion by Mongolian Army troops with armour and artillery support.

The battle had political significance also, of which the IJA was apparently not aware. Stalin, talking to an American commentator in early March 1936, had warned that the USSR was as ready to 'defend' Mongolia then as it had been during the Ungern-Sternberg atrocities of 1921. Then, on 12 March, two weeks before the Tauran conflict began, the Russians formalised an agreement of 1934 with a treaty of friendship which included joint defence arrangements with the Mongols. Colonel Shibuya, in planning his advance for the end of March, thus seems to have discounted the consequent probability of greatly increased enemy resistance. Indeed, it was not until late 1937 that an Outer Mongolian desk was established in the Army General Staff in Tokio; and in 1939 the office and its single occupant were posted to Kalgan in Inner Mongolia whither all enquiries about Outer Mongolia were thereafter addressed.

It cannot, however, be asserted that the Japanese neglected and oppressed their 'subjects' on the scale practised in Russia by the Wehrmacht after Barbarossa. Manchukuo boasted a Department of Mongolian Affairs largely manned by indigenous Mongols. In Inner Mongolia, little Prince Demchukdongrub (Te Wang) from Western Sumid, failing any foreseeable pan-Mongol state free of foreign control, did his best to ensure that collaboration with the occupier would protect his people from Japanese excess as well as from Chinese agricultural colonisation. The Prince was sentenced by the Chinese to a long term of imprisonment after the Japanese surrender, but even that was a kinder fate than those suffered by the Ukrainians, Balts and other victims of the Third Reich, particularly as he was, anyway, eventually released and became a librarian.

Soviet troop strength in Mongolia increased after Tauran in 1936, and substantially so after the judicial assassinations of Demid, Gendun and the main leadership in 1937. (It was then that Ulan Bator accused the Kwantung Army not only of multiple attacks on frontier posts, but of preparing to invade with the help of Mongol traitors within the MPR.) General Damba had predicted in 1937 that, by 1938, the Mongolian Army would number twenty-five thousand men, considerably supplemented by Soviet infantry divisions, motorised brigades and aircraft.

It may be that these Soviet transfers were in response to the 'threat' to Outer Mongolia from Te Wang's puppet 'Inner Mongolian Army', or perhaps to pre-empt any hostile reactions from dissident Mongols to the Stalinist purges. (Defector Captain Bimba spoke of fairly numerous arrests and personnel shifts in the MPRA, and it is possible that the NKVD did not find the dictator, Choibalsan, in adequate control.) Bimba and the other defector, a colonel, on the other hand, alleged that most of the MPRA attacks on the frontier were 'staged' by Choibalsan as a means of acquiring more men and weaponry from the USSR with which to pursue irredentist claims in Manchuria. Certainly, continual border tension was beginning to cause frontier incidents, which transmitted to both sides dangerous sensitivities and led to confrontations on the eventual scale of Khalkin Gol (Nomonhan). Equally certainly, the Mongols had always regarded their geopolitical position as central to Soviet requirements, thus providing themselves with financial and other leverage, inducement, if not blackmail, which they seldom hesitated to apply in alleviating colonial tutelage.

These varying theses are illuminated by the capture in January 1939 of a Mongolian Army junior commander. Attempts by the Mongols to rescue him led to the arrival of Manchukuoan reinforcements, followed by further Mongolian contingents and so on, until the original minor skirmish had expanded to a relatively large set-to. The Japanese then forged leaflets, allegedly signed by their Mongol prisoner, demanding an end to Soviet–Mongol relations. These were used by President Choibalsan as an excuse to execute Prime Minister Amor, a feudal noble but old friend, now described as 'a poisonous snake' in the language of those internecine times.

Although the Japanese seem to have regarded these border affrays as beneath the notice of the Kwantung Army, at most the business of Manchukuo police and border guards, it was at about this time that Russia started to bolster Mongolian units with regular Soviet troops as far east as Tamsag Bulag, south of Lake Buir and the Halha river. These movements, unlike the border incidents and such phenomena as the burning of pasture in the MPR to spread fire into Manchukuo, were reported to the Army General Staff in Tokio. Now the Kwantung Army at last began to believe in the theory of a planned, escalating Soviet–Mongolian campaign against Manchukuo, though whether offensive or offensive–defensive was hard to say.

Nor, in the Greater Mongolia context, should it be forgotten that in 1912 the Barga Mongols of Inner Mongolia (Barguts), including thirty-five out of forty-nine banners, had declared allegiance to the Jebtsumdamba Khutuktu, Living Buddha and Yellow Faith Lamaist God-King of Outer Mongolia, at whose death in 1924 the Russian and Mongolian Communists seized 'constitutional' republican power. Even in 1924, at the Third Party Congress, the Barga representative called for Mongol pan-nationalism: 'Our people in Barga and Inner Mongolia are still like men frantically struggling in the water. We hope that our Outer Mongolian brethren who have managed to reach the bank will do all they can to rescue their brothers of the same Mongol race.' Needless to say, such expressions of pan-Mongolism, incompatible with Soviet interests, did not survive the purges unadulterated. But the philosophy and associated manifestations of Buddhist culture were never quite suppressed, and could be easily observed by observers even before the fall of the Soviet totalitarian regime.

Spring in these latitudes is a trying season, not the joyous rebirth of western Europe, but a time of winds and sand driven against eyes and face and ears. But the ice starts to break for a little while on the streams and rivers, light rains fall on the soda grass and camel bushes, and on grey rocks covered with red lichen. A pale sun shines fitfully through a clouded sky. Dunes border arid sandy clay, gritty, compressed, eroded. Duck, chiefly teal, are found near the rare stagnant pools and shallow dried-out swamps.

After the thaw, when the Halha river receded, patrolling began again for the first time since January and February. On 4 May 1939, the first of several Mongolian incursions took place east of the Kalkhin Gol to the Balshagal Heights, southwest of Nomonhan Burd Obo (Land of the Law Cairn) and north of the little Holsten (Khailastyn) river. The attack was vigorously contested by Manchukuo guards and police, the Mongols taking several casualties but, nevertheless, managing to establish posts with *gers* and transport at Balshagal and Noro. (It will be recalled that neither the USSR nor the MPR regarded the Halha as the frontier; that, they asserted, was some fifteen miles east of the river. The Mongols thus claimed that the east (right) bank was guarded by their troops, although a Japanese general saw none there in early May, while the Japanese claimed that their Manchukuoans were in situ.) Larger units and Soviet aircraft were said to be massing at Tamsag Bulag.

On 10, 11 and 12 May, up to two hundred Mongol horsemen and sixty machine-gunners of the 7th Border Guard were seen and then driven back by Manchurian Barguts who ran deep into the frontier zone claimed by the MPR before withdrawing. An American military observer contended that these troubles might have been initiated by attacks from Bargut troops against pilgrims and traders, escorted by MPR or Soviet soldiers, as they nomadised from Outer Mongolia to the annual fair at a shrine near little Chiangchunmiao north of Nomonhan. Bargut soldiers in Nomonhan are said to have called on the Russian Major Bykov for reinforcement after the Japanese strike on 14 May, an illustration of the ethnic complication of the region.

The Japanese have been accused of 'carrying instructions from Emperor Hirohito to seize Outer Mongolia as a stepping stone to Siberia and the Trans-Siberian railway'. There was nothing that the Kwantung Army would have liked better, but even blowhards like Colonel Tsuji might have considered that more and better troops would have been required for the purpose than the untried 23rd Division, the rest of the Army being on the eastern or northern frontiers. Initially, the Kwantung Army had been concentrating on frontier tactics near non-demarcated borders (demarcated frontiers were allegedly inviolable), admittedly with victory as the aim. One Japanese officer, however, said that the 'provocations' were no more than intelligence reconnaissances, all stopping short of the Halha 'frontier'. General Shtern insisted, however, that the raids on 10, 11 and 12 May were mounted by Japanese, not Bargut Mongols, and that they indicated an imminent full-scale invasion by the MPR. The Japanese deny this, claiming that they could not even *find* Nomonhan on the maps at Kwantung Army HQ. (The Soviets did not credit that.) No one there could believe that 'this insignificant little mound of sand manned by seven Barga guards would become the site of raging battles that made world headlines'.

Lieutenant-General Komatsubara Michitaro, a Soviet expert, had commanded the 23rd Division since July 1938. He was relatively tall, dapper, almost dandyish, literate and cultured. He drank whisky as well as sake, and was a non-smoker. A poet and diarist, he aimed to be a very 'professional' soldier, even a martinet, dignified but rather withdrawn, not loved like, for example, Slim or de Lattre. When he was informed of the fighting at Nomonhan, he despatched Lieutenant-Colonel Azuma Yaozo commanding a reconnaissance regiment, with other Japanese and Manchukuo troops, armour from Hailar and lorries. After an argument with his air commander, he secured fighters and bombers rather than the reconnaissance aircraft which he had originally requested. Tsuji, after a low-level recce flight over the target, had found no enemy in the area except twenty 'military horses' among trees and, although he returned to Hailar with a bullet hole in the petrol tank, General Komatsubara's decision seemed excessive to some.

Coincidentally, the Army General Staff (AGS) in Tokio were covertly considering how to strengthen the western frontier, in case of war with the USSR, in advance of an actual campaign in Russian Transbaikalia. The study was to be thorough but leisurely, not immediate, intended to identify requirements currently lacking in the Kwantung Army. Colonel Inada, a representative of the Army General Staff's Operations Section, was visiting Division at Hailar at the time and displayed concern to officers on secondment from the Army General Staff. They agreed with him that nothing should as yet be done to distract the Imperial Army from its efforts in China, the most important theatre. After he had also spoken to Komatsubara, he then put his arguments to General Ueda Kenkichi, Kwantung Army commander at Hsinking, with hooded eye, British cavalry moustache and long, narrow head. Although Inada was not convinced that Ueda had really grasped the necessity for caution within the parameters of Japan's main Asian tasks, he could not recommend that Azuma's mission be amended or cancelled, nor that the Kwantung Army should cede to the High Command its responsibilities for the defence of Manchukuo.

Azuma's force, about two hundred strong, cavalry, infantry and an armoured company left Hailar on 13 May for the west in their tracked or wheeled vehicles. On arrival at Nomonhan in clear, sunny weather, at last, after the horrors of spring, he learned that most of the Mongolian detachment had retreated westward across the Khalkin Gol on the day before, leaving only a few men behind on the eastern shore. On 15 May, Japanese aircraft operating at low level bombed and machine-gunned either those Mongols at Tsagaan Nur (White Lake) on the west bank who had escaped across the river to the MPR on 14 May, or the Johnny-come-latelies who had only crossed the river after that. (Komatsubara had, as we know, only asked for reconnaissance aircraft, which did not have the range from Hailar to Mongolia including Tamsag

Bulag. Instead 24 Air Group gave him bombers and fighters.) No Soviet air activity took place in reply. About thirty to forty casualties resulted among MPRA troops, losses which may have accelerated Soviet escalation.

The Russo-Mongolians also reported the sighting of 'one hundred lorry loads' of Japanese and Bargut infantry, eight tracked vehicles including one tank and seven armoured cars (possibly tankettes), and an indeterminate quantity of Manchurian cavalry, wearing steel helmets, rifles slung across their backs, well turned-out, booted, and at a gallop. Three hundred of the last-named remained in the sector after the main body of Colonel Azuma's force returned to Hailar on 16 and 17 May. Komatsubara declared that the detachment, including the Manchukuoans, had behaved well.

# 9
# Azuma and the 23rd Division

The Soviets regarded Transbaikalia and Siberia as their most vulnerable areas in the Far East and, from 1937 onwards, had built up their establishment accordingly. (They had also expanded their air, sea and land units in the Maritime Provinces against the Japanese threat to the Pacific coast.) Blyükher's first defence against any Kwantung Army advance out of the scrub of Manchuria into the wastes of Mongolia was based on rows of *tochkas*, concrete pillboxes with gun-ports for 76 mm or machine-guns covered by thick walls. As a deterrent to Nipponese aggression, Russians in this decade would speak to selected audiences in minatory terms of a counter-offensive into Manchuria.

By 1939, Stalin's purges had spread to the Far East. As Chapter 3 showed, the efficiency of Blyükher's command had been adversely affected by the execution of East Siberian railway officials by firing squad, on charges of espionage or sabotage for Japanese Intelligence. Arrests followed, temporarily halted by Blyükher's return from Moscow, among the staff of the Far Eastern Red Banner Front and the Trans-Baikal Military District.

These irregularities greatly encouraged the Japanese Northern or 'Russian' School of the Army General Staff, who sought armed confrontation with the USSR, as opposed to the 'Southern' School advocacy of intervention in South China and South-East Asia. (It was now that General Honma, the Intelligence chief, commented on the possible disintegration of the Soviet Army as a result of the purges.) The June–July 1937 incidents on the Amur river, and the China Incident itself, followed, as did the battle of Lake Khasan or Changkufeng, described in Chapter 6. By 9 November 1938, furthermore, the extraordinary General Blyükher was dead, at Stalin's vengeful order.

On 31 May 1939, Molotov, the Soviet Foreign Minister, had warned Tokio that the Soviet–Mongolian Treaty of 1936 included the USSR's undertaking to defend the MPR frontiers as their own. Patience, added Stalin's oafish creature, had its 'limits', a reference to alleged Japanese border provocations, and now to a major assault from 28 May by two thousand Japanese and Manchukuo infantry, cavalry and aircraft of the JAF.

The Japanese claimed to have identified in 1939 a total of two or three Soviet infantry divisions and the same number of mechanised brigades in Mongolia. One motorised division, according to the IJA, was in the south at Dornod or in the sandy hills of Dalanzadgad, just north of the Gobi desert. One cavalry division and the 36th Motorised Rifle Division were then at Saynshand on the Trans-Mongolian railway, an eight-day journey between Peking and Moscow. This particular station was equipped with a bizarre 'Venetian' campanile and pullulated during the Cold War with drunken Soviet troops, like the bar scene in *Star Wars*. Russian armour and four Corps were at Ulan Bator, armoured cars at Öndorhahn and at other locations. A Japanese writer, Higuchi Toyo, has said that there had been 'four Russian Armoured Brigades near Nomonhan' before the battle, and six brigades with no fewer than 2,500 AFV's in Mongolia as a whole; this was certainly an exaggeration. He added that the Soviet Air Force at Tamsag, Bulag, Sanbiese and Madat comprised two air regiments of bombers and fighters – Dobriya and Tartar – which another Japanese source has enumerated at two to three hundred aircraft. The 36th Rifle Division from Chita had formed the core of the motorised 57 Special Corps at Ulan Bator. Readers will also recall approximate figures (twenty-five thousand) for the Mongolian Army in Chapter 8.

The 23rd Japanese Division, raised in Kyushu, Japan's southern island, almost sub-tropical and many degrees south of Manchuria's chilly plains, was despatched to Hailar under Lieutenant-General Komatsubara in 1938 to guard western Manchuria, responsible to General Ueda's Kwantung Army. It comprised three infantry regiments, plus an artillery, a cavalry, an engineer and a transport regiment, with a nominal roll of thirteen thousand men. The men of Kyushu were solid and reliable, with a considerable reputation in the Imperial Army. The officers of the Division included many who had not attended the Academy, especially those at platoon level, and few with tested combat experience: Komatsubara, for example, had only been glancingly engaged in the First World War campaign against the Germans in Shantung, and his infantry reconnaissance, artillery, transport and engineer commanding officers had had similarly minimal battle histories. Komatsubara and his chief of staff, Colonel Ouchi Tsutomo, were, however, both Soviet 'experts'.

The Division's weapons were often old. The 75 mm guns dated from 1907 and 1908, while much equipment was unmechanised and unsuitable for the speed and mobility demanded by steppe and desert. (The Japanese underestimated their enemy's motorised strength in proportion to cavalry.) The artillery was also marked by age, and by quantity as well; the Division possessed only sixty guns, many of which were designed for mountains, not level steppe. There were not enough machine-guns or anti-tank guns, and the Division's water supply was inadequate.

The 23rd Division had been concentrated, at Hailar, only since November 1938. The appalling cold winter had made training difficult for the warm-blooded men of Kyushu above company or even platoon level. All these deficiencies led to low regard elsewhere in the IJA for the potential of Komatsubara's unit, seen as no more than moderate, comparable with garrison troops. Although the men were well disciplined, General Ueda did not expect from it more than a defensive role against any putative Russian attacks, partly because of the lack in Hailar of brothels and other centres of adult entertainment. (If the Japanese were planning any act of aggression, it does not seem to have been imminent.) And the Kwantung Army believed that its other commitments, on the eastern frontier and internally, prevented the Division's immediate reinforcement. Komatsubara thought that his men needed at least another year before they could be called battle-worthy.

In order to speed up any reinforcements that *might* eventually be required, and to aid troop concentrations, the Japanese added rail track and other facilities on the sector from Harbin via Angangchi and Tsitsihar to Divisional HQ at Hailar, the old Chinese Eastern Railway. According to Marshal Zhukov's American biographer, Otto Chaney, they had also built a railway line 'one or two miles away from the eastern Mongolian border' and parallel to it. The eastern Mongolian border was presumably not that along the Khalkin Gol river line claimed by the Japanese authorities, but the eastern edge of the 'disputed' zone, fifteen miles or so from the river. In that case, this was the railway that ran from Hsinking (Kwantung Army HQ) via Paichengtzu or Taoan and Wuchakon to Arshaan, and Handagai south-east to north-west through the Hsingan mountains, driven to bring the IJA as close as possible to the Soviet positions and, in a curious phrase, 'to Chita' itself. The ultimate destination, not then attained, was Kanchuerhmiao.

These puny, residual railways were but tokens of those planned but never begun, in company with giant stockpiles and motor-roads, to support the Japanese invasion of Russia (Hachi-Go 8), under IJA discussion in 1939 for implementation in 1943, which neither the lessons of Nomonhan nor the desperate condition of the Japanese economy could permit in the event.

Komatsubara's motives for despatching Azuma to the front had not been clear to Colonel Inada of the General Staff, nor really to Colonel Ouchi, Chief of Staff, who, rather, had unsuccessfully sought from Hsinking improvements in weaponry and training before thinking of conflict. Nor was the General's decision to withdraw Azuma's task force any more explicable unless he believed that it had dealt such a wallop to the Russo-Mongolian forces that the frontier question of the east bank of the Kalha had been settled. He was, of course, also aware of the Kwantung Army's wish that military attention should be focused on China, not on Central Asia, a demand which he understood, and of the urgent need for further training of his Division in all arms. He was, at the same time, not complacent about the actual conduct of the encounter, in particular intelligence, air–ground communications, and reconnaissance.

Soviet and Mongol troops were then reported on the east bank in the disputed zone at Balshagal and Noro heights, plus infantry, armour and transport at battalion strength near Tamsag Bulag on the west bank, by a variety of sources, *de visu* agents, aerial observation, a captured Soviet NCO. Soviet units under the mutual-assistance pact of 1936 started to move troops up to the eastern frontier of Mongolia. A Russian mechanised battalion with five hundred men, trucks, anti-tank guns and some armour was sighted at Tamsag Bulag, by which time Komatsubara had already responded to very minor infringements at Noro. The General set out to swat a fly while discounting the swarm of hornets in the neighbourhood. He really seems to have been an impulsive man, and a rather amateurish soldier.

On 22 May, 23rd Division despatched the second expedition, this time led by Colonel Yamagata Takemitsu, commanding the 64th Infantry Regiment. This force included Azuma's reconnaissance regiment (cavalry and armour) of about two hundred men, an infantry battalion of eight hundred men, seven artillery weapons and about five hundred Bargut cavalry, between two thousand and two thousand five hundred men in all. Its aim was to clear the disputed zone east of the river but, as has been said, apparently without much regard to the army 'in being' across the Halha. Firebrand Tsuji remarked: 'Leadership is not scientific; on the battlefield sentiment overrules reason.'

The Russo-Mongols had meanwhile strengthened their contingents at Noro and Balshagal to two hundred men apiece and had built bridges across the Khalkin Gol. Mechanised Soviet rifle and machine-gun units from the 11th Tank

Brigade with a company of armoured cars were stationed on the left bank southwest of the Halha–Holsten confluence, with the Soviet 149th Mechanised Infantry Regiment (26 Division) arriving to the northwest on 28 May. Four 122 mm and four 76 mm guns were eventually sited to the west and southwest of Balshagal, while two regiments of the Mongolian 6th Cavalry Division were to be found southwest of Nomonhan on 29 May. Three companies of Soviet engineers, riflemen and motorised infantry were also on the east (right) bank, as well as near Noro on the Holsten southwest of two enemy regiments from the 7th and 8th Manchukuoan Cavalry. The Russian strength at this time near the river-bank battle-fields has been put at seven hundred infantry, two hundred and sixty cavalry soldiers, forty armoured cars, sixty machine-guns, twenty heavy and anti-tank guns, with supporting gunners, sappers and 'tankists'.

This body was superior in armour and artillery to the Japanese Yamagata force which held between six and eight armoured cars and eighteen artillery pieces. It was numerically much inferior to the initial four or five hundred Japanese and Manchukuoan cavalry and sixteen hundred drivers and infantrymen, the latter not, however, well equipped in comparison with their Communist opponents. The Japanese, furthermore, because of their lack of inter-unit training, were unco-ordinated, short on cohesion, disastrously deficient in the anti-tank, armour and artillery arms mentioned, certainly also weak in reconnaissance and intelligence. Yamagata and his officers also grossly underestimated Soviet and Mongolian qualities, in particular determination, and overestimated the adverse effect of the purges on fighting ability. They would live to regret this contempt.

Meanwhile, five Soviet aircraft were shot down over Nomonhan between 20 and 22 May and Japanese aircraft attacked the 7th Border Guard post on the west bank: a total of eleven Soviet–Mongol fighters and one scout were destroyed between 25 and 27 May. Before these dogfights, the Kwantung Army had responded to a recommendation by Colonel Ouchi for restraint by sending two more fighter squadrons to Komat-subara as defence against increased Soviet aircraft at Tamsag Bulag and in reconnaissance over the disputed zone.

Nevertheless, Komatsubara told Yamagata to wait at Kanchuerhimiao, a trading centre with a Lamaist monastery, until the Russo–Mongolians had secured a deep intrusion into Manchukuo and there by provided a *casus belli* for the Kwantung Army. There was no such penetration. Although Ueda had assured the throne that there was no intention to expand the incident, it is therefore difficult to see, other than alarm at a presumed Soviet offensive, or an arrogant wish to chastise presumption, why Komatsubara on 26 May should have authorised Yamagata to mount an offensive in the politically sensitive disputed zone east of the Khalkin Gol, except as a pre-emptive strike. It seems today politically questionable and militarily inept, and not with hindsight alone. East of Lake Baikal in Siberia, after all, the Soviets were now believed to have between twenty and thirty infantry divisions, five to seven cavalry divisions, six to eight mechanised armoured brigades numbering two thousand five hundred tanks, and two thousand five hundred aircraft. Seven Mongolian cavalry divisions, added to these units, caused the Japanese to be outnumbered by three to one in ground forces and two to one in the air. It was surely clear that Japan's eight divisions in Manchukuo, short of arms and ammunition, were not enough, particularly when the Manchurian Cavalry was included.

On 22 or 23 May, the reconnaissance platoon of the 11th Tank Brigade, which had been in the Hamardaba Mountains since 18 May, had crossed the river and engaged the Japanese on the east bank of the Halha, being surrounded and forced to withdraw into Mongolia on 23 May. On 26 May, the commanding officer, Major Bykov, put two mechanised rifle companies back across the river with a number of armoured cars, a battery of 45 mm guns, his command post and two regiments of the 6th Mongolian Cavalry to positions in the disputed zone, still definable as Komatsubara's 'deep enemy inroad'. But the divisional commander's orders to

Yamagata had been prepared by the early morning of 27 May for execution during dawn the following day.

Komatsubara's plan was one of encirclement from several starting points. The reconnaissance unit under Azuma at Amukulang was told to move from north of Lake Holsten to take the confluence of that river with the Halha, thus cutting off an enemy whom Japanese *hubris* assumed would be in shame-faced retreat. Major Fukumura's 3rd Infantry Battalion of eight hundred men would attack southwards from Lake Manzute. A platoon (Asada) from 4 Company would move westwards to seize a river crossing north of the confluence, and the 10th and 11th Infantry Companies (Goto and Kawabata) would envelop and seal the panicked foe's retreat at four other crossings. A platoon under the gunner Tachikawa was given a roving brief to co-operate with Bargut troops in attacking Russian troops within the battle zone. The front of nearly twenty miles was too extended for troops without artillery or other serious inter-unit training.

All these operations would be supported by the Japanese Air Force and, in the event, the JAF scored brilliant and devastating success. But once the east bank had been cleared, Yamagata's detachment was to fall back on Nomonhan, i.e. there was to be no hot pursuit into the MPR across the dunes, plains and little hills with their low shrub and shrub pine cover. On summer nights, protected against horse flies and mosquitoes only by nets, the men would have been happy to obey.

By 05.30 on 28 May Colonel Azuma's reconnaissance regiment had moved their light armour and cavalry skilfully through the chilly dark of the May night over both desert and hilly terrain to within one mile of their target bridge across the Halha river. Exhilarated by his earlier victory against an almost non-existent foe, Azuma vaingloriously assumed himself to be pursuing a beaten and flying enemy, with his friends from 10th Infantry Company visible on a rise to the north and Colonel Yamagata pelting down to meet him.

But he could not make wireless contact, then or ever,

with Yamagata. His own unit, surprised and entirely surrounded in the blackness and half-light, came suddenly under violent and sustained fire from mortars, anti-tank guns and howitzers. Harassed by infantry and Mongolian mounted cavalry, his own cavalry was unhorsed and scrabbling for cover in the sand. Although they captured a Soviet tank, the regiment by noon had already lost an officer and ten men. The boards inserted to support the sandy sides of hastily dug trenches repeatedly collapsed, exposing the men to yet more shelling. (This was not the soil in which the Japanese Army was later to build those bunkers which, in Burma and the Pacific, became almost impregnable.) On this day also, Lieutenant Semënov captured a map from Azuma's men and Russian self-propelled guns knocked out two Japanese armoured cars protecting the Reconnaissance Regiment.

Elsewhere in that early morning, an important unit under Major Fukumura (Group 1, 3rd Infantry Battalion) of Yamagata's detachment became separated among the dunes from the rest of the force. One of Fukumura's platoons was badly knocked about by one hundred Mongolian cavalrymen. Only five men escaped, who later fortuitously joined Azuma. Another platoon surprised a Mongolian detachment at breakfast, killing sixty of them as they ate. Japanese troops also destroyed two Soviet armoured cars in an otherwise inconclusive action. Twelve Company (Tashiro) could not navigate the treacherous mixed dry and wet soil near the Halha, but 4 Company's guns under Someya put six armoured cars out of business, drove off a hundred enemy cavalry and established a command post further east. Ten Company at 08.00 had freed itself from the dunes and, moving down the Halha, immobilised four armoured cars and two tanks, killing thirty Russians; Yamagata's Group 2 horribly ambushed a hundred and fifty Soviet Buriat Mongols singing military ditties on the march, and slaughtered eighty of them at point-blank range over open sights, taking two prisoners. At 17.00, the 'lost' Fukumura, having at last made radio contact with Yamagata, was ordered to return to the main force.

On the evening of 28 May, Yamagata at last declared his own position three miles north of the beleaguered Azuma regiment at the junction of the Halha and Holsten. Signal wire, which unfortunately could not be brought to Azuma, was at least laid out to Fukumura's 3rd Battalion. Tashiro's 12 Company and Sato's platoon from 4 Company captured a good deal of equipment in a fight with Mongolian cavalry and Russian armour. Although 11 Company's trucks bogged down near the river, they claimed to have killed a hundred of the assembled enemy, in counter-attacks against fast Russian armoured cars and Mongol horsemen. Repeated attempts, however, throughout that day and until dawn on 29 May, to force rifle and machine-gun ammunition through to Azuma were unsuccessful; three separate team failures, one virtually annihilated, another temporarily lost in unknown terrain, and Nakano's platoon from 4 Company fighting to the last man against enveloping Russians. The Azuma unit was thus finally trapped, waging a battle about which Yamagata had meanwhile completely changed his mind, without being able to advise Azuma.

For Yamagata, apart from the division of his force after Fukumura's delay in the dunes, had decided to switch his attack from the confluence to the enemy concentration at Height 733. Nor could he at first get in touch with Tachikawa's unit or 11 Company. All he knew, and that not until daybreak on 29 May, was that Azuma's reconnaissance regiment was in desperate trouble. Azuma himself and his company commanders had been, at that stage incorrectly, reported dead and inaccessible until darkness fell. Tachikawa and Kawabata (11 Company) then rejoined Yamagata's HQ but, although reassuring messages about Azuma were later received, the Soviets then counter-attacked with artillery and armour on battalion scale against the detachment. Russian 76 mm guns had, of course, been targeting Azuma from the right bank since 28 May, while Major Bykov's 1 Company, after a pullback by his 2 and 3 Companies, energetically counter-attacked, driving the Japanese back by 29 May, in front of Bykov and the Mongolians. The Japanese dead were estimated at four hundred, with many more wounded. On the evening of 28 May, a subsequent Hero of the Soviet Union Major I. M. Remizov, led the 149th Regiment of the 36th Infantry Division out of Tamsag Bulag and into battle, supported by two artillery battalions.

General Komatsubara in Hailar was under the mistaken impression that the battle was going according to plan, that early Russo-Mongol casualties and equipment losses were relatively high, that 'cleaning up' was all that was left to do. At 12.30 on 29 May, he therefore ordered Colonel Yamagata to concentrate troops at Kanchuerhmiao and return to Hailar. The latter's accessible effective strength, the rest having been dispersed all over the battlefield, consisted of only a machine-gun platoon, two rifle squads and twenty exhausted signalmen; he believed, furthermore, that a Russian attack that night would result in the liquidation of his headquarters and the loss of the colours. He told the divisional commander that he intended 'to deal the enemy one more blow on 29–30 May'. (It was then that the better news had come from Azuma, and that Tachikawa and Kawabata had rejoined the HQ.) But on 29 May, the GOC, told Yamagata that 23 Division was sending reinforcements and air cover. Yamagata should, after all, now disengage. That Colonel, after talking to Fukumura, went back to his headquarters, where he then heard from the last few survivors that Azuma really was dead, his unit destroyed.

What *had* actually occurred at the confluence since early morning on 28 May? Azuma's men, completely surrounded by superior forces, had been under continual bombardment with simultaneous cavalry and infantry attack from the higher western bank. After six hours, when non-combatants and even the wounded had also had to engage hand-to-hand, no one from Yamagata's main detachment had been seen. Ten Company had mostly pulled back from the nearby rise. No Japanese guns had opened fire at Russo-Mongol troops near the junction. Water was running very short. The blowing sand blocked rifles and machine-guns. No messengers had got back from missions to Yamagata. Radio contact had still not been made. There had not even been time to eat or look after the horses. Captain Kanetake, Azuma's adjutant, braving a hail of bullets found 9 Company at Balshagal with 3 Battalion HQ and the colours of the 64th Regiment. These soldiers would not move, pleading orders. He was still unable, in search of supplies and instructions, to find the force commander.

Late that night, a five-hundred-man Soviet infantry and tank attack under blinding searchlights, preceded by a gun and mortar barrage, fell upon the reduced reconnaissance unit in their trenches. The Azuma regiment, led by their officers, charged into the grenade-throwing mass, capturing armoured cars and trucks but losing yet more men, including their Colonel's two company commanders. Thirty Bargut cavalrymen were also missing; Azuma had now lost twenty killed and seventy wounded. But he refused to withdraw, giving an inspiring address in which he called for defence to the death, appealing to his unit's reunion at the Yasukuni Shrine to the dead after all was ended.

At 03.00, the reconnaissance regiment fought off yet another attack, this time by three or four hundred Russian soldiers, followed by another major artillery barrage from all quarters, almost collapsing the light and precarious trenches, threatening immolation alive. Azuma's car blew up in this hideous din, flinging blazing gasoline over ammunition and the other vehicles, a macabre Brock's Benefit of crimson and golden fire and sparks in the foul and smoke-clotted night.

Six hundred men of the 149th Infantry Regiment and Bykov's rifle troops from the 11th Tank Brigade, supported by tanks and artillery, now encircled the one hundred men still standing in the Azuma Regiment. That body tried to hold the enemy tanks already amongst them with bottles filled with gasoline and other pathetic devices, even hurling back the Russian grenades. Soviet armour retreated momentarily from the disintegrating Japanese bunker. Twenty-five Japanese soldiers survived. With the Russians only twenty yards away in the darkness, Azuma charged with the men who remained, himself mortally wounded in the gunfire. One wounded NCO staggered away, staunching his thirst with blood of his own wounds.

There is some evidence that Yamagata may not have been unaware of his subordinate's plight, and little evidence to explain why he did not try to save him. On 29 or 30 May the aggressive Major Tsuji attacked him personally and bitterly, condemning his 'lack of skill'. After a long discussion, the force commander sent the 3rd Battalion to see what could be done, to collect bodies, perhaps to rescue those still alive, to discover whether resistance was still possible. The business of recovering the bodies in the vile stink of the deserted battlefield continued for three nights, the poor charred and blackened bodies strapped on the backs of horses or carried on litters. Recovery, in the face of continued shelling and imminent attack by tanks and armoured cars, was still incomplete by dusk on 31 May.

On 30 May, Yamagata was again told by 23 Division that reinforcements were on the way. That evening, lorries, infantry, guns, possibly tanks, would be sent. Bombers would fly again. A rifle and machine-gun company, ten heavy guns with inadequate range for the purpose, plus about three hundred men under Major Baba Susumu of 2 Battalion, 71 Infantry Regiment, reported to Colonel Yamagata that evening. Yamagata's strengthened detachment drove off reconnaissance probes by Soviet armoured cars. The accompanying Russian artillery bombardment did not last long. On 31 May, Yamagata was ordered to bring his detachment back to Hailar which, after a succession of Japanese air raids on Soviet armour and guns across the river, he managed to do. The Japanese did not launch a last attack by Fukumura's 3rd and Baba's 2nd Infantry Battalions across the river because, knowing that they were about to depart, their 'aggressive spirit was dampened'. A Japanese artillery bombardment to cover withdrawal scarcely reached the targets on the west bank and, after a final recovery of bodies from Azuma's regiment,

Yamagata left Balshagal for Hailar. Before reaching divisional HQ they were addressed and praised by General Komatsubara. The GOC prayed over Azuma's ashes, warning the men that there would be more conflict to come.

The most significant Japanese 'victories', perhaps the only ones, were those in the air by the existing bombers and fighters of 24 Air Group around 28 May and by the two additional fighter squadrons under 12 Air Brigade reinforcing them. Although Tass reported that only nine Soviet aircraft had been destroyed on the ground at airfields within the Mongolian border, the total number of Russo-Mongol planes claimed on 2 June and by the JAF was sixty-two, against one Japanese aircraft shot down. The Japanese had little or no respect for the tactics, skill and training of Soviet pilots, and still less for the Mongols. They also believed at that time that the construction and technology of Soviet aircraft needed a lot more work which, thanks to the Tupolev and Ilyushin generation, it certainly achieved in due time.

To make assurance doubly sure, three more bomber squadrons at Tsitsihar were assigned to the 23rd Division. The Kwantung Army was also allocated the 1st Fighter troop. No other reinforcements, except air force mobile repair teams and – significantly – caissons and other river-crossing equipment were sought.

In their post-mortem on the battle, the Soviets concentrated on 149 Regiment's excessive original distance behind the front, and on the unprofessional disposition of the Mongolian cavalry on the right bank, permitting an early partial Japanese encirclement. Apart from the aircraft, the Russo-Mongolian forces were estimated to have lost, chiefly against Azuma at the confluence, and against Yamagata's later drive south, about four hundred and fifty dead, twenty tanks and armoured cars, and ten artillery pieces. These losses were from a unit of three hundred Mongolian cavalry from 6th Cavalry Division, from Major Bykov's mechanised rifle and machine-gun battalion of 11 Tank Brigade and, much later, from Remizov's 149 Regiment. Bykov's battalion was in three motorised companies totalling five hundred men, with ten tanks, fifteen (reconnaissance) armoured cars, a battery each of 76 mm guns and 45 mm anti-tank guns and engineers. The guns and the tanks were responsible for most of the three hundred or so missing, wounded and dead Japanese, the weight of whose casualties, one hundred and forty out of two hundred and twenty, fell on Colonel Azuma's reconnaissance regiment.

There were explanations for the Soviet defeat of 23 Division's planned annihilation of the Mongolian People's Revolutionary Army. The first was that Japanese Intelligence and prescience were so feeble that none of the staff, whether in Kwantung Army at Hsinking or in 23 Division at Hailar, seemed to have realised that the Russians would come so heavily to the help of the Mongolian 6th Cavalry. Very few details, furthermore, were known of the actual strength of the entire Mongol forces in the immediate area. Co-ordination among the various Japanese arms – infantry, tankettes (useless anyway except for reconnaissance) and cavalry – was quite inadequate. Kwantung Army also criticised Katsumbara for failing to insist on the anti-tank and artillery guns which might have saved Azuma from the superior ground to the west. Motor transport, as opposed to horse-drawn, was badly lacking, water, as has been said, also short. Wireless communication was almost non-existent, whether between units or to Hailar. Hygiene and supply, as always with the old IJA, were neglected. Yamagata was attacked 'in the messes', perhaps unfairly because he does seem to have gone forward earlier to look at the confluence, for Azuma's failure to break through and the regiment's consequent grisly fate.

Not many of these errors and omissions were corrected before the next struggle began.

# 10
# General Komatsubara Crosses the River

On 2 June, Soviet forces were once again visible on the eastern bank of the Halha – precisely that zone of dispute claimed as Mongolia by the MPR and USSR, and as Manchukuo by the Barguts and Japanese – as well as on the west bank of the river. This presence, and intercepted Soviet requests for reinforcement, were regarded by the Japanese as preparations for a Russo-Mongol counter-attack under Mongol 'cover'.

In Moscow that same day, Defence Commissioner Voroshilov sent for Georgii Zhukov, who had served under him in the 1920s with Budenny and Timoshenko. Zhukov was now deputy commander in Byelorussia and a cavalry leader with no experience in the Far East. This officer, a commander possessing some of Field Marshal Montgomery's attributes, in particular the accumulation of material preponderance, was later to become head of the Kiev military district, Chief of the General Staff, defender of Leningrad, Moscow and Stalingrad, victor over German Army Groups South and Central, Marshal, Russian victor of Berlin, conqueror of Germany, with subsequent post-war promotion and demotion at Stalin's whim, Defence Minister under Khrushchev before final dismissal for Bonapartism. On this occasion, in 1939, Voroshilov sent him by air to Mongolia via Chita, to report on the position and make recommendations for the future conduct of operations.

Zhukov, large, beefy and sweating in his cavalry top-boots and coarse field uniform, arrived on 5 June in the great dry heat of Tamsag Bulag, its three long clay buildings like barns, hundreds of yurts (*gers*) of all sizes. He discovered at once that 57 Corps HQ was about a hundred miles behind the lines, and that nothing had been done to build airstrips or lay communication cable between Tamsag and the river. No one from the staff, except Commissar Nikishev, had even visited the battle zone and, although a command post was planned, Corps Commander Feklenko excused himself from going forward with Zhukov on the grounds that he was 'expecting a telephone call'.

General Zhukov himself then went to the front with Nikishev by air over the yellow-green steppe, goats, sheep and duck scattering below; he reported later that Corps Headquarters was much too far from the battle, and that reconnaissance had feebly interpreted the earlier Japanese 'withdrawal' as an 'advance'. The enemy, however, in his opinion, intended to continue its attacks on the Russians and Mongols. He therefore proposed continued occupation of the east bank and a counter-attack based on the MPR. He advised, for that purpose, reinforcements to include an (incomplete) motorised rifle division, an extra Mongolian cavalry division, one hundred fighter aircraft under such Heroes of the Soviet Union as Smushkevich, later executed, who had fought in Spain, three mechanised brigades; a tank brigade; heavy artillery. Moscow agreed to these substantial commitments, later to become Zhukov's trademark, and also replaced Feklenko as Corps Commander by Zhukov. Feklenko, unlike more apparently deserving officers such as Shtern and Smushkevich, survived and rose to the rank of Army Commander during the Great Patriotic War.

Rumours of reinforcement, and of a Russo-Mongol attack from the right bank, which it was both Tokio's and Hsinking's chief aim to defeat, had also reached Japanese Intelligence. But the IJA did not believe the Russians wanted all-out war. The Russians, in the light of Kwantung Army orders for river-crossing equipment, were, however, not so sure about the Japanese. The latter, nevertheless, claimed that they did not want to weaken Japanese strength in China, even though the Russians were superior to them in Manchuria by a factor of three to one. General Komatsubara's desire for revenge did not discount this argument. But fire-eating Tsuji *wanted* confrontation with Russia, *inter alia* in order to 'frighten'

Britain over the concurrent negotiations with Tokio over the British presence in Tientsin.

The Soviet mechanised build-up proceeded on both banks of the Halha, in day-time temperatures of over 100°F. While several unprovoked sorties by Soviet bombers into Manchuria caused few Bargut casualties, they did destroy stores and gasoline in an area which they, of course, claimed as 'Mongolia'.

Tsuji's arguments now therefore persuaded the staff to prepare an operational plan against Outer Mongolia, ostensibly in order to protect the frontier without escalation to major war. The concept, hopelessly flawed, depended on flank attacks by the crack 7th Division, supported by 23 Division. With hindsight, had Isogai, the Kwantung Army chief of staff, exercised the courage of his convictions, Nomonhan might not have taken place. But the elderly Army Commander, Ueda, later did no more than rejig the plan, giving formal command to the beaten but tearfully grateful Komatsubara and his weak, inexperienced 23 Division, a reduced 7th Division task force attached. Seventy tanks, four hundred lorries, twenty-four AA guns, one hundred anti-tank guns, thirteen infantry battalions and five engineer companies were to take part. One hundred and eighty aircraft in eight fighter, seven bomber and two reconnaissance squadrons were on the establishment. Air attack across the frontier against Mongolian airfields was not, however, then approved by the Army General Staff or, even, Hsinking HQ.

These Kwantung Army intentions were opposed in Tokio by an AGS expert on the Soviet Army on the grounds of probable escalation thereafter. He was the only dissident; his views were rejected. As for 23 Division, their incompetent intelligence staff believed that the enemy, at least at Nomonhan itself, consisted of Mongols only, one thousand of them, with a few vehicles and guns. The Kwantung Army staff rudely brushed aside AGS and North China Area Army offers of five Japanese divisions out of China. 'If you have so many spares,' said arrogant Tsuji, 'take care of your own campaign against the Chinese bandits.'

The head of ordnance in 23 Division shot himself dead, because he knew how inadequate was the Division's equipment. Another officer, who had studied the Soviet Army and who now commanded the 26th Regiment of 7th Division, was horrified at this unit's gross under-equipment in the light of the known strengths of the new Soviet Army. Wheeled transport for 23 Division was so lacking that some regiments marched through the sand towards battle under the terrible continental sun for fifteen hours a day, over four to six days, carrying eighty-pound packs. These were not good indicators for the coming conflict against Zhukov's vast and unknown cohorts.

On 22 June, although, as Alvin Coox confirms, the two sides' claims were irreconcilable, numbers of Soviet and Japanese aircraft were destroyed in the air during dogfights on both sides of the river. The Russians claimed to have shot down thirty out of a hundred and twenty JAF aircraft, although the Japanese alleged that only two of their fighter squadrons, who nevertheless said they had destroyed forty-nine Soviet aircraft, were then airborne. But whatever the numbers, JAF strength was diminishing relative to the Russian plenitude, thereby jeopardising the planned IJA ground offensive. At this stage, General Giga, commanding 2nd Air Division, was still not permitted to attack Russian air power at source on the Mongolian air bases. Convinced that the USSR did not seek major war with Japan, he sought to persuade General Ueda to allow him to destroy enemy aircraft, less than rigorously calcu-lated as between one and two hundred, on the ground at Madat, Bain Tumen and Tamsag Bulag.

Operations Order A1 embodying this permission, although restricted to a few officers and not submitted to the Army General Staff for fear that Tokio would forbid it, in fact rapidly became known to the AGS. Although the air offensive was intended as part of the ground attack of which IGHQ was aware, and which it regarded only as a demonstration in force,

Tokio feared a disporportionate Russian reaction to the bombing of their ally's territory. In response, therefore, the AGS reiterated the need to localise the 'Nomonhan incident', in particular not to spread or escalate it by aerial attack on the MPR itself. It is possible that these comments, not incidentally orders, were not even seen by Ueda or his indecisive chief of staff, Isogai, but only by their 'Young Turks', including Tsuji, in the operations section, who had now estimated Soviet air strength at four fighter, two reconnaissance and one bomber unit, two or three hundred aircraft, although one pilot had 'heard a figure of five hundred'. The AGS's emissary, Colonel Arisue, sent to implement Tokio's 'comments' did not arrive in Hsinking until the afternoon of 27 June, by which time Giga's raid had already taken place.

At all events, the extraordinary fact is that a signal from Tsuji, unauthorised by army commander or chief of staff, ordered the all too willing commander of 2nd Air Division to launch an offensive consisting of the bombing of Russo-Mongolian air bases on the territory of the MPR, a sovereign state. Any Japanese claims on territory applied only to the river and the disputed zone eastward. Tamsag Bulag and the other bases were all on the west bank. There could be no Japanese 'legalistic' excuse or debate over the location of frontiers.

Further dogfights had taken place between 22 and 26 June with loss to both air forces, the Russians claiming sixty-four Japanese kills, but the main Japanese air attack into Mongolia was on 27 June, employing over fifty bombers and eighty fighters. Pilots then reported that the bases contained remarkably few fixed facilities, while most Russian aircraft had scrambled after the first bombing run. In the words of Tsuji, always flat-out to participate in anything going, and a Sergeant Kira, the Russians took off like 'baby fish jumping out of the water', or 'black dots rising like ants through the early mist'. One hundred and fifty were destroyed or damaged, according to Colonel Matsumara, in disorganised panic, 'as easily as twisting an infant's hand', whether airborne or on the ground. The Soviet command would only admit some thirty losses, and duplication as usual undoubtedly occurred. (Bombing of the largely insignificant installations was inaccurate and, according to the pilots, mostly 'useless'.) Zhukov instantly grasped the strategic purpose of the raid but, as he was aware of incoming Soviet reinforcements, his dubious boast of improved Soviet and Mongol performance could be more readily understood.

Emperor Hirohito himself, Changkufeng echoing in his memory, spoke angrily of punishment for the continued arrogance of Ueda and his Kwantung Army. The AGS ordered cancellation of further air offensives, prompting the enraged Tsuji, without superior authority, to demand autonomy for the Kwantung Army in 'trivial' border matters. The AGS, while furious at Tsuji's language, did not dismiss him. Violent command polemics, nevertheless, followed, culminating in IGHQ directives forbidding air attacks on enemy bases in USSR or MPR and restricting action to the border region between Manchukuo and Outer Mongolia, east of Lake Buir. The air raids into Mongolia had exceeded, so continued Tokio, the Kwantung Army's 'defensive mission'. Should similar action ever again be contemplated, Imperial authority was obligatory, to be sought by the AGS. Henceforward, in Tokio, Palace and Executive would alike seek a border 'settlement', or so it was then maintained.

But, of course, the die was already cast and in those baking, waterless wastes, hundreds of Japanese trucks and thirsty horses, and some fifteen thousand increasingly tired men, had already set off more or less keenly on the long arid march from Hailar to Chianchunmiao, heavily burdened. The Russians first met them, the spearhead of General Kobayashi's West Bank 71 and 72 Infantry Regiment units, between 22 and 24 June, in that village, infantry, artillery and armour taking over at night when the AFVs withdrew to refuel. Some Russian armour was knocked out at short (half-a-mile) range by the guns and, as Tukhachevski's joint infantry–armoured doctrine was not followed, significant Russian gains were not made.

The Soviet left on 25 June was at Bain Tsagaan Obo (Fine White Cairn) on the Hara Heights. (These Heights were in fact no more than 'raised pancakes with diameters of three kilometres . . . like sandy beaches with weeds as thin as joss sticks overlying the dry surface soil'.) This cairn was on the west bank of the Halha, the Russian 149 Mechanised Infantry and 9 Brigade laagered by 2 July on the east bank near Balshagal, while the Soviet right wing was to the south at Sambur Cairn on the Hamardaba Heights. One Russian bridge was just below the Holsten, a second northward at the Halha–Holsten confluence and the third near the Hara Heights. Up to one thousand Soviet vehicles were observed east and west of the river in the probable battle area after 20 June, but there was absolute stillness, no activity at all, in the air bases recently assaulted by the JAF. The large Soviet presence, however, at Chiangchunmiao, indisputably Manchukuo territory, indicated to General Komatsubara that his mission to destroy the enemy in the area 'permitted' him to carry the ground fighting to the west bank of the Halha, into Mongolia itself.

Curious reports were received on 29 June of a general Soviet withdrawal to the west of the river. But the Japanese had now decided on an operation to hold and destroy their enemy on the right bank, while despatching across the river Kobayashi's infantry in five battalions, from 71 and 72 Regiments, then the artillery, engineers (23rd Engineer Regiment), three battalions of the 26 Regiment of 7 Division, the tanks and, lastly, the full remaining strength of 23 Division. Crossings would begin on 1 July and be completed on 3 July. By this time, Japanese reconnaissance units operating with difficulty under potential observation from Russian and Mongol troops on the higher western ground, had established that, after rain, the Halha had widened to up to one hundred yards, with a depth not easily navigable by man or beast. In some places, also, neither horses nor soldiers could handle steep river banks or, particularly below the Holsten, extensive bogs and swamps. Unlike Russian underwater bridges, ancient Japanese bridging equipment could not deal with a river width of eighty yards, or handle heavy loads over widths of fifty yards. Their bridges, furthermore, were only two and a half yards wide.

On 1 July, a Soviet contingent of three hundred men with armour and artillery attacked the Japanese columns advancing westward from Hailar through the sand dunes. After the latter had destroyed two or three tanks, the Russians withdrew, leaving light casualties on both sides. On 2 July, a more serious Soviet assault employing infantry, machine-guns, artillery and armour killed over twenty and wounded fifty men in 3 Company of 72 Regiment. The battalion commander, Major Nishikawa, tried ineffectively to commit suicide by standing up in front of the Russian guns and pushing back his tin hat.

Komatsubara, despite his experts' forebodings about bridging equipment and despite unjustified fears concerning enemy foxholes on the left bank, decided to cross the water between Fui and Hara Heights at 17.00 on 2 July, thereafter to move south at dawn on 3 July on the west bank towards the confluence. A tremendous electric storm and topographical errors, such as a launch onto a pond or small lake instead of the river, badly slowed down the crossing. To avoid losing surprise, postponement was not acceptable. Two battalions of foot soldiers from 71 and 72 Regiments slid down embankments 'the height of a tall building', often into bog, thence, from 03.00 on 3 July, to be sculled and poled by boat and pontoon, fifteen men and light artillery to each craft. Sun was up by 05.00 when the eighty-yard bridge, whose erection had already begun on the east bank, was started, also in broad daylight, on the enemy-held west bank without any friendly cover at all. The bridge components were extremely old, almost from the war of 1904–5, and lacked enough spare pontoons. The gravel riverbed and the current militated against a solid foundation, certainly one which would take armour or even horses. That it functioned at all was a tribute to the Emperor's engineers.

Across this narrow, inadequate structure nearly two hundred trucks had now to pass, preceded by divisional HQ and Kobayashi's last battalion, then followed by Sumi's 26

Infantry Regiment, the whole lot bunched up 'like flies blackening food'. No beach masters nor traffic controllers were present. Priorities had to be negotiated in resentful chaos and disorder. Only one truck could be permitted to cross the bridge at a time and, then, an engineer ruled that each had to be unloaded and the guns dismantled, before the vehicle could proceed. Komatsubara, now aware that night would fall before the last two of Sumi's three 26 Regiment battalions could get over, ordered that those would then have to fight in unmotorised mode under Kobayashi and not with their 1st battalion which was safely across.

It is remarkable that the *only* Russian sighting of this shambles was by Colonel Afonin, a Soviet adviser with the MPRA. He had watched Japanese infantry rout Mongolian troops, the 6th MPR, before dawn on 3 July; and then hurried to report to General Zhukov without, however, absorbing the full potential of the inadequate Japanese bridges. The 6th MPR Cavalry, the Japanese having by then seized with superior force the Bain Tsagaan mountain area, retreated to the north-west of the mountain.

The Russians, for their part, had already interpreted the JAF's earlier increased activity as the precursor of the second period of the Nomonhan incident. Zhukov read the Kwantung Army's objective as to surround and rout Soviet and Mongol troops east of the Halha river, to occupy the west bank and destroy Russian reserves, then to expand the bridgehead on the west banks ahead of further advances. He accordingly sent the 11th (reinforced) Tank Brigade under the brilliant Yakovlev to outflank Kobayashi from the north, supported by the 24th Motorised Regiment under Colonel I.I. Fedyuninski and an artillery battalion from the north-west. The 7th Armoured Brigade under Lesovoi, with an armoured battalion of the MPR 8th Cavalry Division moving up, would attack from the south. The 15th Mongol Cavalry Division covered the 9th Soviet Armoured Brigade on the east bank.

Zhukov himself, now Commander in Chief, arrived

at Bain Tsagaan early in the morning of 3 July with the
Military Council of his new 57th Special or Rifle Corps, later
1st Army Group. Heavy guns from 185 Artillery Regiment
opened fire on Japanese troops at the Heights, followed by
artillery from the east bank, and then the entire available
strength of the Soviet bombing force. The C in C claimed
that his forces approaching the mountain included only twelve
hundred infantry and fifty guns, against ten thousand Japanese
at Bain Tsagaan or Hara Heights with a hundred guns and
fifty AA guns. But he admitted that the 11th Tank Brigade
disposed of one hundred and fifty tanks, while the 7th
Armoured Brigade and the battalion from the 8th Mongol
Armoured Division had another hundred and fifty, with 45
mm guns. The Japanese immediately started to bomb their
enemy's armour in the treeless open. 'For hundreds of kilometres around, there was not even a bush in sight,' said Zhukov,
and Colonel Shishkin added that Mongolia proper at this point
was 'a flat and sandy plain, devoid of natural camouflage or
hiding places'.

Zhukov decided therefore that the main attack, led by
the armour of 11 Tank Brigade with maximum air support,
must therefore go in at once against the Japanese mass. The
decision was executed at his order at precisely 10.45 on 3 July
1939. Armour, aided by artillery and aircraft, was to form the
Soviet hammer until the reserves could arrive. 'Our trump
cards were the armoured detachments (including tanks camouflaged as *tochkas* or pillboxes) . . . and we decided to use them
immediately in order to destroy the Japanese troops that had
just crossed the river, not letting them entrench themselves
and organise anti-tank defence. It was impossible to delay a
counter-blow once the enemy saw the advance of our unshel-
tered tanks.'

The General had rapidly reorganised the chain of
command, improved Army Group communications, sharpened
and developed reconnaissance, finally combined armour, artillery and motorised infantry to go for the weaker
(Manchukuoan) units on the flanks. Encirclement was the

objective, conducted with the speed and brutality which later won the Great Patriotic War against Germany, isolating, dividing, breaking up, exterminating, Cannae over again.

# 11
# Sorge and Other Russian Spies

Richard Sorge, a German citizen born in 1896 to expatriate parents employed in the Baku oilfields, moved to Berlin in the Fatherland when he was two years old. He fought and was badly wounded as a German patriot in the Great War but, seduced by the October Revolution and sickened by the Great Betrayal, he joined the Communist Party in 1919 and was co-opted by the Comintern in 1923. In 1929, he was recruited into the Fourth Department of Soviet Military Intelligence, later known as the GRU, which posted him under the cover of a German journalist to Shanghai and, subsequently, to Tokio.

His original marriage having collapsed, the dark, moody and dangerously handsome Sorge had already begun a long series of drunken love affairs, including an extended romance with Agnes Smedley, champion of the 'colonial oppressed'.

Sorge, by 1939 probably the most important Soviet agent in Asia, had not only constructed a comprehensive espionage network among Japanese politicians, civil servants and soldiers, but had won the complete confidence, as a 'well-informed Nazi journalist', of General Eugen Ott, the ambassador of Germany, Japan's principal ally among the Western powers, with access to Japanese and German informants at the highest level. Sorge's reporting to Moscow, although sometimes constrained by local circumstance and, in the Kremlin, by disbelief and weak assessment, included the prediction of *Barbarossa*, the Nazi invasion of the USSR in 1941, and of Japan's intention after Nomonhan to forego plans to invade the USSR via Siberia in favour of Strike South against South-East Asia, Indochina, the Philippines, Indonesia, Malaya, Burma, Singapore and the British Borneo colonies. Stalin ignored the first of these *tuyaux*, but grasped the second with sufficient confidence to move units from the Soviet Far

East to defend Moscow, Stalingrad and Leningrad against the Western aggressor, a real contribution to Nazi defeat.

Sorge, in 1938, had already been able to obtain from Ott and clandestinely despatch to the GRU most of the Abwehr's interrogation in Tokio of the Soviet defector, General Lyushkov. He thus provided the Russians with German and Japanese estimates of Soviet morale, capacity, intention and weakness, even of potential Japanese armed action by the Kwantung Army along the borders of the USSR. In June 1939, furthermore, in response to the GRU's request for intelligence indicating that Tokio sought confrontation with the Russians, Sorge's agents reported to the Soviet High Command, and thus to Zhukov, the Kwantung Army's Order of Battle in Manchukuo with subsequent troop and material reinforcement. The same sources also recorded their conviction that the IJA would ensure that border clashes were localised. A Japanese prosecutor at Sorge's eventual trial reasonably claimed that this put the Russians 'at a great advantage in the battle of Nomonhan'.

But the Soviets could not believe thereafter that Japan's defeat there had caused Tokio to abandon all earlier plans to invade the USSR. The GRU therefore ordered Sorge to maintain intelligence gathering on Order of Battle (OB) and military industrial production. This requirement was still current in 1941 when Sorge, quoting Ott among others, continued to maintain that the Japanese Government had 'decided not to go to war against the USSR . . . and that Japanese attack against the USSR was out of the question'. In October 1941, nevertheless, he warned that Japanese aggression against the Soviet Union might not have been abandoned, only postponed to a date when the Wehrmacht could have suitably reduced Russia's ability to fight on two fronts.

But, at least on 3 July 1939 at the Halha river, Japanese capabilities and intentions were strategically transparent to the Russian Commander in Chief, General Georgii Zhukov, conscious that his career, even his life, depended on the next move against Japanese aggression in the Nomonhan incident. One detailed and disturbing indicator of Soviet pre-knowledge of Japanese intentions was the markers that the Russians had established as early as 30 June for artillery fire against the putative Japanese lines of advance. Another, although sourced not to Sorge, but to a Russian double agent in Harbin, was misinformation allegedly 'from Yakovlev to Zhukov' to the effect that, 'because of muddy conditions, Soviet units near the Halha–Hosten river confluence had withdrawn for repairs'. They had not, and the Yasuoka detachment were the losers from this piece of deception. Common sense would have shown that that sort of sand does not liquify when wet, but packs hard.

The Kwantung Army also included the Asano Brigade, formed from White Russian refugees, expanded from an original seven hundred men. The Brigade had been employed on scouting and reconnaissance duties under Komatsubara at Nomonhan in 1939 but, as the years wore on, particularly after the German invasion of Russia, the intake became less enthusiastic. *Émigrés* increasingly sought Soviet citizenship through the consulate at Harbin or suffered penetration from that office. Tokio's hopes for the Brigade as the military component of a future non-Communist Russian Government were correspondingly diluted.

In fact, the Brigade Commander, an Armenian called Gurgen Nagolen, may have been an officer or at least an agent of the GRU. The commander of the Hailar Asano detachment was shot by the Japanese as a Soviet spy in August 1945. The Japanese dissolved two Asano detachments as 'unreliable' in 1945, and it seems likely that many of the troops had secretly adopted Soviet allegiance by that time, if not sooner. When the origins and leadership – Semënov and Kalmykov, the paranoiac Count Ungern-Sternberg, Admiral Kolchak – of the first Cossack and Mongol Asano volunteers is recalled, the Japanese were fortunate to retain their loyalty for so long.

# 12
# Zhukov into Battle

The Soviet estimate of Japanese strength at Nomonhan by the end of June included the 23rd Infantry Division, part of the 7th Division, two tank regiments, two artillery regiments, AA and mountain gun detachments and several Bargut cavalry regiments. The entire formation was broken down into thirteen infantry battalions, one hundred anti-tank guns, nearly five hundred vehicles of which seventy were armoured, and two hundred aircraft. Opposing this force, the Japanese claimed to face three Soviet rifle divisions, five motorised and/or armoured regiments with eight hundred armoured vehicles, two Mongolian (MPRA) cavalry divisions.

At 11.00 on 3 July, only fifteen minutes after Zhukov's order to attack the enemy with armour, artillery and air power, five hundred Soviet tanks and armoured cars had been sighted on the horizon near Komatsu Heights. The Japanese observer was a Major Hamada from 72 Regiment. He stopped counting at that figure and thought that the armour might have totalled as many as a thousand vehicles.

Before this sighting, smaller encounters had taken place with light petrol-driven Soviet tanks, which overheated in direct sunlight and burned freely when hit. (They were later to be replaced.) In 71 Regiment's sector, 'dozens of chunks of iron from tanks etc lay strewn around the area and smoke from blazing armoured vehicles clouded the sun. It looked like a steel works at Yawata . . . or the factory district of Osaka . . .' These earlier confrontations waged on the Japanese side with grenades, Molotov cocktails, even sabres, as well as elderly field guns, had led to considerable Soviet losses, perhaps twelve out of fifty vehicles in an hour's fighting.

These successes around Hara Heights – 'the black pillars of smoke reminiscent of the sea battle off Tsushima' – were not repeated in this sector during the afternoon, when 'several scores of tanks attacked unexpectedly, causing chaos . . .' Horses stampeded, neighing, dragging gun carriages with them . . . morale fell extremely low . . . Japanese soldiers could be heard saying: 'terrible', 'sad', 'ghastly'. Although 72 Regiment fought stubbornly, it began to withdraw. Elsewhere 71 Regiment suffered casualties, retiring in a battlefield 'black with enemy armour' to foxholes from which only their heads could be seen, waiting for the night.

We have seen that, outside the Kobayashi task force, only Major Adachi's battalion of 26 Regiment was across the Halha by 3 July. This regiment's task was to advance with 71 and 72 Regiments, destroy enemy resources and pursue the fleeing Russians. When Colonel Sumi, slight, even weedy, bespectacled, but a good leader, commanding the regiment, without contact with Komatsubara at Division, saw from high ground at Bain Tsagaan on 3 July some one hundred and fifty tanks in the distance, he moved his other two battalions across the river from the right bank. As many troops as possible carried *Kaenbin* or Molotov cocktails, carbonated soft drink bottles now filled one third with sand and two thirds with petrol, tied with string to their waists. Each bottle had a 'wick' but as they were as difficult as cigarettes to light in the steppe winds, the men often simply threw the unlit bottle against the targets.

Then, as the bottles burst, the gasoline would spread and, in the heat of the day, the flames would burst upward from the base of the vehicle, 'like a burning newspaper', giving the additional impression that the very earth was on fire. As the fire reached the ammunition, bullets shot out in all directions. Escaping Soviet tankists, many of them burned, struggled through the hatches, to be shot down or bayoneted as they crawled and staggered toward their own lines. As many as seventy vehicles may have been destroyed in these hand-to-hand attacks but, without artillery support, 26 Regiment took two hundred casualties on this day alone. Meanwhile the tanks would smoulder on through the night, their cannon rounds exploding into the sky like a fireworks display.

But without artillery support, Sumi's infantry could not advance. Adachi had already been held up and was out of ammunition. The 2nd and 3rd Battalions disposed of one infantry gun, one box of ammunition and just thirty-six cocktails. Sumi, after sending forward to Adachi, with orders to fall back on the regiment, an NCO whose name he forgot to ask, prepared to 'change direction'. His motive was as much to protect the regimental colours as to escape from his, and especially Adachi's, exposed positions. Indeed, in preparation for a defence of the flimsy bridge, if not retreat across the river, he sent the colours over the water escorted by an entire company.

By dawn on 4 July, although Sumi saw troops from Colonel Okamoto's 71 Regiment falling back on his left, Adachi's first battalions still had not rejoined 26 Regiment. The nameless NCO had apparently not got through. In the meanwhile, Sumi persuaded a reluctant Okamoto to give him a wretched twelve more fire bottles, believing that when they were gone, his entire regiment was doomed to annihilation.

At the 1st Battalion's position, where at noon the heat was so fierce that to touch a steel helmet burned the hand, the NCO probably had reached Adachi, who was preparing to withdraw by the night of 3–4 July. In the darkness, however, the Major's split and isolated battalion was then jumped and overrun by a much larger Russian motorised attack, lights blazing. Adachi, sword drawn, with mainly headquarters troops, led his final charge against armour, 'a tiny black dot aboard a Russian tank, illumined by an enemy flare, grappling with tankists at the hatch', shot by tracer from another AFV, falling back and crushed to death under the tracks. Messages from his successor, Captain Kondo, extracted a few supplies from Sumi, which did not get through. At the battalion, there was nothing left to eat except dry biscuits and no water to drink. Six Japanese even mounted a bayonet charge against Russian machine-guns in order to get at the water coolant, though undrinkable, filled with chemicals, nauseating.

At night, mosquitoes swarmed incessantly around the unprotected men. Kondo prepared for a charge toward Lake Buir to die, if need be, in the sweet water, thirst assuaged, under enemy fire. (Meanwhile, the Japanese Air Force dropped ammunition for guns which the battalion no longer held.) Sumi, with over three hundred men under Major Kikuchi, reached Kondo before the latter could depart on his bizarre journey and, exploiting Soviet distaste for the bayonet, evacuated as many dead and wounded as he could. But since to remove one dead man required four soldiers, all some families later received was a lopped-off hand.

The 3rd battalion, the remnant of the 1st and 26 Regimental headquarters, reached the bridge in the early morning of 5 July. The 2nd Battalion was at the command post under Major Kawai. Major Kikuchi was mortally wounded during the pull-back, and this crack regiment of the 7th Division had thus lost two battalion commanders, one hundred and forty-one officers and men killed, including half the company commanders, and two hundred and seventy-eight wounded.

Tsuji, with hindsight, ascribed the relative fiasco of operations to failure to give the lead to 7 Division rather than to the inexperienced 23 Division, while admitting Intelligence's original underestimate of the joint Soviet–Mongol force. The Chief of Staff Operations on the Army General Staff was horrified by 23 Division's planning, especially the division's dispersal, including the arrival of the artillery on the left bank without its commander! Others referred to anti-tank and field artillery deficiencies, arrogance, overconfidence, shortage of trucks and radio communication equipment, weak direction at both Division and Kwantung Army level, not enough food or, especially, water.

Westbound, General Komatsubara had crossed the river impatiently on 3 July in his smart black Buick, when he was promptly bombarded at two hundred yards by tanks which he had taken to be Japanese. He and his staff had to lie face down in the sand, saved only by old Type 38 guns. The Buick, in which he subsequently escaped to the Kobayashi Force, was destroyed that evening by Soviet artillery. That night, three Soviet tanks with flame-throwers got within ten yards of the bridge before the engineers halted one of them with charges. A sergeant hauled out the wretched driver and Private Kaida bayoneted him.

But this 'triumph' and much more, the remarkable losses in Soviet and Mongol armour, perhaps three hundred vehicles, to 71 and 72 Regiments were, in the end, outweighed by Japanese near-starvation, thirst and exhaustion, by lack of surprise, by shortage of artillery, by reliance on one shaky bridge, by the failure to use air power. The left bank offensive, in the words of 71 Regiment's history, had only *nearly* succeeded. At 16.00 on 4 July, the General ordered the Kobayashi group to pull back, cross the bridge and regroup at Fui Heights on 5 July, the order to 26 Regiment following. The soldiers moved hurriedly in the black night, bright tracer and brilliant starshell far away over the desert, past burnt-out tanks and over the bridge, again packed with anxious horses, trucks, batteries and infantry into a vast bottle-neck.

When 71 Regiment (Okamoto force) crossed the bridge, the first of the three infantry regiments, its attached field artillery battalion took heavy casualties among men and horses, the shelling like 'raindrops jumping from the surface of the water during a shower'. The regiment was still within enemy range when well east of the bridge, but both 71 and 72 were at least across by 02.00. The last to come was 26 Regiment, dragging its dead on ropes, or with the bloody faces of dead comrades sticking out of body bags, the 'rescue' of Adachi's 1st Battalion more or less accomplished. The bridge was then blown, perhaps only the centre span, but there is no record of its later use by the Soviet Army. Tsuji, who had otherwise abandoned himself to abusing Sumi falsely for 'leaving Adachi in the lurch', nevertheless imaginatively claimed that enemy tanks had been on the span when it blew . . . One man only, Lieutenant Negami, an Olympic swimmer, managed to cross against the current by swimming.

Had the division remained on the west bank, it would have sustained a great and humiliating defeat. Instead, some Japanese were able to convince themselves that they had achieved their purpose and others, as we have seen, that they *nearly* succeeded. The fact is that they did not again try to invade Mongolia.

The Russian verdict is final, illustrated by their commander's extraordinary adaptability, for example in the use of tanks hull-down in sand: 'Tanks and motorised troops with air force and mobile artillery are a decisive means for carrying out swift military operations . . . mobile armoured cars can be effectively employed in attack *and* defence.' The Russians emphasised combined tactics, infantry–armour–artillery, and trained accordingly. The Japanese, accustomed to fighting Chinese armies largely bereft of tanks, neglected the infantry role in favour of armour alone, pretending that mobile offensives would only be slowed down by infantry support.

These characteristics were to be demonstrated to Soviet advantage both before and after the Japanese retreat to the east bank.

It was on 5 July, as the Japanese scuttled back across the bridge, that General Shtern had been appointed commander of a Front Corps in Chita, incorporating Zhukov's 57 Rifle Corps from Mongolia, the Pacific Fleet based on Vladivostock, the two Red Banner armies and troops in the Trans-Baikal military district. On 19 July, Voroshilov appointed Zhukov as commander of the First Army Group, formerly his 57th Rifle Corps, the latter reporting directly, not through Shtern, to Voroshilov and Stalin.

By the date of his counter-offensive in August, Zhukov had four times more armour, twice as much artillery and aircraft than the IJA, with ratios of 1.7 to 1 in machine-guns and 1.5 in infantry. Down seven hundred kilometres of rough dirt roads, the supply organisations in the USSR sent him, via

Chita and Mongolia, twenty-five thousand tons of fuel, six thousand tons in airborne projectiles, eighteen thousand tons of food, against the hopelessly inadequate totals dispatched from Tokio and the Kwantung Army to Japanese troops in the field.

# 13
# Tamada's Night Assault

The Kobayashi task force, 71 and 72 Regiments under Colonels Sakai and Okamoto, the 3rd Battalion of the 13th Field Artillery Regiment, Colonel Sumi's motorised 26th Regiment, the River crossing covering unit (one battalion and company of 64 Regiment, and the 24th Reconnaissance Unit), on 5 July joined the Yasuoka Detachment on the east bank. In the latter formation, Lieutenant-General Yasuoka Masaomi commanded 3rd and 4th Tank Regiments under Colonels Yoshimaru and Tamada, the other two battalions of the 64th Regiment under Yamagata, 2nd Battalion of the 28th Infantry Regiment under Kajikawa, 2nd Battalion of the 13th Artillery Field Regiment and the 24th Engineer Regiment.

The 26th Regiment was on secondment from the 7th Division, but all the units named above remained responsible to the GOC 23 Division, Lieutenant-General Komatsubara Michitaro. Few of the Japanese participants, although recognising deficiencies in equipment and attitude, believed that the Halha crossing had been a defeat, at worst a draw which could be rectified next time by more and better training, communications and artillery. Kobayashi even considered that Komatsubara's order to withdraw was premature, if not incorrect, and that a night attack on 3 July, using 26 Regiment properly, would have won the day. He did not believe that this view was negated by superior Soviet armour and fire power.

The use of armour was not originally part of the Kwantung Army's plan for the battle of Nomonhan. In early June, the only existing armoured unit, supposed to be doubled in August by medium tanks from Japan, was the Yasuoka armoured brigade originally for deployment in battle on the *eastern* frontiers, not on the steppe. It consisted of about one thousand men in 3rd and 4th Tank Regiments with four medium type 97s, thirty-four medium 89s, thirty-five light 95 tanks, ten 94 and some 97 tankettes. The 97s with a range of 210 km and a speed of 38 kph were the best, while the 89s, range 150 km, speed 25 kph, inferior armour and machine-guns, the oldest and worst. All in June lacked spare parts and reserve crewmen.

Yasuoka was fifty-three at the time of battle. He was described as 'haughty, like a feudal lord', a fighting soldier, concerned with his men. In appearance, he was 'balding' but powerfully built, tall; like many Japanese he smoked, and drank freely. He was, however, calm, a master of detail, easy to work for. Colonel Yoshimaru was a 'pure samurai', loved and respected by the troops, gentle, considerate, a good leader, favouring the 'attack'. Tamada was not a professional tankist, although thorough, abstemious, intellectual, a sound learner and teacher.

In mid-June, as tensions grew on the western frontier, Tsuji proposed the use of Yasuoka's armour with motorised infantry, artillery and engineer units, to replace the main body of the 7th Division and incorporate the units named at the beginning of this chapter. The first intention, that the detachment should cross the Halha and cut off escaping Russians, was now changed to direct attack on the right bank only, because of the deep, fast, wide river, the weak, single, over-crowded bridge and the grave shortage of fuel. General Yasuoka himself did not know about this decision until 29 June. Colonel Sumi's 26 Regiment, originally supposed to cross the river with the General, was still digging up roots and herbs near Lake Dorot on 26 June to supplement inadequate rations, only next day to follow the Kobayashi unit into Mongolia.

Meanwhile on 20 June, the Detachment had moved out by rail from Hailar on the single-track Paichengtzu line, the trains heavily laden and liable to slip backwards as they climbed. One officer complained of dysentery in his platoon, and also of a failure to check equipment. Apart from Arshaan, the roads had no tarmac. Heavy rain turned the brown, lightly indented steppe tracks into muddy quagmires. Tracked vehicles could move, while wheeled trucks had to be towed or dragged by men and tractors, vehicles up to the axles, and men up to their calves in the morass. A Japanese first lieutenant, desperate for reconnaissance, borrowed a pony from a Bargut cavalryman in the Manchukuoan Army, only to be ambushed by Russian troops. 'Imagine,' said a brother officer, 'a tank officer killed on horseback', instantly assuming that he had committed suicide on capture.

Progress was so slow that the staff proposed to 'forget' about the trucked infantry, to dismantle the tanks' machine-guns and, with them, to fight the Soviets on foot. It was at this time that rumour 'confirmed' the earlier misinformation that the Russians were retreating. They were not. Yakovlev's 11th Tank Brigade was moving *towards* the river; the sand of the Halha area had not been churned into liquid mud as had the low, soft steppe. The moon was down, the night dark and full of fog, until cut at dawn by the hot rising sun.

On 30 June, Captain Kitamura of 4 Regiment was killed in an unnecessary ambush, his tank destroyed by an anti-tank gun. A handsome young Russian was captured. His mouth blown away, he was still able to give away the existence of the 11th Tank Brigade, Bykov's armoured unit, details of Russian anti-tank shells and the fact that the right bank was held not by Mongols, but by Russians. It was also plain that the Russian gunnery was very accurate and their ammunition, although the Japanese killed ten lorry-borne infantry, better than the Kwantung Army's.

On the same day, a Japanese aircraft dropped a communication tube with orders to Yasuoka from Komatsubara at 23 Division to move to Chiangchunmiao in order to support the Division in its crossing of the Halha. Yasuoka was then to Strike South from Fui Heights toward the Halha–Holsten confluence, supported by Manchu cavalry against Balshagal and Noro Heights, thus cutting the Russian 'retreat', which all Japanese still seemed to anticipate as inevitable. The artillery and 1 and 2 Battalions of Yamagata's 64 Infantry were attached to Yasuoka. The Kajikawa battalion was late; other units kept removing its trucks and contact was lost with it on 2 July.

All units of the Yasuoka Detachment left Chiangchun-miao for the front at 04.00 on 2 July, except for 64 Regiment, which had already left and been in action on 1 July. Although Yasuoka's orders were to assault the confluence at dawn on 3 July, the General wanted to start at 18.00 on 2 July, despite Yamagata's obvious exhaustion after his long march. But Yama-gata leant on his sword and the three colonels drank to victory in 'cider'. Komatsubara now spoiled the pattern by substituting Iso's (13th Field Artillery) ancient horse-drawn guns for 1st Field Artillery (Miyao) new, long 75 mm's which the C in C had appropriated for the cross-river attack against the left bank.

Japanese intelligence was customarily bad. Two Russian divisions were *believed* to be in position, as was heavy wire, but the Japanese did not even know whether the Soviet vehicles observed were trucks or tanks. Despite great effort, no prisoners were taken and *de visu* sightings were blocked by sand dunes. Nevertheless, commanders and men were cease-lessly urged to 'charge, attack, rush to the Halha, to Tamsag Bulag' and so forth. 'Arse', as they say nowadays, 'was relent-lessly kicked.' The armour went forward: 'Snowstorm', 'Flying Dragon', 'Falcon', named too after flowers, mountains, rivers, a tiny crimson rising sun on each turret. Morale was high. One platoon had a last meal of tangerines and beer. A company commander claimed to his men in the grotesque old Japanese way that each tankist's pitch-pine coffin would be worth a hundred thousand yen. The soldiers laughed dourly.

Tamada's 4th Tank Regiment, in 'an unknown military situation and terrain', left at 18.10 on 2 July, ahead of Yoshim-aru's regiment and, led by light tanks, hurried towards an unpredictable destination.

The Russian 15 cm howitzer barrage from Hara Heights that night was more fearful than anything experienced by Japanese troops in China, 'like lightning bolts or buzz saws, dense smoke, kicking up pillars of sand' against a 64th Regiment exhausted by days of forced march. Dog-tired and thirsty, Yamagata still hoped to reach and cross the bridge, to pursue an enemy 'in flight'. Confronted by a thick bolt of wire, however, the 64th stopped and dug in to miserable foxholes lined with grass. Under machine-gun fire, to the sound of hostile armour, the thunder rolled and the rain poured down on this unhappy infantry, damply catnapping in the darkness. Gunners of 13 Regiment, without even foxholes or tents, lay out in the open throughout the stormy, drenching night.

Yamagata's 64th had started well, 'like a pursuit', before running into the barrage. Nor did Russian cannon and howitzers from the left bank deter Yoshimaru's tanks ('we passed through pleasantly'), until that artillery was supplemented by Soviet anti-tank guns and armour only half a mile away. Although some Russian armoured cars caught fire and were abandoned, so too were some Japanese tanks destroyed. Colonel Yoshimaru pulled back to a dip near Heights 731 as dusk fell, bringing with him a captured Russian armoured car and a 57 mm gun. But two of his medium tanks and a tankette were found immobile or burning, another two were bogged down. A shell had broken one driver's thigh and the drive shaft of another tankette.

In the dark and the driving rain, there was confusion. Russian wireless transmissions frequently blotted out the Japanese radios, making communication on the air with other formations impossible. Messengers lost their way. There were no landmarks in the night. Artillery fire was a danger and a deterrent. Units went round in circles. The 3rd Regiment had great difficulty in reassembling. Maps misled. Compasses went awry.

For the first time, Soviet piano wire, like 'green grass', was encountered, enmeshing the first Japanese AFV to become trapped in these terrible entanglements. (Lieutenant Koga, in his tankette, committed suicide.) Wandering about purposelessly in the thunder, tankists fighting on foot with their dismounted machine-guns took to lying on the soaking earth and 'lapped up muddy water', collecting it too in their tin hats in which they soaked handkerchiefs to suck. Behind Yoshi-maru, but out of contact, Tamada's 4th Regiment moved southeast in the dunes, instead of south to the confluence. Neither regiment was in contact with General Yasuoka. Both patrols sent by the General to find them were unsuccessful, one getting lost, oversleeping, disappearing until 4 July. Contact, furthermore, between the 3rd Tank Regiment and Yamagata's 64th Infantry on 3 July was brief.

Tamada faced the same difficulties, (including compasses which did not function properly) as Yoshimaru who had been fiercely engaged near the target confluence. In the dip where his tanks had been parked, Tamada's second-in-command, Major Ogata, sought to redeem the deficiency and the regiment's earlier failures in China and in the Tauran fight by proposing a night attack, an action almost unheard of for a tank regiment unaccompanied by infantry, in this case the 64th Regiment. Ogata's aim was, chiefly, to save the unit's honour. He persuaded Tamada that enough knowledge of the terrain had been acquired for success, even at night when armour usually remained at rest behind infantry protection, which protection was quite absent there.

Tamada's regiment included forty light tanks with 37 mm guns, and a company of medium tanks under Captain In with his 57 mm guns. The total complement was thirteen officers and three hundred men in four companies, of whom only one officer and eight men were lost during the battle that followed. Facing him, although he did not then know it, were four-gun Russian batteries of 75 mm field guns, 10 cm cannon and 12 cm howitzers, seven anti-tank guns, five mortars, twelve motorised machine-guns, twelve AFVs, many trucks; it was Bykov's mechanised brigade.

In an emotional address to company commanders, Tamada demanded that they 'for the honour of the regiment, push forward at the risk of annihilation'. Then they advanced, the silence broken only by clanking tracks, medium tanks leading, with Ogata navigating aboard In's tank at only five kph, each flying the Japanese flag. The night was black, under huge storm clouds, no moon, 'the first armoured night attack in military history'.* The clouds burst at midnight, thunder and rain so intense that tank commanders could only breathe or see through gas masks. On the other side, only when the armour was lit up by lightning did the Russians realise that they were under assault.

Then, with the Russian positions illuminated by headlights as well as by lightning, Tamada charged, his tanks suddenly accelerating, six metres apart, his four companies themselves separated by thirty metres, like wild bulls enraged, firing point-blank from a starting range of one hundred metres, more like a destroyer flotilla than any land formation. The lead medium tank platoon (In), hatches open in the downpour, crashed a thousand metres into the Soviet infantry, overran twelve Russian guns, killing the crews and observation troops and, without Soviet artillery resistance, exploding the enemy's ammunition with cannon fire. Matsumoto's 1st Company ranged too far to the left. When 2 Company's lead tank with its commander, Lieutenant Ito, was struck in the ammunition locker by a Russian shell, it stopped the tank and badly burned Ito and the crew. The three wounded men stumbled off, leaving the tank burning, an act of desertion forbidden in the IJA, to be picked up by other 2 Company tanks under Second-Lieutenant Niikura. Ito himself was blinded.

Tamada, his tanks scattered, mistakenly thought that the night attack had been a disaster. In the words of a famous civil war commander in 1877 who also sought suicide, he said to Ogata: 'How about round here now?' But In's 4 Company now rejoined the Regiment, rallied by an enormous Japanese flag on a pole. Matsumoto's 1 Company followed, then Tamaki's 3 Company, and more stragglers from 1 and 2 Company. But Tamada would still not permit Tamaki to risk all by taking the Russian artillery positions or removing their

---

* Two British armoured night attacks in the Great War, one at Bucquoy and one described by Liddell Hart as 'a very significant demonstration of the potential of tanks in night attack' were on a very minor scale, one of five tanks only accompanied by five infantry platoons.

guns. Nor was the regiment ready to mount another offensive; instead it moved back in line with the column. At the laager, Tamada was fully rejoined by 2 Company, including the wounded Ito in Niikura's tank. Although a search produced no sign of Ito's missing vehicle, it was shown later in Soviet propaganda pictures, surrounded by gloating Russian soldiers. What punishment was later awarded to its commander in hospital is unknown.

In the early morning of 3 July, Ogata reported to General Yasuoka's headquarters on the 4th Regiment's dashing night of action. 'That's a relief,' said the General, although shocked by its irregularity, and agreed that Tamada should start off once more for the confluence. Ogata was told that Yoshimaru's 3rd Regiment had meanwhile lost five officers and sixteen men. The Russians admitted that the Yasuoka offensive had, in its 'objective of covering the Kobayashi strike group', broken through the defences of their 149th Infantry Regiment under Major Remizov and the 9th Mechanised Brigade. By dusk on 2 July, the Japanese had forced back the Russo-Mongol left flank towards the south-west, cut into the defences, and reached the Soviet artillery positions.

The rain had stopped by 3 July, the day clear under the blue skies and golden light of Central Asia. On the left bank of the Halha, Russian tanks were burning in black funeral pyres in the bright air, encouraging General Yasuoka's illusion that the Soviets were in terminal difficulty. He determined to block their envisaged retreat and destroy them on the right bank. Unfortunately, Iso's horse-drawn artillery made slow progress, and Yamagata's infantry was stalled, still thirsty and overtired. Artillery-infantry-armour co-operation remained inadequate. When Colonel Yoshimaru's 3rd Tank Regiment went forward, he met hull-down Russian armour in quantity, as well as infantry and anti-tank guns. But he also ran straight into the 'piano wire . . . thin, flat, strong rolls; unbreakable by artillery shells, resembling carpets, vertical nets, mainsprings, electric coils', according to location. Tanks, especially if they tried to turn, became caught in the spirals, the wire entwined into the tracks; they lay there motionless, unable to move forward or back. Stuck fast, in static line abreast, outranged by superior armour-piercing Russian anti-tank shells, Yoshimaru's own tank was caught and the Colonel killed by concentrated fire. (The shattered bodies were not found and recovered until 6 July.) Only a few infantrymen surmounted it by covering the wire with canvas.

Although elsewhere on the front the Regiment claimed the destruction of sixty-seven Russian armoured vehicles and the capture of much equipment, these dubious figures were insignificant, given the Russian capacity for resupply. The 3rd had lost sixteen per cent of its manpower, while the Soviets claimed to have knocked out thirty Japanese tanks, seven in the 'piano wire', and to have taken eleven prisoners. The Japanese had not 'chilled the innards of the enemy'. Yasuoka ordered the unit to fall back until dawn on 4 July, a withdrawal not made happier by the absence of air force retaliation to attacks by I–16 fighters, nor by the knowledge that Japanese shells bounced off Russian turrets and that suicide fighters were flung off the revolving turrets to which they clung.

At dawn, Tamada's 4 Tank Regiment also moved toward the confluence, initially destroying or driving off Soviet armour on his left flank. Believing that the enemy was not in flight, he did not immediately obey Yasuoka's order to cross the river with field artillery and Yamagata's 64 Infantry. Two battalions of the latter, although Tamada did not know it, had just taken Heights 731 where Kajikawa's refound 2nd Battalion of 28 Regiment was engaged. When Tamada eventually found Yamagata that evening, they agreed that the infantry was not yet ready to support a tank offensive, a decision conveyed to the General on 4 July.

A Russian assault combining all arms developed at a half-mile range against Tamada at 06.00 that morning, continuing in sporadic fighting until dark and exposing the Holsten flank. That evening, in heavy low cloud and darkness, plus earlier problems with radio and compasses, Tamada could not pursue the enemy, whose losses he put at seven AFVs and two guns; but he had also driven off Russian infantry on several occasions during the day. When he learned that the 23rd Division was recrossing the river from the west bank and making for his sector, he was all the more determined to remain where he was. On 5 July, in return for repelling armour and artillery who were attacking a Manchukuoan Bargut cavalry unit, Tamada was presented by the Manchurian horsemen with presents of sheep, the nomad's principal resource. The usual optimistic orders were received from Yasuoka that afternoon (based on a Russian 'retreat' between the Halha and Holsten) to attack the line of retreat with the returned Kobayashi force of one artillery and three infantry battalions.

Russian infantry dug in as close as 200 yards to Tamada's position just before dawn on 6 July, 'crawling forward, with light artillery, heavy machine-guns and rapid-fire weapons in the front waves', quickly destroying four of In's medium tanks and a tankette. Heavy artillery barrages accompanied the attacks, and Japanese infantry, earlier rejected by Tamada as unnecessary, took time to come up. Soviet armour joined the battle and, although Japanese tanks overran and drove back the Russians, the Regiment lost another five tanks to rapid-fire guns, with machine-gun bullets killing or disabling tank crews through the vision slit or the open hatches.

Losses in armour, infantry and guns were inflicted on the Russians by all four companies of the Regiment, sometimes at a range of fifty metres. Soviet advances were at least held in the early morning and afternoon. Iso's artillery opened fire for the first time at 11.00; Fukomura's 3rd Battalion of the 64th Regiment arrived at 08.00. At 13.00, Russian reinforcements of all three arms threatened encirclement, driven off by Tamada's main force two-company sortie fifty minutes later, and by the 1st Company at 15.00. Heavy losses were incurred on both sides, Tamada losing twelve tanks, eighteen men killed and twenty-four wounded on that single day.

At 16.00 on 6 July, Yasuoka ordered the 4th Tank Regiment to be replaced by the infantry which had returned under Kobayashi's command 'in order to collect lost tanks, maintain vehicles and recover combat strength'. At the same time, he told Tamada to support the 72nd Infantry and the 3rd Tank Regiment to perform that function for the 64th Regiment under Yamagata. On 8 July, six or seven tanks of the battered 3rd Regiment, spontaneously and without orders, attacked a larger force of Soviet armour, destroying four, stopping another and driving the others away.

About his withdrawal from combat, Tamada said: 'My unit was almost surrounded by attacks [on 6 July], yet we repulsed them all . . .' He knew that his role was over at Nomonhan.

# 14
# Yasuoka's Armour Goes Back

The territorial claim of Russia's Mongol allies on the east bank of the Halha was too important to ignore. Yasuoka's armour, outgunned, slow and restricted in range, had now lost half its tanks. No further losses, because of the intention to create a mechanised corps, could be accepted in this core unit. Despite loss of face and morale for the whole Detachment, General Ueda, in command of the Kwantung Army, on 9 July ordered that the tanks should return to Kungchunling before a planned infantry offensive by Komatsubara with artillery reinforcements. The officers and men did not understand. All were shocked by the affront to themselves and their commander. Neither, since the Russian right bank bridgehead still held, was Ueda's order that 23 Division should pull back eastward to Kanchuerhmiao, Fui Heights, Balshagal, Noro Heights and Handagai, comprehensible to the troops.

Maximum offence having been given, the orders were rescinded but, because the tanks were required for the new, larger armoured unit, their departure was only postponed, not cancelled. Despite Yasuoka's achievements, nevertheless, both the return of 23 Division to the east bank and the need to conserve tanks for the future justified for some officers the 'deactivisation' of the Detachment. (The so-called failures of 64 and 28 Infantry sometimes made the last consideration irrelevant.) Everything had been improvised almost as if the battlefield were to be in China, not on the Mongolian steppe. Intelligence and reconnaissance seemed discounted in favour of the commander's wishful thinking. Proper maps were lacking; communications collapsed. IJA tanks were much slower than the Russian ones and their armour too light against armour-piercing shell. Short-barrel guns were inferior in direct combat with Russian long-barrelled tank artillery. Ventilation was inefficient and ammunition, food, spares, water and, most seriously, fuel, all ran out at various times. Resupply took too long. Tank treads fell apart. The Russians deployed amphibious vehicles, heavy armour, and flame-throwers. The Japanese did not.

In general, the Red Army disposed of more and better vehicles, including tracked or wheeled armour, always supported by artillery and infantry, whereas the Japanese 4th Tank Regiment had made its desperate advance into the wire unsupported by any infantry or, indeed, by anything except *samurai* spirit. The Soviets fought skilfully, if with less *bushido* dash, using ambush and deception, exploiting technical and numerical superiority through good organisation, beginning with artillery barrages under which tanks and infantry mounted co-ordinated assaults, professionally and without bravado. The Russians conquered by speed, long-range fire power, reverse-slope and hull-down fire. They also won by forethought and training. On the other side, even Tamada's gallant and successful night action suffered from bad logistic planning, since shortage of fuel precluded follow-up pursuit.

But the departure of the Yasuoka tanks would still be remarked with pleasure and relief by the Russians, and with regret by a Japanese infantry that had looked up to its armoured brother.

# 15
# Trying It With Cold Steel

Coox's chapter titles in *Nomonhan* are graphically helpful: The trap on the Halha, The Kwantung Army's unauthorised air offensive, On to Mongolia – a bridge too far, The Halha river crossing, Retreat from the river, Trying it with tanks, Tanks dare the night, Foiled by piano wire, End of the Yasuoko detachment are then followed by Trying it with cold steel . . .

After returning to the east bank on 4 July, General Komatsubara still sought to attack the Russians at the Halha –Holsten confluence, but this time from the right bank. At his *eventual* disposal were the reduced 3rd and 4th Tank Regiments, Sakai's 72 Infantry, the 64th Regiment, the battalion of 28 Regiment under Kajikawa, Sumi's 26 Infantry, 1 and 13 Field Artillery, the 71 Infantry under Okamoto, the Sappers.

Kajikawa's battalion, together with the 'hollow-cheeked and glassy-eyed' veterans of 64 Regiment, tried to blow up a Russian bridge at the confluence. Soviet tanks were engaged, of which five were destroyed. Three hundred Russians were claimed dead, many after hand-to-hand fighting. Japanese posing as Russians placed charges near the bridge; this caused confusion, damage and collision among the enemy. The raiders hid in the bushes nearby, cutting enemy telephone wire on the way home. Next day, companies of 'tall, strange men in unfamiliar greatcoats, innocent and chattering' were jumped in a bloody charge, 'the happy slashes of bayonets and swords . . . desperate sprinting away by hunched-up enemy soldiers'. Over a hundred Russians were 'found on their backs, large figures sprawling in black blood', field guns smashed and machine-guns captured.

Japanese losses were heavy, and Kajikawa made now familiar complaints about 'artillery, co-operation, communication, ammunition and terrain'. Saké and sweet bean jelly were issued to the troops. Russian armour, infantry and artillery attacked Tamada's 4th Tank and Sakai's 72 Regiments. There was concern about Manchukoan cavalry weakness: 'not too good . . . a tendency to be overwhelmed by the enemy'.

Komatsubara really believed that the Russians did not like 'cold steel', the bayonet and the sword, alleging indeed that they ran screaming in tears from Japanese sabres in the close-combat night attacks preferred by his countrymen. He thus planned to assault at dusk, 'when goblins haunt the mind'. A Russian build-up of up to eighty tanks was spotted by reconnaissance aircraft. The Soviet ground attack on 7 July was preceded by artillery barrages, to which Miyao's guns mounted ineffective counter-fire in the rain. The 64 and 72 Infantry (now Kobayashi's Left-wing Unit) moved out at dusk on 7 July in a black drizzle, Sakai well ahead of his battalions. Their advance was not substantial: twelve officers and two hundred and eighty Japanese were killed or wounded, mostly by gunfire, against a claim of two hundred and fifty Soviet dead. The Russian 149 Regiment, losing their commander, Major Remizov, took most of such shock as the Japanese provided, with one infantry battalion right up against the line of mortar and artillery shells.

South of the Holsten, Okamoto and 71 Regiment were in the wrong location, and had overestimated Russian strength at their target, Noro Heights; they were as far off their goal as were 64 and 72 regiments. Komatsubara's joint dusk offensive against the confluence was a chimera so far. But the General blithely congratulated everyone, and the air force once again swore that the Russians were on the run. They were not and, instead, attacked Hinomaru Heights, firing tracer and shouting 'Hurrah!', presumably 'Horosho!', until checked by Kajikawa's battalion of 28 Regiment, their barrels red hot, though losing two-thirds strength. But the Japanese killed one hundred and fifty Russians, including ten slaughtered by a single master swordsman.

Several more raids by parties from the infantry regiments and the engineers, before the planned main attack on the night of 8–9 July, were mounted against the Russian bridges across Holsten and Halha rivers. Russian troops on sandbanks challenged the raiders before the latter, replying in pidgin Russian, poured petrol and deposited explosive on the planks of one bridge, destroying it and thus preventing Russian retreat or advance. Another was blown by the electrical detonation of sixty kilos of explosive placed by engineers with support from a large infantry platoon. In the darkness the flames shot up to a height of a hundred feet. These bridges were often hard to spot, identifiable only by the sound of the water as the vehicles crossed their submerged spans; time, stealth and, often, hand-to-hand fighting with sabres were necessary before they could be reached.

At midnight, 72 Infantry Regiment set off in moonlight for the confluence, and returned at 04.30, leaving a company behind with gun platoons in support. Yamagata's 64 Regiment seized a howitzer position, suffering and inflicting casualties, one battalion failing to demolish a bridge, another reaching Heights 733. The Russians were not abandoning the region but they *were* now pulling back north of the Holsten, and Colonel Sumi's 26 Regiment, his machine-gunners firing through their own infantry, captured equipment as well as seizing Soviet positions. 71 regiment, now under Colonel Nagano (*vice* Okamoto) was further east than it had thought when marching off at 17.20, at once badly hit on its way to Noro Heights by artillery from across the Holsten. The regiment took, not Noro, but the 'Boat-shaped Hill', Funagatayama, at 21.15.

On seeing five Japanese corpses, and eight dead saddled horses with their legs in the air, Komatsubara was reminded of a picture in a Moscow gallery. 'It tells of the misery of battle,' he remarked. The C in C was dissatisfied with his offensive, blaming poor co-ordination between 64 and 72 Regiments for their failure to reach the river. Yasuoka, however, believed that the failure was due to superior Red Army fire power and to the IJA policy of returning the main body to its jump-off points, leaving only small units at the target, a sort of 'grandmother's steps'.

On 9 July, as we have seen, the Yasuoka Detachment was deactivated. Then, also, Sumi's 1st Battalion moved to the battalion of Kajikawa's 28 Regiment on the right flank. On Hinomaru, the Russians continued to attack. That evening, traversing a series of dunes, Sumi took ground a mile west of Heights 731. His 1st Battalion occupied a dip south of Hinomaru, where the Russians had incurred a hundred casualties and lost two tanks. But three hundred Soviet riflemen, infiltrated into the sector with machine-gunners in attendance, did severe damage at dawn on 10 July to a battered company of 26 Division. Yamagata's 64th took off late on 9 July. Before dawn on 10 July, one battalion had to abort the destruction of a bridge. The other at least forced a temporary retreat on a large combined Russian force.

# 16
## Firming the Base for August

The Red Army was now less active against Sakai's 72 Infantry on the left front, but Soviet artillery on the right bank itself had increased after the Japanese built 'Old Engineer Bridge' across the Holsten. From the Bargut Mongols 71 Infantry under Nagano learned that the Russians to their left now mustered about thirty armoured vehicles and two or three hundred men. His regiment's rations arrived safely but, in the great heat, the water supply was quite inadequate even when supplemented using biscuit tins from puddles.

Nagano was told by Division that the Russians on the right bank were weak, and had been losing fighting spirit since morning. Then 71 Infantry arrived at what they took to be Noro but was, in fact, Height 758, two miles away, called Funagatayama (Boat-Shaped Hill). Kui Heights was the next objective, but held twenty Russian tanks and two hundred riflemen. It was now that Komatsubara, convinced as usual that the Russians had been 'seriously weakened', ordered the tanks to be withdrawn and 23 Division to be reallocated eastward, his own division to subsume all Yasuoka's non-tank units that had not returned to Hailar.

The bitter struggle continued at Hinomaru Heights under substantial fighter battles overhead, white parachutes like jellyfish in the sky. At 23.00 Kajikawa and a Sumi 26 Division battalion went forward successfully under thick smoke against very light resistance. (On the left, both Yamagata and Sumi's teams failed to blow the bridges.) In 'broiling heat' on 10 July, two Russian infantry companies, six motorised guns and heavy machine-guns, the crews bawling 'Hurrah!' (or 'Horosho!') penetrated close to Nagano's HQ. Fighting went on all morning until the Russians were beaten off, uniforms torn, faces blackened with oil and cordite, limping away from their abandoned dead.

At Hinomaru, the gunfire was comparable to Verdun. Some of Sumi's units previously in 72 Regiment's sector started to return, although his 3rd Battalion took off at 21.00 and conquered 'Boat-shaped Hill' an hour later. On the right, Russian artillery almost buried men of Kajikawa's battalion under sand, and in the south they blew up a Japanese ammunition truck near General Kobayashi's HQ, the projectiles cartwheeling in all directions, white (ordinary) and red (tracer) shells.

The 1st Battalion of Yamagata's 64th Regiment had at last crept to within five hundred yards of the confluence before being almost cut to bits by armour and the main guns. (Its first company, however, had set light to a Soviet tank with fire bottles, the troops shouting '*Banzai!*', killing the Russian crew mercilessly with sword and bayonet.) No less than one hundred and thirty Russian tanks were at this bridgehead; the Japanese battalion was encircled by infantry and falling thick and fast to gunfire. 'Dying or wounded soldiers lay pleading for water or groaning. Little movement was possible through 12 July.' Sakai's 72 Regiment and a 38-man company under Lieutenant Hayama near Kikugata came under severe attack. Hayama, after beating off the Russians, disguised himself in a private's uniform and mounted a deep, gallant reconnaissance, repeated on 12 July, which revealed Soviet Order of Battle as including twenty tanks north of the confluence.

South of the Holsten, Nagano's 71 Regiment on 11 July at last forced the Russians to withdraw. Hours behind schedule, he then mounted an offensive in which 'his troops lost heart and the advance ceased'. Although he claimed to have pressed the enemy to the Halha, none of 71 Regiment's objectives was really achieved, not the rescue of a company which, it emerged, had saved itself, nor the suppression of enemy batteries, nor the destruction of Russian bridges. A gun lay wrecked and overturned, an armoured car caught by mines, a burned packet of cigarettes, dead and twisted bodies.

Sporadic torrents of rain fell, turning the earth to thick, sticky mud, up to the knees of the living, while mud in the eyes and ears, mud in the rations, mud in boots and clothing, quite buried the dead. No aircraft could take off so long as the rain lasted, no tanks advance. When the mud dried, the Russian tactic, practised also in the 1939–45 war by the Germans, was to lay out minefields, dominated from such heights as existed by artillery, mortars, anti-tank guns and machine-guns in hidden pits. Then nothing could move until the sappers, in great danger, had cleared the mines. Only then, and after the air force had brutalised the area, could the tanks and infantry advance, toy figures, no more than little dots, sometimes animated.

The Soviets regarded the attempt on their bridgehead by the 1st Battalion of the 64th Regiment under Yamagata as the most dangerous moment. 'Cut off my finger and take it home', shouted Second Lieutenant Miura, as he charged to his death by sniper fire among collapsing foxholes and his yelling men. But now, perhaps under Iso's artillery, the Russians suddenly withdrew, treads clanking. 'I am delighted', said General Ueda to Komatsubara, 'how you have chastised the Mongols and Soviets, and secured the frontier.'

But the Red Army tanks and infantry were still in full cry, 64 Regiment casualties stood at nearly fifteen hundred, the Russian bridges had not been blown, artillery still thundered from the left bank, two Russian infantry battalions and two hundred tanks faced the Japanese.

Komatsubara then ordered all attacks to cease, and all units, including the 64th, to withdraw. The Russians had lost three hundred men, three anti-tank guns and forty-five tanks; guns and machine-guns had been captured; but Yamagata had lost sixty killed, about a hundred and ninety missing and wounded. One company was down to fifteen men from the original one hundred; Tokio could not afford such a loss, although withdrawal was ordered unfortunately at the exact moment when the Russians and Mongols were outnumbered.

Sakai's 72 Regiment launched a night attack on 12 July, suffering three hundred and thirty casualties, while Sumi's 26 Regiment, fighting off the white men with hand grenades, was assaulted by armour and riflemen. Without orders, Sumi went to the bridge at the confluence under a hail of three hundred Soviet shells a minute: Division, to his rage, told him to pull back, in spite of him having reached the target itself for the first time.

The 28 Regiment could not ford the Halka river and Kajikawa, after conflicting instructions, made to join Sumi. Kajikawa – 'our tall and slim battalion commander, on the crest with his binoculars, his cheeks hollow, eyes shrunken, straggly beard streaked with grey, Master of the sixth *dan*, holding the Order of the Golden Kite, leading his independent unit through the entire combat.' He and his men dug in on 18 and 19 July under a terrible sun. Elsewhere, Russian troops attacked 72 Regiment with two hundred men, a similar number against the heroic Lieutenant Hayama and his worn little platoon. The Yamagata Regiment could make little further progress. Now 71 Regiment under Colonel Nagano made for the two bridges connecting Noro Heights with the Holsten. 'The sky was wonderfully clear', deepest blue with flat bottomed Mongolian clouds, 'the sun glared down on the fleeing enemy, and our morale soared along the whole front', taking the empty Soviet trenches around the northern river bridge beside 'Mongolian cliffs seven storeys high, Maxims firing from "the windows"'. The bridge was wide, made with cement like a road. The sappers exploded it, but only half the (11th) raiding company survived to pull back: a second bridge was blown that night. 71 Regiment retired to Noro Heights.

Five bridges in all had been destroyed; the Japanese were finally in Red Army territory, claiming seventeen hundred Russian dead, forty prisoners, over four hundred armoured vehicles out of action, forty-one guns and forty trucks captured. In ordering a withdrawal, Komatsubara *might* have ruined a real chance of defeating the enemy within a few days. But, although the infantry behaved superbly, the Red Army guns were superior: 'Hell in daytime, paradise at night.'

A 72 Regiment officer observed, 'It was the others

that couldn't keep up. You've advanced too far, they would tell us . . .' (Too much time was also allowed the Soviets for bridge repairs.) Of the eight thousand Japanese troops in action by 12 July, over two thousand had been killed, wounded or were missing.

These night attacks were preceded by gigantic feasts of rice. The men then crawled forward on their stomachs, each touching the leg of the man in front. Traversing fire followed and hand-to-hand combat with bayonet and sabre, the main Russian response being at dawn or dusk with artillery, armour and, in the end, the foot soldiers withdrawing when Japanese resistance was fierce enough. The elimination of the Russo–Mongol forces on the right bank needed heavy artillery to complete the damage in night assault on Soviet infantry and armour. The guns were not there.

The 3rd Heavy Field Artillery Brigade in Japan under Major-General Hata Yuzaburo had already been mobilised. It consisted of two motorised heavy military regiments, one with two battalions, the 1st under Colonel Hishima, four batteries of four 15 cm Type 96 howitzers each, one battery commanded by an Imperial Prince. The other, the 7th Field Artillery Regiment under Colonel Baron Takatsukasa, was armed with sixteen 10 cm cannon Type 92. The Brigade did not arrive at Hailar until 19 July. A motorised heavy artillery regiment (Colonel Someya) with four 15 cm Type 89 cannon and a motorised Artillery Intelligence Unit were detached to the western front from the Kwantung Army, the whole responsible to an artillery corps commanded by Major-General Uchiyama Eitaro. Colonel Ise commanded existing artillery forces at the 'frontier', and Hata led the new arrivals in the field itself.

Komatsubara reluctantly agreed to Uchiyama's request on 11 July that the 23rd Division suspend their (infantry) attacks, and evacuate territory taken near the river, until the artillery had destroyed the enemy's guns across the Halha. At *that* point, the infantry should mount a terminal attack, their earlier inaction serving to keep the Russian guns within

Japanese range and to give the Kwantung Army guns a free field of fire.

The corps began emplacement, camouflage and ammunition storage on 17 July. D–Day on 23 July started at 08.00 with sudden and overwhelming fire, tacitly anticipating victory and the infantry's advance on D–Day plus 1, wishful thinking *à outrance*. The day, after earlier rain, turned out clear and very hot. The 15 cm guns, despite vigorous counter-fire, were successful in flinging Russian 'bodies and fragments of guns and wheels in the air'. The barrels turned red hot. The crews wrapped them in damp cloth and poured water on them. Ise's Type 38s fell short and the 12 cm howitzers stayed in their pits. Each piece in the 3rd Battalion fired a hundred rounds on D–Day. A total of eleven thousand four hundred rounds were expended by batteries under Mishima, Takatsuka, Someya, Miyao, and Ise. Two or three Red batteries were thought to have been destroyed and five or six more damaged, but when the infantry went forward at 11.00, they were met by withering fire from resited and otherwise sheltered Soviet guns.

The enfeebled Japanese air reconnaissance formed an adverse view that day of IJA artillery skills, yet Komatsubara ordered the infantry to continue the offensive at dawn on 24 July, the heavy artillery to move up in support by two kilometres. Hata objected. 'It is both unwise and sinful,' he wrote in his diary, 'to sacrifice precious subordinates because of self-advancement by commanders or staff officers.'

The batteries did better on 24 July, but the guns drew 'torrents of enemy bombardment'. Komatsubara, visiting the scene, had tears in his eyes. Mishima lost three 15 cm howitzers and other batteries suffered casualties. Ammunition expenditure was reduced. Eight of Takatsukasa's sixteen 10 cm guns were out of action and one of Miyao's Type 90s. Three Japanese field, four mountain, nineteen rapid-fire, five infantry and two anti-aircraft guns, eighteen heavy and forty-four light machineguns were lost; twenty-four Soviet guns were destroyed and ten 'neutralised', out of seventy-six. Blue-silk balloons were used for spotting until a Soviet I-16 shot one down in a scarlet flame, 'like a hawk swooping on a sparrow'. The infantry made little progress, although Hata believed that, by 25 July, they were beginning to advance.

On 26 July, Kwantung Army at Hsinking ordered that 23 Division was to suspend the offensive at once, 'an admission that the much heralded general offensive had not really succeeded.'

The Japanese infantry had been modestly reinforced on 14 July by replacements, *inter alia* of victims of amoebic dysentery contracted from fouled water, patients with temperatures of 102°F and fifteen visits to the latrine in five hours. The number of troops allotted to the general offensive was nevertheless no more than had been available before the C in C suspended the night attacks on 11 July. Komatsubara hoped that Sakai, Sumi, Nagano and the others, aided by the 15 cm and Type 90 guns and by air cover, could clean up after the supposed destruction by artillery of the Russian right bridgehead. Uchiyama's Artillery Corps believed that results had been splendid, and that the infantry were on the point of taking the confluence. The C in C knew that this was not so. Heavy Soviet losses in men and material were certainly sustained, but damage to the Russian artillery was consistently overestimated. Japanese casualties were heavy and morale low. 'Men were falling around . . . for example, a figure in a white shirt could be seen waving a sabre until he toppled to the ground . . . a second lieutenant just returned from infantry school.' The loss by 26 Regiment of one hundred and thirty-five men between 23 and 24 July was disproportionately heavy among officers. Someya fell, leading 4 Company of the incalculable 1st Battalion of 64 Regiment; 'his throat on fire and breathing difficult . . . his greatest regret to have lost the chance to climb Komatsu Heights into Outer Mongolia'. The noise and volume of the Red Army artillery remained three times greater than Uchiyama's. There was also no doubt that, whether from Sorge or more perishable intelligence, the Russians were dangerously forewarned of Japanese plans and movements. But still the men moved into the terrible gale of the Red Army's bombardment.

One platoon commander was hit in the jaw by a shell fragment, teeth knocked out, tongue nearly severed, lying flat in a hole until a tourniquet was applied, when he staggered back to the command post. 'I knew that I was dying,' he said, 'but I was opposed to that.' A young doctor cut a hole in his throat and saved his life by inserting a banana-sized rubber pipe. He then sewed up his tongue. A Russian officer in close combat bit off the thumb of a sergeant in the 26th Regiment. In 72 Regiment, the second battalion lost three hundred out of five hundred men, while in other battalions, companies were down to sixty, even thirty men. General Kobayashi's HQ was hit by artillery fire on 25 July and trenches caved in wholesale under Red Army gunfire.

Little had been accomplished by suspending the night infantry attacks that had pierced the Soviet–MPRA shore defences, by abandoning the territory taken at such cost, and by starting afresh against a rejuvenated enemy. The Russian artillery was better made, better trained, better disposed, more plentiful, with more ammunition, using better spotting techniques and preregistration. The region seemed like nothing less than one vast Russian firing range. The unfortunate Japanese infantry was further from the Holsten–Halha confluence on 25 July than they had been before Generals Uchiyama and Hata arrived. Many officers and men were ill, most were exhausted, and the majority was frightened. They lacked superiority in the air, in armour and in artillery. They were, however, still overconfident and, in consequence, tactically idle and unprepared, another cause of great losses.

The Russians simply explained that in the face of the main Japanese artillery offensive, they held their fire until the enemy mounted what Moscow considered an unco-ordinated ground attack which, because not 'concerted', the Red Army was able to repel. The bridgehead held and the river frontier held. The Japanese were forced to the defensive. It was exactly to achieve that objective that General Zhukov had defied the IJA's incessant but inconsistent assaults, beating off the night attacks against weak gaps by shifting units fast from one to another sector over huge distances at immediate notice. The base was firm for August.

# 17
# The Kwantung Army Goes Over
# to the Defence

On 25 July, the Kwantung Army effectively ordered the abandonment of 23 Division's offensive in favour of protracted defence. Komatsubara, in saddened response, recorded his private regret that he had ever pulled back his infantry in favour of artillery barrages. Fortifications were prepared immediately, using ammunition boxes, crates, cans, captured *matériel* including stakes from Russian barbed wire, fuel drums, lots of junk, poles, grass for fodder. Sand was used to strengthen concrete blocks, which finally ended up as Japanese tombstones. Uchiyama returned to Kwantung Army. General Hata, on succession, believed that *he* now had the men's confidence.

On 27 July, 71 Division was the only infantry unit to fight actively, chopped up in rain and fog by Russian mortar and 12 cm howitzer fire, with the IJA artillery soon out of ammunition. A 'heartrending and ghastly battle' took place against a charge by four hundred Soviet riflemen, supported by fire 'like a seething blast furnace' from the Red Army guns.

Construction of defences continued along the existing forward lines, as if to secure the right shore, if not to cross the river. The Kwantung Army, remembering the past month's losses, stubbornly refused to consider discarding the Halha as a frontier. The policy was to build field works which would hold for a month or so including housing, and wells, at Kanchuerhmiao, Amukulang, Fui, Noro and Nomonhan. Modest reinforcements from 7 Division, two battalions from 28 Regiment, a Mukden battalion, were to be brought forward, air defence and Manchukuoan cavalry strengthened.

Fire-eater Tsuji surprisingly opposed proposals for a new offensive in September, which was even to have involved a river crossing. Wintering, he said, in temperatures of −60°F, was incompatible with an offensive. Positions should be established before the real winter set in. No one, it seemed, was considering the possibility of a new *Soviet* offensive in August.

At Hailar, the newly created 6th Army under Lieutenant-General Ogisu Ryuhei, one class senior to Komatsubara, formerly in action in both Taiwan and China, took command of the old and new units at the front. His chief of staff, Major-General Fujimito, had joined the 6th Army from an air force command at Pyongyang in North Korea, where his senior staff officer was Colonel Hamada, a veteran of Manchuria. Ogisu's Army was responsible for the entire Hsingan province, not the Nomonhan battle alone and was therefore behind the front when Zhukov moved in August.

On arrival, Hamada recorded despondency at the imbalance between Red Army and IJA resources. 'If the Japanese army were serious about winning, the size of our forces would have to be increased greatly . . . the fighting should be settled politically.' The threat of winter, as opposed to that of the enemy, was plain to the Intelligence staffs. Neither equipment nor Japanese troops, even from Hokkaido in the north, could handle temperatures to which many Russians, on the other hand, were accustomed. The Japanese military attaché at Moscow, for his part, strongly advised that powerful fortifications be pushed right back from the border. But what was built, the Nomonhan 'apartments', dugouts with curtains, beds and desks, had walls only of light planks and ammunition boxes, hardly designed against the cold, and certainly not against the Red Army. Up against the river, within Soviet artillery range, the Kwantung Army seemed condemned to a most painful end.

# 18
# Zhukov in August

The Russian and Mongolian armies were conscript bodies engaged not only in military training, but responsible, with other State institutions, for the defence of frontiers and for internal security; they were also used to disseminate the Communist doctrine throughout the USSR and the MPR.

The Red Army comprised regular and, in 1939 on a diminishing scale, territorial troops. Regular units included a permanent cadre of officers and senior NCOs, the rest being conscripts serving for two years, then transferring to the reserve. The estimated strength of the Soviet Army, including the air arm and territorials, was about two million men in one hundred and fifteen infantry, thirty-five cavalry divisions, five mechanised corps or light armoured divisions, posted in fifteen Military Districts and two Military Commissariats, the majority located in frontier districts. Except for special units such as the Far Eastern 1st and 2nd Independent Red Banner Armies, the highest fighting formation was the Corps. One wartime Army would contain from three to six Infantry Corps with cavalry and other arms as required.

The wartime complement of an Infantry Corps was two to three infantry divisions, two artillery regiments, one anti-aircraft group, one Sapper and one Signal battalion, a two-flight squadron of reconnaissance aircraft, administrative troops and the Corps Headquarters, totalling some sixty thousand men. Each Cavalry Corps had a war establishment of seventeen thousand, at least two cavalry divisions, administrative troops, a signal group, and so forth.

An infantry division of the ordinary kind held a headquarters, three infantry regiments, two field artillery regiments, Sapper, Signal, Tank and Reconnaissance battalions, anti-tank and administrative troops, a war establishment of eighteen thousand. Mountain infantry divisions differed slightly from this description, as did the five mountain cavalry divisions. The *normal* cavalry divisions, of which there were thirty, included divisional Headquarters, one mechanised and four horsed cavalry regiments, a horsed artillery regiment, Sapper, Signal and administrative troops. Five cavalry divisions were exclusively Cossack.

Soviet Armoured units were brigaded, at least until October 1939, but there were no brigades then in the Soviet infantry. *Regiments* included about three thousand five hundred men, eight hundred horses, three hundred vehicles. Each regiment had its headquarters staff, an artillery group, forty mounted scouts, sniper, signals, sapper, camouflage and chemical platoons, medical and veterinary detachments, a political section and a supply company. Normal, as opposed to mountain, regiments held over a thousand rifles, six 76 mm guns in two batteries, ten 37 mm or 45 mm anti-tank guns, six mortars, eighty light automatics, eighty grenade-throwers, seventy-five machine-guns and four AA machine-guns.

Cavalry regiments consisted of a headquarters, four sabre squadrons, anti-aircraft, chemical and sapper troops, medical, supply, veterinary and political sections, totalling one thousand two hundred men, thirteen hundred horses, six MT vehicles, four 76 mm and two 37 mm guns, twenty machine-guns, three AA machine-guns, forty light automatic guns, forty grenade-throwers. A sabre squadron was formed from four troops of two sections each, a headquarters staff and an administrative troop.

Each infantry or cavalry regiment had, as we have seen, its own regimental artillery group distinct from Army artillery, the latter ARGK or 'artillery at the disposal of Higher Command'. (All Army Artillery had been mechanised, tractor drawn, by 1939.) The ARGK consisted of super-heavy, heavy and medium-field guns, howitzers and AA guns, often train-mounted, in regiments, groups, batteries and armoured-train units, their guns over 122 mm and howitzers of 152 mm, employing chiefly HE, gas and smoke shells.

As for armour, Zhukov's approximately five hundred

AFVs at Nomonhan itself were drawn from the 6th and 11th Tank Brigades, 7th, 8th and 9th Motorised Armour, plus a company of flame-throwing tanks. Overall, the Soviet total of armoured, mechanised formations comprised, firstly, the mechanised corps, in size more like armoured *divisions*, each with HQs, two mechanised brigades of light-medium tanks, one motorised brigade of three infantry and machine-gun battalions, mechanised engineering, signal and administrative units, a flight of Corps aircraft. The total also included mechanised brigades originally with T26, now BT tanks, with three companies of three platoons of three tanks plus one Corps HQ tank, one reconnaissance Platoon of S-7 amphibious tanks, one training battalion, one reconnaissance company of sixteen amphibious tanks, a 'BO' or ancillary battalion; motorised brigades of mechanised Corps (holding units with three motorised infantry and machine-gun battalions, one (training) motorised infantry and machine-gun battalion, a BO battalion, a recce company with amphibious tanks, an infantry and machine-gun battalion); independent mechanised brigades with BT tanks, formerly T26; TRGK units, at the disposal of Higher Command, containing one training and three tank battalions, a BO battalion, a recce company; heavy tank brigades with three tank battalions. In 1940, throughout the USSR, the estimated number of Soviet tanks was ten thousand.

Under 'tactics and training', Soviet military regulations emphasised surprise and all-arms – armour, air, artillery and infantry – co-ordination and, perhaps because of a Russian tendency to do nothing under stress, initiative. Attack, whether direct or flank, was aimed at destroying all defensive systems in depth, initially by heavy bombing and mechanised forces. In defence, emphasis was on anti-tank systems.

Attack had to be on as broad a front as possible in divisional strength, with a strike group of artillery and tanks, and a decoy and defensive holding group. Offensives would, of course, be preceded by air and ground reconnaissance before concentration of superior forces, followed by air and artillery bombardment of the reserve and throughout the whole enemy depth; by armoured (long-range tank) penetration; by infantry assault with tank support; then by cavalry operating with mechanised brigades against the rear flanks, the whole crushing blow aiming to destroy the enemy and seize his *matériel*.

An infantry (rifle) division would attack on a front of 2500 to 3000 m, a regiment one of 1200 to 2000 m, a battalion 500 to 600 m, and a company 250 to 300 m. Between 75 and 200 tanks should be deployed per division; two gun batteries would cover a kilometre of front. Moving barrages, unsuccessful, incidentally, against the Finns in Karelia, were preferred in support of long-range tanks, whereas in support of infantry and armour, fire was directed against anti-tank and small arms weapons. 'Artillery preparation' involved destruction of enemy artillery, defensive works and tank obstacles before the Red attack went in.

*Armour*: The Russians used tanks in huge quantities, either at long range, or as infantry support, or as cavalry support. Due to faulty staff work, the essential artillery support was not always adequate and, at least in the Finnish War, tank fire on the move was also inaccurate, while infantry support tanks were too lightly armoured.

*Air Force*: In the attack, aircraft were either low flying (Storm), light bombers, fighters or bombers. The first two categories struck the enemy rear before D-Hour and, to turn withdrawal into rout, all types assaulted those troops who had evaded outflanking in the main attack.

Soviet defensive doctrine was the mirror image of the offence. It was designed to meet superior, co-operating forces of all arms, destroy the infantry, prevent an enemy armoured breakthrough or break it down with anti-tank weapons, counter-attack with tanks and other arms including mines, artillery, obstacles and chemical weapons.

★ ★ ★

At Nomonhan, although Japanese defence construction seems to have discounted an early Russian offensive, at least one part of the Kwantung Army believed that the Soviet armies of the Far East would be ready to take the offensive by mid-August. Soviet radio and other methods of deception, designed to convince the enemy that the build-up was defensive only, was negated by high-grade Japanese *de visu* observation of two Russian rifle divisions and eighty guns entrained and proceeding eastwards; by an air attack on a strategic Japanese bridge at Fulaerchi; by aggressive patrolling; and by an accurate – but ignored – intelligence summary.

On 3 August furthermore, four hundred Russian soldiers out of one thousand men were killed in an attack on 71 and 72 Regiments under Colonels Nagano and Sakai, hardly a defensive manoeuvre. Ten tanks were also lost. Similar losses were suffered on 8 August against the 8th Border Garrison Unit, largely through awe-inspiring Japanese grenade attacks. More were killed north and south of the Holsten by other units of 23 Division. A Mongol cavalry division fled in 'laughable disarray', two men on one horse, and others running away naked.

But, on 5 August, 23 Division casualties included over fifteen hundred sick and four thousand wounded. Available Soviet strength, on the other hand, was estimated at two hundred and fifty guns, seven hundred and fifty armoured vehicles, thirty-five infantry battalions, twenty cavalry squadrons, over two thousand machine-guns, greatly exceeding Japanese numbers. All were brought out of Russia by truck, except the riflemen, most of whom marched to the Halha from Borzya. Meanwhile, the High Command in Tokio, seeking to avoid major war with the USSR, had temporarily forbidden any air attack against bases in Mongolia, a grievous handicap for Ogisu and the Kwantung Army.

Zhukov planned to start the campaign no later than 20 August, incidentally coinciding with the signature of the Nazi–Soviet Pact, preceding it by air reconnaissance and deception, the whole directed at the encirclement of the Japanese flanks which, although fortified, lacked mobile reserves. To achieve surprise, transmitters broadcast false information and recordings of non-existent armour and air activity. Conversely, to mask *real* movement, tanks had their treads removed and ran on wheels; the exhaust mufflers were taken off trucks to drown even the reduced sound of the armour. A leaflet, 'Reminders for the Soviet Soldier on the *Defence*' was printed and 'just happened' to reach the Japanese in the field. Additionally, scheduled flights and firings disassociated routine from specific actions in the mind of the enemy.

Unobserved, the Russians began to cross the Halha on the night of 17 August, no movement detected until a Japanese aircraft on 19 August sighted armour hidden among the willows. Northwards, at dawn on the same day, 'Soviet troops in black greatcoats' followed by armour and artillery 'kicking up dust . . . like on parade' were seen in rank after rank encircling Fui Heights.

In fact, the Northern offensive went in against Bargut cavalry five miles further north. It was mounted by the Russian 7th Armoured and two battalions of the 11th Tank Brigade, one regiment of the 82nd Rifle, and the 6th Mongol Cavalry Division, aiming for Nomonhan via Fui Heights and for the destruction of the enemy north of the Holsten. Also directed at Nomonhan, but from the south, were the 8th Armoured, 6th and 11th Tank Brigades, three regiments of the 57th Rifle Division, 8 Mongol Cavalry, all under Zhukov's deputy, Colonel Potapov. The Central force contained 602 and 603 Regiments of 82 Rifle Division below the Holsten, 24 and 149 Regiments of 36 Motorised Rifle Division north of the Holsten in the Remizov Heights near Balshagal, aiming to vanquish the enemy above that river in direct frontal assault.

The 212th Airborne, 9th Armoured and a battalion of 6 Tank Brigade were in reserve on the left bank of the river. Also on the left bank were 122 mm and 152 mm guns and howitzers providing long-range support for regimental artillery stationed with the three groups on the right bank. A dawn bombing offensive from three bomber regiments opened the proceedings, 'the first bomber-fighter offensive in Soviet Air Force History', followed by an artillery bombardment of some three hours' duration. Red rockets fired all along the front signalled the order for the mass of tanks and foot soldiers to go forward at 09.00 precisely under the roar of the guns.

South of the Holsten, by nightfall on 20 August, two regiments (127 and 293) of 57 Division, the 8th Mongol Cavalry, the 8th Armoured Brigade and 80th Regiment had reached the frontier claimed by the MPR at Great Sands (Heights 780–91), at Height 757 and, at the far right, achieving advances of some eight miles. The opposing 71 Regiment, now commanded by Colonel Morita, had been engaged against some fifteen hundred riflemen and two hundred armoured vehicles, with Russian fighters and bombers 'running wild . . . it was a veritable circus overhead and we suffered rage and frustration'. The Central force under Potapov was less successful on the first day, 602 and 603 Regiments of 82 Division gaining less than a mile against Hasebe's 5th Border Garrison Unit (BGU) and Kajikawa's battalion from 28th Infantry. The Japanese claimed that, against their own insignificant losses, although Manchukuoan troops deserted to the enemy, the Soviets had suffered three hundred and seventy casualties. 'The Red Army lacked fighting spirit.' Nevertheless, a pattern was established of Soviet air attack followed by artillery, then armour and, last, the riflemen, so that Japanese supplies of water, food and so forth were soon interrupted.

In the north, the 2nd and 8th Manchukuoan Cavalry Regiments were beaten and sent flying, isolating Colonel Ioki's eight hundred cavalry and infantry at the 'raised pancake' of Fui with its trenches and log bunkers. Ioki was opposed and encircled by 601 Rifle Regiment, the 7th Armoured and part of 11 Tank Brigade, under continual bombardment. 'Smoke blanketed the area and reduced visibility to a couple of metres; earth and sky throbbed like the incessant pounding of drums . . . or like the gongs of hell.' Most of the horses were killed on 20 August. Trenches collapsed. Bunkers were smashed. Men fell dead as they emerged from shelter. In the great heat, destruction of the few, pitiful hand-dug wells meant no water at all. 'Men used towels to wipe up night dew, and chewed on the cloth.' The nearest unit to Fui, at Honiara, was a battalion of Sumi's 26 Regiment under Major Ikuta, a company of which lost sixty-five out of eighty-five men. 'To be killed is all that remains,' said a survivor.

North of the Holsten, the Soviet 36th Motorised Rifle Division, 5th Machine-gun Brigade, 149th Rifle Regiment, 24th Motorised Infantry and a tank battalion took on Yamagata's 64th, Sakai's 72nd and Sumi's 26th Regiments. Russian aircraft 'swarmed like mosquitoes or dragonflies . . . shimmering on high', the Red Star often visible. Russian infantrymen were within thirty yards of the 64th Regimental lines, grenade duels rained all around. The 72nd Regiment too came under artillery, tank and, finally, infantry assault, their positions thin and porous. In the air, despite destruction of many Soviet aircraft, both on the ground and airborne, the Red Air Force had begun, because of relative ease of resupply, to achieve command or, at least, superiority. Even after permission was given for heavy attacks on Tamsag Bulag within Mongolia proper, General Giga, the Japanese AOC, admitted that one hundred and eighty Soviet fighters and fifty bombers were still active on 21 August. Better dispersal, more frequent patrols and new AA batteries had all improved Russian defence capacity since the successful Japanese raid on Tamsag in June.

By 21 August, the Russo–Mongol forces had moved east along seven routes of advance. The Japanese 6th Army under Ogisu did not set up its forward HQ until 23 August. Ogisu's Chief of Staff, Major-General Fujimoto, then went to see Komatsubara at 23 Division HQ. The two officers disagreed. The Red Army and its Mongolian ally were in full, destructive cry. The Japanese could not stand passivity, and the 6th Army sought to destroy the enemy from the rear, south of the Holsten. That required the disposal of one battalion of Yamagata's 64th Regiment and two BGU battalions along the lines, transferring ten battalions southwards. Komatsubara, because 23 Division was so weak, wanted to send only five battalions, leaving Morita's two battalions of 71 Regiment and a battalion of BGUs on the left, 26 and 64 Regiments on the right. The five would be Sakai's 72nd Regiment and an IGU battalion under Yotsuya. Major-General Hata, the artillery man, had to act as conciliator in the debate between Fujimoto and Komatsubara, in which words like 'personal honour' were fiercely brandished. Eventually, Komatsubara agreed to implement the 6th Army's plan to attack the Russian right rear, south of the Holsten river, the Japanese start point being south of Lake Abutara at Lake Mohorehi; the artillery role, involving the movement of 10 cm and 15 cm guns, was prepared in support of the offensive scheduled for dawn on 24 August.

But, from 22 August, the Russians were pressing hard frontally on Colonels Morita and Hasebe with artillery and flame-throwing tanks. Sumi had already been obliged to divert part of his 26 Regiment to both Ioki's cavalry reconnaissance at Fui Heights and the Ikuta battalion. The 6th IGU took over from him, and Sumi was 'returned' to a brigade of 7 Division, also on the left wing, after some plain speaking with Komatsubara. The latter deployed Kobayashi's Right-wing Infantry Group, battalions of the 71st and 72nd Infantry Regiments, field artillery, and so forth, and the Left-wing Unit of *General* Morita's infantry brigade, the 1st and 2nd Battalions of the 26th and 28th Regiments, more artillery and Sappers. Yotsuya and the IGU battalion were on the latter's left.

Most of these formations were, in Alvin Coox's words, 'tired and lacerated', except for General Morita's brigade HQ and two new 28 Regiment batteries. The Red Army still surrounded Fui Heights. Colonel Morita's three battalions were hammered by over a hundred tanks and fifteen hundred men. The Ikuta battalion was severely bloodied at company commander level downwards. Soviet satisfaction at the isolation caused at outlying or holding sectors by Japanese concentration around Mohorehi was considerable.

General Ogisu at the 6th Army, aware that Tokio wanted to avoid major war and therefore wished to localise the battle at Nomonhan, had been reluctant to ask the Kwantung Army to unleash the main body of 'crack' 7 Division. The decision to commit that formation, with river-crossing equipment, but under Hsinking's direct command, was taken on 23 August by the Kwantung Army without prior intervention from Ogisu. In the meanwhile, General Hata had had serious difficulty in moving his 10 and 15 cm artillery to cover the offensive due on 24 August. There was in the thick fog or the dark much confusion. The guns were not all ready by dawn that day. Some of the cannon and howitzers were in position, but the Type 90 field guns had not yet arrived. Bombardment, therefore, could not be synchronised.

On 22 August, Russian armour had 'overrun a quartermaster's dump, ripping up food and clothing . . . burst barrels of pickled apricots drenched the soil with red juice that looked like blood'. Near Heights 753, two rifle companies from 72 Regiment had to be deployed to destroy and drive off forty or fifty Red Army tanks which had encircled 7 Heavy Field Artillery and some infantrymen from 71 Regiment in foxholes nearby.

In dense fog, 28 Regiment reached the assembly point and ate their last supper, of 'cold, half-spoiled rice', and 'cider' which they drank from the bottles and then refilled them with gasoline for use as Molotov cocktails. Trucks to transport 26 Regiment were ninety minutes late. Sumi was thus not ready to go until 07.00 and his exhausted troops had to start fighting in daylight. Colonel Morita in 71 Regiment never received General Komatsubara's full orders for the unit, and his 3rd Battalion was cut up on 23 August.

Russian armour, infantry and artillery had annihilated the garrison on Sankaku Hill – 'heaped with Japanese and Russian dead . . . a gloriously tragic scene' – and on Fui, where Ioki's brave garrison, after suffering 51% casualties against one hundred tanks and 30,000 shells a day, got out on 25 August to the fury of the Kwantung Army. The peripatetic Tsuji was eating a 'delicious dinner of boiled rice, a pickled apricot and a few pieces of pickled radish' with General Morita when he heard the news of Fui and, typically, abused the messenger. He, nevertheless, condescended to drink a toast to victory with General Ogisu.

General Morita, for his part, did not receive 23 Division's instructions until 23.00 on 22 August and then did not know the location of 26 Regiment. In the Kobayashi group, 72 Regiment did not get their orders until 19.00 on 23 August. When they advanced, it was not at dawn, but in thick fog, at 09.30 on 24 August. Ahead lay flat, open country. 'We will be annihilated,' said a young second-lieutenant. 'But we are Japanese soldiers' was regimental HQ's idiotic response.

In the attack, the right (Kobayashi) wing had to proceed with only two battalions of 72 Regiment, and the left (Morita) wing commanded but two battalions of 28 Regiment, now under Ashizuka, and Yotsuya's IGU battalion. There had been very little reconnaissance or preliminary bombardment by air or artillery. The offensive was not in darkness and it was, unusually for the Japanese, a frontal confrontation. As Coox has wisely said, the differences between it and the Russian assault on 20 August, were 'pronounced ... the last gasp effort by Ogisu and Komatsubara was doomed from the start'.

# 19

# Cannae (1)

The Russian response to the counter-attack launched by the Japanese on 24 August was successful for several reasons. On 20 August, when the Red Army had begun its own advance, General Zhukov commanded over a hundred thousand men against the battered and reduced Japanese seventy thousand, the Soviets had, in fact, over two hundred aircraft, eight hundred AFVs, forty-five thousand men in three rifle divisions, two hundred heavy guns. At the end of this fighting these numbers were greater still, with seven hundred aircraft, several more regiments of artillery and an additional rifle division.

Their C in C planned to encircle the enemy south and north of the river Holsten within a solid ring and smash them, first on the south and then on the north of the Holsten, covered from outside the ring. The IJA, beginning on 24 August, intended to break this encirclement, initially against the 8th Armoured Brigade and the 80th Rifle Regiment of 57 Division at the Great Sands. But since General Kobayashi's Right-wing Unit lacked most of Colonel Morita's 71st Infantry, depending heavily on Sakai's 72 Regiment, and since General Morita's battalions from Ashizuka's 28th Regiment and Yotsuya's IGU started so late from south of Moherchi, Komatsubara's offensive failed. Kobayashi and the right, unsupported until late by artillery, suffered fifty per cent casualties, while General Morita's unit was slow as well as late. Both wings, on entering the sand dunes, after severe bombardment from Russian heavy artillery, were then devastated by tanks and infantry.

The Russians, stationed amongst scrub and willow in the open plain, had initially quailed at the grotesque spectacle of 72 Regiment advancing in open order across the wastes. At one position they had even fled, leaving their weapons behind, no doubt at the sight of some Japanese officers crawling 'like rats' while 1st Battalion commander Nishikawa stalked forward, the hilt of his drawn sabre bound in red. Nishikawa was soon hit, but shifted his sword to the other hand and went on under the ferocious sun, even a glint from his field glasses catching the eyes of Soviet snipers. In Kokura's 2nd Battalion at Ipponmatsu, men dug shelters with their hands among grass blazing from flame-thrower attack. In the 1st Battalion, only one company commander was left alive.

Wounded soldiers halted packed ambulances by lying in front of them. Both Colonel Sakai, and General Kobayashi who had been hit by machine-gun fire and then stamped on by his fleeing men, had to be evacuated. Officers fell like flies. One body of forty or fifty men 'ran like mad' until Tsuji gave them grenades and turned them round. This odd man then sprinkled his last drops of drinking water on a dead friend's face. Death was especially common in the 2nd Battalion, whence five trucks bound for the rear held a hundred and forty wounded. The battalion had evacuated 54% of its strength, or seven hundred men, by 25 August. One wounded officer who could neither stand nor sit, but only crouch, shipped himself to Hailar only to protect his men's morale from the sight.

On the left, 26 Regiment being absent, Ashizuka's 28th Infantry buried their belongings and prepared, as members of 7 Division under General Morita, for battle. Hotta's 1st Battalion and Fujioka's 3rd were in the line on 24 August. At first, 'they heard what sounded like birds chirping in the grass . . . machine-gun bullets whizzing overhead'. Men fell everywhere in the noise and smoke. The General, although forty-seven, managed to run for two thousand metres, the men rushing fifteen metres at a time with rifles and shovels, before throwing themselves down. Hotta's battalion was pinned by gunfire. The Regiment's colours were only just saved by a battery which knocked out four tanks while itself suffering more than twenty casualties.

Losses were grave, only thirty men surviving in one of Hotta's companies. Two hundred soldiers were killed in Fujioka's 3rd Battalion, which also became 'entangled' with

Yotsuya. Here, a truck parked because it did not have enough fuel was loaded with wounded and sent off to get as far back as it could. Sumi, leading 26 Regiment, arrived and, also aged forty-seven, ran four kilometres before digging in, in ignorance of Ashizuka's or even Morita's position. One of his companies was within three hundred metres of the Russians by evening. Yotsuya's unit, however, badly hit and with morale low, withdrew despite admonition from Sumi.

Colonel Sumi advised that Soviet weaponry was first class, but that the Russians did not like to be attacked by infantry at night and, therefore, that the Japanese should shun 'costly, ridiculous daylight parades'. Neither Ashizuka at whose command post corpses were stacked up like cordwood, nor Morita had the stomach for night attack, and the 26th Regimental commander's extensive experience was ignored that evening. On 25 August, in daylight, Russian shelters were so impervious to artillery that no advance by division HQ could be made, although Type 90 field guns, now arrived, countered some of the armoured element of the main Red Army offensive. Morita's unit, under tank and artillery fire, without food and water, could not move under the bombardment, 'the most furious that Sumi could ever remember: the cross-fire over his head sounded like the thumping of a windmill'.

Komatsubara had ordered an advance for first light on 25 August. Under devastating shelling, the 1st Battalion of 28 Regiment in Morita's Unit bound for Heights 780 could not advance at all, assaulted in the rear by tanks only just beaten off by a sergeant's platoon. The 3rd Battalion also could not move after the death of its commander, Major Fujioka, against immense fire power from guns now protected by barbed wire. In Sumi's 26 Regimental attack east of 780, Nakano's 2nd Battalion, advancing on flat terrain in broad, sunny daylight, took terrible casualties, including his own death and that of many other officers. A corporal took over one company, and a lieutenant the Battalion.

Nakano's 7th Company did penetrate to within fifty metres of the Soviets who, for a short while, started to retreat.

But the company was down to thirty-five out of an original seventy-five men, including one platoon of thirteen men, and one of only four without even grenades. As they dug in, 'in the light of the setting sun, the silent battlefield looked desolate'. The counter-offensive begun on 24 August had reduced the Japanese infantry from a maximum of seven to four battalions. (Artillery fire had, however, improved by 25 August.) Nevertheless, a Russian company ferociously assaulted on 26 August by no more than thirty men, believed that they had been struck by an entire battalion. But the Soviet guns continued to work, killing eighteen and wounding fifty-four men of 26 Regiment, who made gains of only a hundred metres. Young officers, too, 'had a tendency to stand, not crouch, and snipers were accurate, even by moonlight'. And when Red Army tanks were immobilised, they were always quickly replaced.

Sporadic fighting followed until 29 August, General Morita's regiments in their light-weight uniforms shivering at night in the cold winds of approaching winter, when they were then withdrawn from the attack on Heights 780. Tsuji reported that Molotov cocktails were no longer effective against new or protected Soviet armour and that there were not enough rapid-fire guns, the only other effective anti-tank weapon. Proposals were made for reinforcement by either the guns or the entire establishments of 2, 4 and 5 (now in China) Divisions, and by 59 Air Group. (7 Division was imminently expected to join 6 Army.) It was thought that the despatch of 2 and 4 Divisions might unacceptably weaken the strategic defence of Manchukuo, but when Tsuji saw General Ogisu, the latter gloatingly believed that they were about to be assigned to him. Tsuji was disgusted at this empire-building, also noting puritanically that there was a whisky bottle on the General's desk.

When General Kunisaki's 7th Division arrived on 27 August, it was not deployed in support of 23 Division and the forward defences, but mainly put into 6 Army reserve. (Kunisaki was, however, described as 'shy as a maiden at the outset, but bold as a lion in the end'.) These reinforcements, anyway, were trivial compared with the current Russian total of five rifle divisions, six or seven tank brigades and several artillery regiments, units four or five times greater than the Japanese force.

On 26 August, Colonel Potapov in the south, sent his 6th Tank Brigade against the 26th and 28th Regiments, checked by Ashizuka, but breaking Sumi's battalions and inflicting serious losses in the process. The Japanese escape routes eastwards were now completely blocked, while Soviet aircraft in ten strikes claimed to have destroyed seventy-four JAF aircraft between 24 and 27 August as well as rendering relief from Hailar impossible. Soviet 127 Infantry had contacted 8th Armoured by 24 August and 293 Infantry was advancing northwards.

Ioki's reconnaissance unit had already retreated from Fui in the northern sector, having suffered six hundred casualties. South of the Holsten river, Colonel Hasebe's unit, the 2nd Battalion of 28 Regiment under Major Kajikawa, two BGU battalions under Sugitani and Mijazawa, plus Colonel Morita's poor, tattered remnant of 71 Regiment, had 602 and 603 Regiments of 82 Rifle Division to contend with. The Japanese were originally savaged by the Russian artillery: Kajikawa's battalion held *fifty* survivors by 25 August, of whom only sixteen could fight. Three machine-guns, a grenade launcher and rifles were all they had to fight with, the heavier guns smashed and twisted, nothing left but 'cold steel'. (But even the wounded were required to resist, unless murdered by Russian bayonets as they lay.) Colonel Morita believed himself immune to bullets until taken off by three maxim rounds as he stood up in full view of friend and foe. When Higashi succeeded him, the 71st had lost five hundred killed and three hundred wounded in the previous four days. An attempt by a Japanese battalion to break out eastwards on 27 August was halted by 127 Regiment who destroyed part of the formation, the rest eliminated by 9th Armoured Brigade as they escaped north of the river.

North of the Holsten, the 24th and 149th Regiments of the 36th Motorised Rifle Division attacked the Balshagal Heights. While 601 Regiment of 82 Division and the 9th Armoured Brigade went for Komatsubara's men from north and east, others, including some from 36 Division and 293 Rifle Regiment, drove on for Barunishi Heights, which was eventually taken by Fedyuninski's 24th Mechanised Rifle Regiment. Then 293 Regiment annihilated an escaping IJA formation of four hundred men after their commander had contemptuously refused to surrender.

Ten kilometres south of Fui, Kanaizuka's 3rd Battalion of 64 Regiment and Ikuta's battalion from 26 Regiment, were surrounded. 'Only rifles remained' in defence of positions wholly surrounded by up to sixty armoured cars, ten heavy guns firing at ranges of a thousand yards, and a thousand riflemen. The Japanese grenade launchers had no ammunition. Every officer in one company had been killed; privates commanded the platoons. The survivors made a last bayonet charge, the wounded committing suicide. Soldiers had been earlier buried alive in collapsed trenches, where smoke and dust made even breathing difficult. Kanaizuka did not eat for seven days although, at one point, a Russian bakery truck had been seized, giving pleasure at least to the men.

Colonel Someya's 15 cm cannon batteries had been the first artillery units destroyed on 25 August, the survivors' bodies blackened by flame-throwers, their commander killing himself. In the 1st Heavy Field Artillery Regiment, under a storm of fire which exploded their ammunition and drove the gunners to take shelter, the men were so tired that they even slept through bombardments. Their acting commander made a farewell speech exhorting them to die 'like beautifully falling cherry blossoms', to meet after death at the Yasukuni Shrine. The soldiers then faced towards Japan and gave three *banzai* for the Emperor. The gunners, at the last barrages and impending ultimate tank assaults, smashed their secret lenses and range-finders, while the regimental commander shot his wounded men with a revolver at their own request, 'sending them to heaven'. During this period, this battalion had lost eighty per cent or two hundred and fifty men, of its establishment. It received a citation for a 'glorious ending', the acting commander was cited a 'war god', although chiefly because the circumstances of this battle had deprived the artillery of infantry protection.

Near Heights 742, 'a gunner heard Japanese soldiers singing the national anthem, then shouting cheers for the Emperor, the prelude to mass suicide'. Soviet rings or cordons tightened across the whole battlefield, at a time when the Japanese lacked weapons, ammunition and, increasingly, men, the latter not only dying but sometimes running for their lives. The Russian radio broadcast injunctions to surrender: 'You fellows won't get any food or ammunition . . . stop your useless resistance, lay down your arms and give up.' In one battery, 'each man took a sip of the last saké and passed the bottle round . . .' Elsewhere, 'men could see the desperate struggle and the heart-rending scene of wounded men being stabbed with bayonets'.

The guns had to defend themselves without help from other arms, fighting off the enemy with rifles alone and even medieval weaponry. Men committed suicide or fought to death or were killed or withdrew. Some fled. One man, from 5 Battery of Ise's 3rd Field Artillery, wrote: 'Battery commander, sir: I greatly regret dying today, hit by a shell fragment. The Soviet army does not deserve to be feared, so please fight on to the last. I am very glad to become a falling petal on the borders. I will continue to defend the frontier here for ever. Please don't release this news to the homeland until the war is over. Long live the Emperor!'

From 20 to 27 August, the Red Army had mounted a co-ordinated offensive with the MPRA of infantry (80th Rifle), armour and artillery, seizing the higher ground from the start, dispersing and digging in professionally with good camouflage before launching paralysing artillery barrages. The Japanese, on the other hand, failed to co-ordinate, let alone communicate with one another, made few preparations, artillery or other, acted piecemeal, lacked resupply facilities, depth or resources. Their close-quarters qualities were almost inapplicable when such assaults had to be preceded by marches of more than two miles, in daylight and open country, against an enemy of overwhelming technical and numerical superiority.

# 20
# Zhukov 'At Home'

In the second half of August, Zhukov's headquarters at Hamar-daba were on an eminence on the left bank of the Halha river, approached by a rather steep incline surrounded by deep ravines, not unlike the Upper Don, but without trees. Fortified bunkers had been built into the ravines. Yurts, or *gers*, stood on the upper ground, camouflaged by grass and covered with nets. In the propaganda section of the HQ, the poet Konstantin Simonov found the earth floor littered with photographs taken from Japanese corpses. They were a miscellany, Mount Fuji, snaps of parents, wives, children, cherry blossom, all that heart-break in the huge, military machine with its grand, pitiless movement of events, trampled by the feet of white strangers.

Simonov crossed the river by a tiny, narrow bridge from which a few *gers* and trenches were visible on the east bank. The steady din of the guns was audible from the battle-field eight kilometres away. When he reached the nearest artillery battery, the guns under their netting were firing at Golden Sands, the hillock some three kilometres away. The top of that hill was concave and constantly erupted like a volcano under the weight of Russian shells and the flash of enemy guns.

Fedyuninski, commanding 24 Motorised Infantry, later a General of the Army, had been wounded at the base of the spine. The regiment was now led by little Major Beliakov, dirty, unshaven, great sunken eyes, apparently undernourished, in tin hat and filthy greatcoat, his belt so twisted that it made him look like a hunchback. Many wounded passed on their way back westward across the river, one group led by a swearing sergeant with his arm in a sling, all of whose officers had been killed, and who cursed the Japanese. The faces of recumbent Russian dead, at first thought by Simonov to be resting, were covered by their greatcoats, more than matched in numbers by the many Japanese cadavers on the hill, under it, in trenches, and in the open.

That night, the men slept in little hollows near the trenches, among low bushes. A half-buried Japanese lay in the same dip. The offensive started again at dawn. At the target, the enemy began to jump out of the trenches on top of the hill, retreating over the crest to another rise where the Russian guns caught them. One shellburst caused a soldier literally to disappear. Thirty minutes later, the Soviets had taken the summit of Golden Sands and, by the evening, had occupied the whole hill.

The Russian battalion spent that night amongst the IJA corpses, fans, papers, little bags, very small dry Japanese biscuits and tiny dried fish. The corpses smelled of creosote.

On the next morning, under fierce Japanese artillery fire, the Russians went into the attack against the next hill, and took that too, its trenches stuffed with enemy dead; even later, in the Second World War, the poet was not to have seen so many. At this sector, although firing could still be heard, killing in the fortified communication trenches was by bayonet. A Red Army soldier, knowing that an enemy private pretending to surrender had just killed a Russian company commander, was prevented from rushing another who, with hands high, his face and neck covered with blood spattered bandages, was trying to give up. The smell of creosote persisted from the dead Japanese.

The evening sky turned green and then red, the fighting, broken by occasional rifle and machine-gun shots, began to die away. Japanese, finished off over the next three days, wandered in small groups among hillocks and on the open steppe. 'Skeletons' of damaged tanks and AFVs stood out in the gathering dark. The front wheels of one small tank were jammed in a Japanese trench, a crewman's boots sticking up out of the sand, the gun barrel downwards, the rest of the crew buried. A temporary monument in cyrillic read: 'So you got there in the end, old lad . . . got to the trench, but died at the very last moment.'

On the black steppe, heavy rain in small drops driven by strong winds began to fall, almost parallel with the ground, beating on the felt of the *gers*. The storm in the darkness completely obscured the tents so that one had to feel one's way between them by guesswork and memory and, even when the curtain was opened, there was only a black 'room' without windows. The days were windy, too, but usually dry. The night winds cut to the bone. In the hills, the dead bodies stank of rot and corruption.

The fighting stopped when the Russo–Mongol version of the Mongolian–Manchurian border was attained, flags were raised, barbed wire and anti-personnel obstacles installed, invisible trip-wire laid in the pasture which ensnared and halted men and vehicles. The Red Army was, allegedly, under strict orders not to cross the frontier. Nevertheless, there were sporadic shoot-outs and, at night, the IJA started to fight their way out from behind the Russian rear. Combat had been engaged for months now in the endless grass-covered desert under conditions strategically superior for the Russians, but tactically inferior. Whereas Hailar was only fifteen kilometres from the Japanese position, the nearest Russian railhead at Borzya was seven hundred kilometres away. Yet the Kwantung Army, for its part, had to build a railway line to Arshaan through the Hsingan mountains from southeast to northwest, close to the large arc of Mongolian territory. It had also to take over a strip of territory along the Halha river and its surrounding hills, within Russian field-gun range, to build a vital, strategic railway line from the point where the old line ended, just short of Tamsag Bulag.

Eastward from the Hsingan Ridge, there were bushes, but no trees, on the hills. The deep, narrow Halha was cut by the winding Holsten brook. To the west lay another range of hills, then the endless steppe to Tamsag and another three hundred kilometres to Bain Tumen, and so on to Urga, today known as Ulan Bator or 'Red Hero'.

Buir Nur, Lake Buir, lay to the north, surrounded by very green, low bushes and yellow sand outcroppings. Here was the Japanese border guard post where the fighting had begun, then south to the Khalkhin Gol, where a little house and tower oversaw the Japanese post. The limitless, unprotected steppe ran from left to right and, only here, in the fifty to sixty kilometres along the hills, were there field fortifications, and they were light at that. Outflanking by cavalry should have been very simple. There was, reflected the poet, something odd about a desert war in which Russian tanks, in order to arrive at all, had to make a four-hundred-kilometre journey from Öndorhahn in Mongolia, and in which troops had to march hundreds of kilometres across the empty, baking steppe, all the way from Borzya to join battle.

Simonov believed that the Russians had indeed commanded three infantry divisions, but that the two Japanese divisions, each in any case larger than its Soviet equivalent, were supplemented by special battalions, police, railway troops etc. The enemy thus had had twice the number of infantry, but were outnumbered and outclassed in armour and artillery. Only once did the Japanese, with their technically inferior tanks, mount a real armoured assault; they were not wholly successful even then. By the third month of battle, the Soviet Air Force had also achieved superiority and, on the first day of the August offensive, put a thousand aircraft into the air.

In the sectors nearest to the front, no birds or animals moved but by the Soviet headquarters was a Chinese slaughter-house surrounded by huge piles of foul, rotting entrails, with bustards and eagles perched expectantly on the telephone lines. Duck and geese swam in or flew in their thousands over the salt lakes beyond Bain Burt and Tamsag. The Mongolian government had moved the entire nomadic and other population of the locality westward into Mongolia as a measure against espionage. Only one *arat* (peasant) family, an old man and his wife, were seen trudging doggedly through the wastes with heavily laden camels.

Accommodation for Zhukov's staff and ancillaries was in *gers*, narrow iron beds in a circle against the round felt walls, with a table in the middle where the propaganda writers worked. (The headquarters, as well as housing a hospital, had printing equipment in a long tent.) Sometimes the poet had to compose in his car, a red-hot inferno filled with mosquitoes, all of which had to be squashed or smoked out before work could begin. In the *ger*, the ropes tying the felt to the structure burst regularly, causing the rain and hail to pour in. Frenzied activity to resecure the tent, with a good deal of cursing, ensued, helped by Major Mihailov, later to become a Colonel and to be killed at Kalinin: under his mild smile and wild, angry eyes, the Red Army at Bain Tsagaan had stopped Japanese encirclement and decided the outcome of the first fighting.

In his yellow shirt and trousers, General Zhukov sat at his desk in the corner of the C in C's office, a fortified trench probably built in the last day or two from wood just cut from telephone poles behind the outflanked Japanese lines. The trench was spotless, with curtains and a corridor. The General was not tall, but broad, massive, with a huge white chest. During the discussions, he listened silently, and looked, his thoughts seeming elsewhere, until the commander of the divisional reconnaissance unit claimed that the Japanese were deploying six divisions. Zhukov regarded him with lazy, angry eyes: 'You are lying. There can't be six divisions. They only have two. They're trying to *pretend* to be stronger . . .'*

'I don't *know* if the Japanese will mount another offensive. I personally don't think so,' said the General. 'I think we could leave here tomorrow.'

---

* Two British armoured night attacks in the Great War, one at Bucquoy and one described by Liddell Hart as 'a very significant demonstration of the potential of tanks in night attack' were on a very minor scale, one of five tanks only accompanied by five infantry platoons.

# 21
# Cannae (2) and Komatsubara's Last Charge

On 26 August, despite the deplorable losses already suffered, General Ogisu, commanding the 6th Army, ordered the 2nd and 7th Divisions to resume the offensive. And 23 Division was to continue its offensive, a concept which, under persistent bombardment and without the means even to resist, was quite beyond its power.

Nevertheless, on 27 August, Komatsubara ordered a 'last charge' across the Holsten, deploying 71 and 72 Regiments, Yotsuya's battalion of the 6th IGU, Sappers, Signallers, HQ staff and a field artillery unit. Because of the numbers already killed, wounded and missing, the force probably comprised between five and nine hundred men only, including walking wounded, and with no weapons larger than machine-guns. The General encouragingly ended his final address to the officers: 'I am prepared to die. All of you should share my resolve and carry out this mission with a sublime spirit of sacrifice', a dreadful rallying cry to be heard repeatedly over the next six years, from Kohima to Okinawa.

His ostensible objective was to join whatever remained of Yamagata's 64th Regiment on the Holsten and secure the positions necessary to the 6th Army's planned offensive, an impossible task with the pathetic force at his disposal. If, remarked one of his officers, his real motive was to march to his death, there was no need for him to 'take his subordinates as companions'. Alternatively, if the operation had had any real purpose, the 6th Army should have reinforced it, instead of hugging 7th Division to its own defence.

The party, carrying the severely wounded on stretchers or on litters made of staves, paired rifles, twine and mats, went straight forward to Old Engineer Bridge, losing Sugitachi, the *third* 71st Regiment Battalion Commander to be killed. Dim light trickled upward from trenches which housed sleeping Russians under canvas. The Japanese, intent on silent transit of the river, quietly tucked down the edges and moved on, to be joined, before a cold dawn, by three hundred men under Higashi from the 2nd and 3rd Battalions of 71 Regiment, with only six guns and nine machine-guns.

A dozen Soviet tanks were initially driven off by 71 Regiment, but ten lorries were destroyed and thirteen of seventeen men killed from Hamada's transport company. Kusaba's 7th Field Artillery of three guns destroyed no fewer than ten tanks and killed most of their crews. Ammunition exhausted, trucks unmanageable on the rain-soaked earth, their commander dead, the battery then returned to artillery HQ. Komatsubara, under armoured and artillery attack during daylight, advanced, much slowed down by the wounded, in the drizzling moonless night westward to the supposed position of 64 Regiment, observing *en route* the wrecked and abandoned 10 cm and 15 cm guns of unfortunate predecessors, and bombarded by noisy Russian folk tunes. At 03.40 that morning, Suzuki, one of 23 Division's staff officers, found Colonel Akai's 1st Battalion of 64 Regiment, the unit closest to the river.

Three Red Army infantry regiments including 127 and 293, an armoured brigade, a machine-gun brigade and, finally, Fedyuninski's 24th Motorised Infantry had been unleashed on Remizov (733) Heights since 23 August. Here Yamagata and the 2nd Battalion, aided by Ise's guns, had held the line until 29 August, having lost telephone and radio contact with the Division which had been expected for 28 August. On that day, the Soviets had reduced Yamagata's strength to one hundred and fifty fit men armed only with grenades, rifles and explosives against an enemy thirty yards away. He ordered Akai, commanding the 1st Battalion nearer the river, to mount a diversion at Jugan Heights and then gave orders to all three battalions including the 3rd under Kanaizuka, to make for Nomonhan; 'only a few men' at HQ 'were still unwounded'. At 03.00 on 29 August, the gunners, Yamagata's infantrymen and the Sappers left Heights 733; Higashi's 71 Regiment arrived nearby at 06.00.

After Staff Officer Suzuki had found 64 Regiment's 1st Battalion under Akai, the latter, after discussion and even an order to remain from Komatsubara, took his men out to join Yamagata towards Nomonhan, whether to protect the colours or to show the Regiment's resentment at the Division. Yamagata, in retreat, missed the 23 Division relief force and was caught, men and guns alike, in 'the jaws of Zhukov's Central and Southern' tanks, artillery and machine-guns, his destruction not then total only because of Miyao's Type 90 guns. Ikuta's residual battalion from 26 Regiment, with two machine-guns, was encircled near Old Engineer Bridge. After reciting the Meiji Emperor's precepts, he gave three *banzai* cheers, and led the charge, his men trying to shield the wounded from the tanks. But the armour squelched the wounded in their litters just the same. Only a handful reached the other bank, to be abused as cowards by a 7th Division officer just arrived at the front.

Soviet armour, the guns having smashed the Japanese standard, closed in at last on the trench where Yamagata, Ise and three other survivors had just burned the colours. The two colonels committed suicide with their pistols, one between the eyes, the other through the temple. A wounded sergeant escaped to tell the tale. In answer to Yamagata's order to rejoin the regiment, Kanaizuka in the 3rd Battalion had told his commander that he could not yet leave the wounded. For five hours, under remorseless tank and rifle fire, the Russian infantry charging with grenades, bugles blowing, flame-throwers burning the enemy to death, Kanaizuka's men fought on with decreasing ammunition, guns, water and medicine. 'Wounded soldiers were catching pneumonia, weakening and dying . . .' Further resistance *within* the ring was pointless and the unit, now three hundred men, with very few hand grenades, cartridges or anti-tank charges, broke out 'in the dazzling moonlight' of the early morning of 30 August, the gleam of their bayonets camouflaged under grass. As dawn approached, having evaded Russian sorties, the men passed by heaps of Japanese corpses over which hunched the black, hideous, man-sized *tass*, the giant Mongolian griffin-vulture.

Kanaizuka had lost one hundred and twenty-nine casualties. 'The battalion's survivors amounted to the equivalent of one able-bodied company', one company of wounded, and another of sick. The entire 64th Regiment now comprised only six hundred and fifty-nine men, 'many wounded, all exhausted and tattered'. General Komatsubara saw Kanaizuka on 31 August, and when he discovered Kanaizuka's intention to commit suicide, said: 'Leave your lives to me for a while. We are going towards a new offensive and you can meet death then.'

On 29 August, Russian snipers, tank artillery and infantry hammered Higashi's 71st Regiment north and south of the Holsten. The 2nd Battalion lost seventy men in half a day, the standard bearer having already wrapped the colours round his own body. The 2nd Battalion of the 72nd Regiment had, over the same period, lost up to forty men. In all, the division suffered two hundred casualties that day. General Komatsubara sent messengers to the 6th Army for help and reinforcement and to report that he intended 'to accomplish his mission and die in the graveyard north of the Holsten river'. One of his officer couriers who had shared, at their request, his last hard-tack biscuits with his divisional commander and Chief of Staff Okamoto before leaving, was upset by the chanting of Buddhist prayers among Japanese soldiers, provoking enemy grenade attack.

General Ogisu at the 6th Army, quite drunk according to Tsuji, was upbraided screaming by that officer for allegedly hoping that 'Komatsubara would die'. But rescue, only possible by a 7th Division itself unacquainted with the terrain, would be difficult. Air drops, runners, bomber support, radio contact, nothing worked to save the beleaguered five hundred men of 23 Division now under orders to pull back. In his command post, under mortar and 12 cm howitzer shelling, listening to the moans of his wounded and dying men in that living hell,

Komatsubara ordered all units to withdraw toward Nomonhan. Russian encirclement in the dip by tanks, grenades, and snipers who blew off heads or any other organ exposed, could not be breached in daylight.

The General and his officers destroyed their insignia, buried their uniforms and burned the order books. Komatsubara had to be restrained from leading a suicide charge, sabre raised. Communications, after a last order from the 6th Army, broke down completely even between HQ and Higashi, eighty metres apart.

So 64 Regiment 'disappeared', leaving a gap for Russian tanks between the 1st and 2nd Battalions of 71 Regiment, now outflanked and surrounded. Japanese, never good at the defence, now began to panic; even officers discussed *sauve qui peut* as twenty tanks and eight hundred men closed in. 'The dark-green Russian tanks seemed huge ... blood dyed the dunes; all we could do was fight with an iron will transcending human strength', in combat which included grenades, bayonets, even shovels. Higashi's orderly said: 'We hadn't eaten for a week and our faces and bodies were so misshapen that we no longer looked human.' The colours were then burned, three cheers were given for the Emperor, and Higashi with sword drawn led a charge in which almost every man was killed out of the fifteen colour guards, headquarters troops and other soldiers in the tiny, heroic group.

On 30 August, Komatsubara's headquarters was again assaulted by grenades and snipers. Okamoto lost a leg under surgery with only local anaesthetic. At dusk, Soviet tanks pulled back until daylight and, although unable to remove all the screaming wounded in the command post, 23 Division joined by Hanada and the hundred men left of the 1st Battalion of 71st Regiment, navigated eastward following the North Star, perhaps two hundred men in all, followed by the 2nd Battalion under Takada. Only thirteen of the latter reached Nomonhan.

The two 'battalions' left from 72 Regiment under Captain Hirowatari, faced by five hundred Soviet riflemen, twenty tanks, guns, machine-guns and mortars, also withdrew and arrived at Nomonhan on 31 August. *En route*, apart from damaging encounters with the enemy, they tangled with 71 Regiment and changed course. They would have been even worse off, according to Sapper Colonel Saito, if the 'stupid' Russians had not been so easy to evade by stealth and silence.

The pleading in the moonlight of those wounded and abandoned – 'Are you going to leave us behind . . . please take us with you' – haunted for ever the memories of the survivors. But, against tracer, flares and machine-gun fire, the few fit men 'left their fates to the gods and ran and ran until their unit lost all formation'. The wounded, supported by their mates or hobbling on sticks, limped with them; two corporals held Komatsubara's arms to prevent him from shooting himself as he staggered along.

At one moment, a group of 71 Regiment soldiers actually strayed onto a secret airfield, used by low-level fighters, the crews of which they mistook for Japanese, shouting questions at them. They were totally ignored by the Russians and crawled silently away, inch by stealthy inch.

When, at dawn on 31 August, Japanese trucks were sighted which then took the General to the 6th Army, Suzuki remained behind with the troops to put some order into them, beaten men, shabby, down-at-heel, laggardly. He stayed at his task for two hours. Now 71 Regiment had four officers and two hundred and fifty fit men with only two machine-guns. Companies were commanded by sergeants, even private soldiers. The whole 23 Division comprised perhaps four hundred men. All, or almost all the men, had been incandescently brave. They had, however, been beaten, after a final intervention full of drama and 'honour' but devoid of intelligence; in Coox's words, 'The Death of 23 Division'.

General Ogisu and Komatsubara embraced. 'I am sorry,' said the Commander of 23 Division, 'that I have lost so many of my men. I thought that I ought to have died, but I was ordered to return. I broke through the tight encirclement and came back. Now I'll do my bit to rebuild the Division and restore its reputation.' His aide, tears streaming down his cheeks, said that the General's hair had turned entirely white, his face filled by an indescribable sorrow.

The battlefield was extremely quiet and both the ground and sky looked still.

# 22
# Cease - Fire

Zhukov's armies were now defending a front forty-eight kilometres long, and about ten deep from the forward edge to the
Halha river. This mass, defensive in mode since winter was
only six to eight weeks away, thus precluding an advance into
Manchuria, eventually became virtually impenetrable by ill-
equipped Japanese forces matched against the vast aerial and
ground superiority of the Red Army. Tsuji spoke of new
tactics in such circumstances, specifically night operations for
ninety-six hours in four five-to-ten thousand metre clandestine
advances, in darkness, digging in by day until the unlikely
event of a 6th Army breakthrough on the fifth or sixth day.
Training began of tiny, 'special' infiltration squads, accustomed
to night movement and possessing anti-tank expertise. But no
one had thought of a renewed Soviet onslaught by the mechanised and rifle Corps against these grandmother's steps, or of
the probability of a seven-month stalemate in the iron winter
of the Central Asian steppe.

In fact, the Soviets described the final hostilities at
Nomonhan as consisting, firstly, of an assault by two battalions
of the Japanese 2nd Army on 4 September against an eminence
at Eris Ulyn Obo, driven back by the Southern Force, 'leaving
three hundred and fifty casualties in the field'. A smaller four-
company-sized attack on 8 September was also said to have
been repulsed by heavy casualties. (These examples presumably
referred to the taking of Heights 970 on 4 September by
Colonel Kashiwa's 30th Regiment, and Heights 997 by Miyazaki's 16th Regiment on 8–9 September, both part of General
Katayama's new task force.) Casualties at 997 against the Russians and a Mongolian cavalry regiment numbered up to three
hundred dead and wounded, as opposed to seventy Russo-
Mongol corpses, twenty tanks and several guns immobilised.

The Soviets did not at all mention another action, that

by a Colonel Goto of the 4th Division who, from 10 September, in snow, rain and rising waters, succeeded in pushing a bridge across swamp and river and, with it, the second battalion of his 1st Regiment. The 6th Army believed that Goto had swept the Russians across the river from the south flank, and were very pleased; Goto was ordered to withdraw between 11 and 13 September on replacement by IGU troops, in order to take part in the 6th Army's planned main offensive.

An odd consequence of these encounters was the construction of stone markers by masons in Miyazaki's regiment as a carved memorial along the Japanese front line, later recognised by the joint demarcation committee as forming the frontier between the Mongolian People's Republic (MPR) and Manchukuo.

Zhukov did not now intend anything other than the retention of the territory to which the MPR laid claim, the flat lands to the east or right bank of the Halha. The Japanese, on the other hand, were determined on yet another major offensive, a hammer blow, but this time from the Arshaan–Handagai region southeast of Nomonhan. To that end, Ogisu's 6th Army proposed to deploy Lieutenant-General Yasui's 2nd Division, Kunisaki's 7th Division, Lieutenant-General Sawada's 4th Division, parts of 1st and 8th Divisions, tank, howitzer, anti-aircraft, transport, Sapper, motorised railway (trucks) and other units plus the (later augmented) four hundred survivors of 23 Division. Although all these additions, plus the suggested release of the 5th Division to the 6th Army, tripled that Army's numbers, the force would still be light in men and fire power. Staff officers feared that the IJA divisions would be wiped out just as 23 Division had been; 'an atmosphere of death' permeated 23 Division HQ, even though four divisions and a number of anti-tank units had been alerted even from General Sugiyama's sacrosanct North China Area Army. And 14th Division had also been proposed by the Army General Staff.

A principal motive for the offensive was the need, already mentioned, to recover the dead and wounded, and the colours and imperial crest of 71 and 64 Regiments, suspected lost, before winter forced a halt to all movement until the spring of 1940. But Tokio by 29 August, afraid of a Russian drive deep into the heartland of Manchuria, sought to curb the Kwantung Army and to permit Ueda only to 'hold out with minimum strength in the Nomonhan area'. Imperial General Headquarters (IGHQ) Order 343 indicated the High Command's wish to end the Nomonhan 'war', and to evacuate the disputed areas. The order was delivered by General Nakajima from the IGS to Generals Ueda and Isogai, both smartly at attention to attend the Imperial will. As the 7th and 2nd Divisions had already been posted to the 6th Army, Ueda asked, as a favour, to mount a 'limited, finite' operation to recover bodies, wounded and colours, employing also the 4th and 5th Divisions and three new air groups. Nakajima did not reject Ueda's plea, awed as so many others were by the fire-eaters of Manchuria.

The AGS therefore found itself obliged to draft and send, again via Nakajima, Imperial Order 349 suspending *all* offensive operations by the Kwantung Army, other than air sweeps and actions in self-defence. Colonel Inada of the AGS had not dared himself to carry the message to Hsinking: 'Tsuji would go after me with a sword.' Nakajima, on return to Manchukuo, also transmitted a message from the elderly Prince Kan'in, AGS Chief of Staff, demanding prudence from the Kwantung Army. Japan, it was explained, in the light of the hectic European situation – war had been declared on 3 September between Britain and Nazi Germany – sought diplomatic negotiations with the USSR. No argument could change Nakajima's attitude, murmuring 'it's too bad' in a low, mournful voice, head low, chin in hand.

On his departure, final telegraphed pleas from the Kwantung Army to clear the battlefield were rejected by the AGS after reference to the Throne. Ueda's signalled response 'Our hearts chilled by the iciness of command' was 'soaked and smudged by Tsuji's tears'. The letter ended with the C in C's request for immediate relief. All operations were suspended on 6 September by imperial command, a decision perhaps ratified by the comment from Doi, the Japanese military attaché at Moscow, who believed that the USSR did not intend any major war with Japan. It was certainly influenced by the navy's 'pressure on the Army Ministry and General Staff to deny armour and aircraft support and reinforcements to the 6th Army in order to avoid a wider conflict'.

Ueda, Isogai (Chief of Staff), Yano (Deputy Chief of Staff) and Colonel Terada were relieved. Tsuji was sent to Hankow in the 11th Army, his 'funeral march'. Ueda retired in 1939, Isogai became Governor of Hong Kong, subsequently to be convicted of war crimes, Yano retired in 1943, and Terada, Kwantung Army Operations Chief, eventually commanded Armoured HQ as a Lieutenant-General. Nakajima died in a Djakarta prison in 1949, while Tsuji, after a long career of atrocities, went underground and then, cleared by the American authorities, became an MP, disappearing in 1961 during a visit to Laos.

The whole 'shake-up' was described by a Major Hayashi as 'merely for the sake of appearances . . . Most of the *staff* officers really responsible at Nomonhan were transferred to sinecures, and then obtained important posts with the High Command . . . Even if punishments were meted out, it was only for form . . . while proponents of a prudent approach were treated like cowards . . . [This] fostered a foolhardiness that [provoked] successive disturbances . . . the officers responsible for the Nomonhan débâcle became strong advocates for launching the Pacific War.'

This did not apply to Nomonhan *fighting* soldiers, particularly the commanders, many of whom were rigorously, and most unfairly, disciplined. Yamagata, Ise, Higashi, Umeda and Someya were all driven either to actual suicide or to 'suicide charges' by the 'interpretation' of regulations. The gallant Colonel Ioki, after Fui Heights, was remorselessly harassed until, despite the intercession of friendly officers, he shot himself. Komatsubara and Ogisu also forced the gentle Hasebe to kill himself, after he had removed his uniform coat to prevent the stains of dishonour. Colonel Sakai of 72 Regiment put a bullet through his own jaw. General Morita was retired; Okamoto, in disgrace, was sabred to death in hospital by a lunatic fellow officer; Sumi, who had commanded 26 Regiment, and many other colleagues, none staff, all front-line, were dismissed, Sumi for daring to 'slight' Komatsubara; Takatsukasa, who lost some 10 cm guns and withdrew to the 6th Army, had his title of Baron and privileges removed before being retired; all of them, including Air Force Generals Giga and Ebashi, without court martial or even official record.

Prisoners committed suicide, since to return alive meant disrespect to the Throne and the Yasukuni Shrine, and because they had mocked the Gods. In the 1st Heavy Field Artillery, those encircled were required to kill one another in pairs by the bayonet, standing in the trenches. Elsewhere, survivors tried to bite off their tongues, the Russians having removed their belts. No matter how gallant, or how implacable the circumstances, returnees were court-martialled under the rules of the Imperial Rescript.

Some were locked up by the Russians, like wild beasts in barred cages. Others were found much later with Russian names and married to Russian women in Siberia and the Primorski Krai. One, a baker in Komsomolsk, tagged pigeons, weeping before he released them to a Nippon he would never see again. One Japanese captured in Manchuria in 1945, at the end of the war, found a *ger* containing five or six men, all 'dead soldiers' from Nomonhan. 'We are no longer Japanese,' they said. 'We are Mongols.' And many ex-prisoners lived and died in Ulan Bator. In 1985, Coox's sources believed that there might have been as many as a thousand prisoners of war living abroad in helpless exile, fearful of their fate at the hands of a supposedly unregenerate Army.

One Japanese soldier, however, had a sense of humour. Captured by Pedyuninski's regiment while spying on the Russians from the reeds, he had earlier endured, motionless and for hours at a time, incessant attack by mosquitoes until his eventual surrender. Zhukov himself gave him half a glass of vodka as inducement to 'talk', to which he surprisingly replied:

'Please will you take it first because I am afraid of poison. I am the only son of my father who has a haberdashery shop, and consequently his sole heir.' When the interpreter spoke of the usual Japanese insistence on death rather than dishonour, the private chuckled: 'Father told me to return home alive, not dead.'

In the 1960s, at least General Morita grinned: 'Thanks to Nomonhan I am still alive today! Since I was really an excellent officer, I'd undoubtedly have died in the Pacific War, or ended up as a war criminal.' He and his fellow victims were scapegoats for the failure of Nomonhan and had to take the blame, a waste of gallant trained and experienced leaders.

Meanwhile, on the ground in September 1939, there was uncertainty in Zhukov's Headquarters over Japanese intentions. Unless the enemy admitted defeat, the main Soviet defences against outflanking, apart from the Soviet air force, lay temporarily in the hands of the Mongolian cavalry. At Hamardaba, this was the 8th Division, initially knocked about by Miyazaki. General Zhukov himself, according to a younger Soviet cavalry general who had known him since 1921, was confident that he could encircle the Japanese without bothering to call for assistance from Shtern. (The latter, in the uniform of an Army Group Commander, with shining well-polished boots, accompanied by Air Corps Commander Smushkevich, his long, sad face under a hatless, curly head, and wearing sandals because of feet injured in an aircraft accident, had attended an award of medals at Hamardaba.) Certainly, the General had made fairly short work of the 2nd Division battalions at Heights 970 and 997.

At HQ, luncheon was served in a hospital, anti-mosquito coils burning at each side of every plate. Mutton was the basis of all dishes, *booz*, a delicious meat and garlic dumpling, *hushoor* or mutton pancakes, and rich, greasy mutton soup, on a steppe which already reeked of sheep. Officers and men with coat collars up, hats and gloves on, protected themselves in the late summer heat against the insects. In the nearby shop, a bow-legged Mongol co-operative trader in huge felt boots, sold condensed milk and cigarettes against tugriks, the local currency, with which Soviet pockets were well provided.

Apart from the actions of 2nd and 4th Divisions at the Heights and the river, Handagai having been exempted from the Imperial order suspending operations, air battles were the sole continuing activity. General Ogisu even said on 28 August that the Air Force was 'the only thing the 6th Army can depend on'. Between 23 and 29 August, the Japanese had claimed sixty-five destroyed out of three hundred and forty-five Russian and Mongolian aircraft. On 30 and 31 August, they claimed a further forty, another forty on 1 and 2 September and forty-five more on 4 and 5 September. The Soviet claim for the last week of August was four Japanese bombers and forty-five fighters, twenty-nine pilots killed or wounded in August, and Giga's 2nd Air Division reduced to one hundred and sixty aircraft even after the arrival of two new air groups from China. Most of these claims were exaggerated.

On 5 September, Giga was ordered to turn his command over to Lieutenant-General Ebashi and to relocate from Hailar to Mutanchiang. 'Suddenly I was unneeded,' this highly experienced Kwantung Army Air Commander complained. Ebashi, when fully reinforced from China, now disposed of some three hundred and twenty-five aircraft, mainly fighters, in four wings totalling thirty-five squadrons, to be fit for action by 11 September. Snow fell on that day and Japanese bombers withdrew to Hailar, leaving the 12th Air Division fighters forward.

The Soviets also reinforced. Eighteen heavy bombers and twenty fighters were spotted at Bain Tumen on 12 September, sixteen bombers and sixty fighters at Tamsag Bulag, plus sixty fighters at secret airfields on the west bank of the Halha. Rumours of paratroops circulated and trucks had started to move up from Borzya to Buir Nor. But the last battles of the Khalkin Gol war occurred in the air on 14 and 15 September, in a Japanese attempt to destroy the Red Air Force and its bases, when the usual conflicting claims were made, totals shot down amounting to more than the actual numbers of aircraft deployed on either side. Poor training, and lack of trust, precluded the participation of *many* Mongols, except as Soviet air crews. Indeed, one Mongol pilot defected with an I-16 to the Japanese.

On 24 August, the Nazi–Soviet Non-aggression Treaty shattered Japan's confidence in her German ally, and in the Anti-Comintern Pact of which she was a signatory. In Central Asia, by 31 August the armies of the Soviet Union had effectively castrated the Kwantung Army. On 3 September, Great Britain declared war on Germany. On 1 September, Germany, followed by Russia, had invaded Poland. It was on 22 August that Adolf Hitler remarked: 'Let us think of these people [the Japanese] as lacquered half-monkeys who need to feel the knout.'

As early as 18 July, the Japanese Ambassador at Moscow, Togo Shigenori, had been instructed to begin negotiations with the Soviets for border demarcation and an armistice. Both he and the Kwantung Army believed that negotiations should wait upon an improvement in the 6th Army's position. The instructions were therefore not carried out until the Nazi–Soviet Non-aggression Treaty was signed, when the Tokio cabinet fell and the new Prime Minister, General Abe, facing the alarming facts, ordered Togo to begin negotiations immediately.

Togo was later Foreign Minister twice, and tried for war crimes. (His earlier tenure of the Berlin Embassy had been ended by a reference to Hitler as an upstart.) Addicted to Saville Row tailoring and to striped shirts, as well as, until his doctors in 1945 advised otherwise, to alcohol and cigarettes, on 9 September he called on Molotov, Foreign Commissar and Stalin's loyal creature, to negotiate a cease-fire and to settle other issues including frontiers. The Kwantung Army, until the arrival on 8 September of their new commander, General Umezu, who 'took no guff' from Tsuji and his like, had naturally proposed different ideas to Tokio, such as complete freedom of action to maintain the Halha line as the frontier, and military measures to divide the MPR from the USSR. Doi, in Moscow, had recommended 'greater efforts to perfect war preparations', including readiness to counter-attack.

Molotov agreed to discuss a frontier settlement, a border commission also covering Sakhalin and Kamchatka as well as the Manchukuo–Mongolian frontier, and a commercial agreement. He insisted, however, that the entire disputed area, less a small exchange of territory for the construction of a railway, belonged to the MPR. On 14 September, Togo proposed that 'the situation at Nomonhan and south-west of Arshaan' revert to that on 1 May, that hostile action be suspended, prisoners and wounded exchanged, and agreements concluded locally. A general agreement, including a cease-fire, was accepted next day, neatly permitting the Russians to ease their concern about a two-front war and thus invade Poland on 17 September as a delayed consequence of the Nazi–Soviet pact. The agreement was criticised by Japanese hard-liners who, nevertheless, had to admit that the Soviets, far from imposing a defined frontier, had left it to a frontier commission.

Not all Japanese officers and men were so confident of victory on the rebound, or second time around, as to feel sharp disappointment and sadness at the cease-fire, the vain deaths, the postponement of revenge and the uneasy recognition of defeat. Coox, in describing a Soviet officer standing openly on a crestline, the lining of his cape bright scarlet, green pennons along the Russian lines, 'their vindicated claim to the frontier paints the reality of the IJA's failure, the unhappy end of the Nomonhan war for eager, patriotic, ambitious men outclassed in battle by a despised foe'.

# 23
# Negotiations and a Peace Treaty

The Japanese Ministry of War in 1945 admitted that IJA casualties numbered eighteen thousand, of whom eight thousand had been killed. (War Minister Hata in 1945, when confronted by this figure, said: 'At least.') Zhukov gave his commanders an estimate of about fifty thousand. The American Consul at Mukden, 'from authoritative sources', hazarded thirty thousand. Given a total strength of seventy-five, as opposed to the official and incorrect fifty-eight, thousand and accepting the astonishing seventy-five percent casualties in 23 Division (ninety-three per cent in 71 Regiment), something like twenty-five thousand casualties, chiefly by shelling, is not implausible.

The Soviets at the 1945 War Crimes Tribunal would not admit to much more than nine thousand Russian and Mongol casualties. But, even allowing for huge Soviet superiority, the figure seems low measured against anecdotal evidence at the time and against Zhukov's notorious indifference to his own losses.

The two five-man local military delegations met on 16 September among low sandy hills and narrow ravines, one of which held a single crooked tree. The weather had become cold and wintry, with an icy wind which flattened the grasses. Toward the grey and yellow outcrops of the Hsingan hills, smoke rose from fires, corpses burning or Japanese field kitchens. Over the horizon, shone a dim, watery sun. Three large tents had been provided for the Russians, and a ceremonial silk tent (*maihan*) for the meetings, like those in Prince Igor or Turandot or the medieval Princes' tents in children's books.

Colonel Potapov, promoted to Major-General, later to be commander of the 5th Army, wounded and captured in the 1940s by the Germans, received the Japanese in their winter greatcoats with huge, dog-fur collars. These, bizarrely accompanied by a camera crew, and led by a General with two or three colonels, saluted the Russians with sabres. A soldier opened the curtain in the silk *maihan*, revealing a wide table, two dozen chairs and two armchairs. The Japanese major acting as principal interpreter, tiny, giggling, a bespectacled Asiatic cartoon figure, spoke very rapid literary Russian in a strong Japanese acent, using endless proverbs and sayings. The officers smiled in a stressed mode as if trying to placate or to imitate 'civil' Westerners. The other ranks, sensible peasants, did not smile at all.

The main points were for resolution in Moscow. Discussions at Khalkhin Gol concerned demarcation, an end to combat on 19 September, and the mutual exchange of corpses, wounded and prisoners. Most of these, except forty Mongols killed in Manchuria during encirclement, were put out of action in territory firmly claimed by the MPR.

The Soviets believed *at this time* that between twelve and fifteen thousand Japanese had been buried where the last fighting took place in the last days, according to a 'chart' held by a bandaged Kwantung Army lieutenant against the actual evidence of the corpses. The Kwantung Army sought to recover as many bodies as possible without official enumeration or, although the Japanese newspaper *Asahi* had already published a figure of fifteen to eighteen thousand casualties, without alarming the public at home. The Russians for their part did not want the Japanese digging in 'their' territory, but also did not want 'their' boys to do Nippon work on up to fifty sites in MPR lands. They accordingly agreed to ten one-hundred-man groups of Buriers, the officers bearing side-arms, rifles for the other ranks, officers carrying swords, the men daggers. As to the corpses, any firearms recovered became Red Army booty, the Kwantung Army trousering the contents of dead men's pockets.

In the 'corpse' tent, where the bodies lay, the interpreter showed reluctance to drink from bowls filled by three pretty girls from the Russian Military Trade Organisation until persuaded that drinking was mandatory from vessels filled by females. Quite soon, every one became very drunk indeed. A Japanese Major-General had already grotesquely opened proceedings by intoning: 'Today's moon shines upon our pleasant gathering, and sets as the gathering ends.'

Next day, he gave a dinner before the transfer of corpses got under way. The bodies were taken in ten columns of yellow/green Japanese vehicles flying white flags and piled with stinking blackish cadavers, through ten passages in the barbed wire. After ten days digging, over eight thousand corpses had been recovered (Coox says over four thousand) and, if time had been allowed, more could have been removed. At first, the diggers formed up, bowed and put on resin-soaked bandages across their mouths but, after a return of hot weather with its terrible stench of death, they had no way of breathing. At the side of new, gaping graves, Japanese soldiers sat, helmets off or on the backs of their heads, bandages across their noses, while half-rotten rags were flung without much respect on the poor bodies below. The officers stood apart, marking off the finds on their 'charts', mouths bandaged.

Behind a range of hills on the flat steppe the Japanese were pouring gasoline on corpses found in a trench six feet wide. As they lit the gasoline, ammunition and grenades exploded on the bodies. The Russians wondered whether this represented a sacred burning, the ashes, or those of their horses, to be placed in urns, returned to next-of-kin. They felt pity for the dead, repugnance for the living.

On 2 October, the exchange of wounded followed. The walking wounded were at one station, and the seriously wounded at another where aircraft could land behind the Russian left flank. Two hundred lightly wounded and bandaged Japanese walked away to Manchuria, thirty drove by lorry. Four Russian and four Japanese aircraft landed; three of the Russian aircraft were empty, the fourth containing twelve badly wounded, emaciated, dirty, unshaven Soviet soldiers. A senior sergeant disembarked, grey-bearded, his eyes sunk in his head, chest bandaged, leg in a splint, half-burned military tunic with no sleeve, wounded in the arm. Food was brought from the Russian hospital, chocolate and condensed milk.

A Soviet aircraft later brought Japanese wounded, all on stretchers, in clean Japanese uniforms, underwear, blankets and greatcoats, 'in full military order', seized by the Soviets from a store during the battles, given then to their prisoners. The Japanese commander, Hamada, whistled with rage. His men hurled the stretcher cases brutally to the ground: these prisoners wore thick, white, paper bags or sheets like flour bags over their stretched necks and raised heads.

The odious Hamada smiled, his lower lip pulled back in an arrogant grimace, then nodded towards the prisoners. 'We put them on for their benefit, so they wouldn't be ashamed to look into the faces of officers and soldiers of the Imperial Japanese Army.' The poet Simonov said 'au contraire', without hope of being understood. Eighty Russian tankist prisoners marched silently by, followed by open cars containing Japanese who waved their wounded limbs to the Russian doctors and nurses who had welcomed them. General Komatsubara wept as he inspected his dead soldiers.

The exchanges of corpses were fairly free of confrontation although, at the beginning, Soviets in immaculate uniforms rather shamed less soigné Japanese, in particular when they complained about the IJA's behaviour in waving the Rising Sun. The meetings also were amicable, marred by the stupidity of a Japanese sergeant in asking his opposite number whether he didn't think his enemy had been brave. 'No,' replied the Russian, in Japanese, 'don't be such a jerk, we won the war.' Later, one Kwantung Army soldier, after 'brainwashing', had shouted: 'Long live the Japanese and Russian proletariat.' Most, however, were downcast and ashamed, but the Russians seemed 'happy, elated and proud', at least *before* returning to the USSR.

The Soviets returned the Japanese banquet with one of their own, 'champagne', caviar, hors d'œuvre, dancing with Red Army girls. An NKVD general chatted in French with Colonel Inada from the Army General Staff. Relations became more friendly in direct ratio to the length of time taken by the exchange.

The searches covered four main areas including Fui and found dismembered bodies, bodies crushed by tank treads, incinerated bodies, decapitated, all decomposing, vilely smelling. The bodies of Yamagata, Ise and Higashi were dug up. Under Yamagata were part of the standard and the tassels of the 64th Regiment colours, the chrysanthemum globe of which was buried in the legs of another corpse. No trace of the 71st Regiment colours were ever found.

The Imperial precepts prescribed 'never, by failing in moral principle, fall into disgrace and bring dishonour on your name'. An imprisoned soldier disgraced his Emperor, his family and his cavalry and was to be despised and shunned as a coward. It is thus the more remarkable that up to three thousand Japanese prisoners, according to Japanese medical records, are alleged to have been captured, 'thousands' seen on a train from Ulan Bator to Chita in 1939, and 'five to six hundred' in a Chita compound in 1940. Only eighty-seven Russian prisoners were handed over at Hamardaba, and the final exchanges were not completed until April 1940 in Chita. On that occasion, many of the pathetic Japanese kept their eyes down before General Fujimoto's staff, several blind anyway, many without arms and legs as they tried to support one another. Nakayana Hitoshi, a private captured at Nomonhan, was put on a stretcher and eventually made to sit up, astonished that he was not shot there and then. He imitated cutting his throat. The Russians would not follow, giving him water instead. He tried to seize a pistol and shoot himself, but was prevented. A Mongol nurse offered him a drink. He thought it was poison and, again, acted the slitting of his throat. The nurse, laughing, drank from the glass herself. Later, upon returning to his unit for court martial, Nakayana was sentenced to only twenty days' imprisonment, then posted to a 'secret' unit building bunkers in Manchuria until his term of service expired.

In Moscow, Molotov told the Supreme Soviet on 31 October that 'peace had been fully restored on the Mongolian–

Manchurian frontier'. A Soviet Ambassador was appointed to Tokio. Agreement between Togo and Molotov about a mixed commission on demarcation of the frontiers was reached on 19 November, to begin at Chita and continue at Harbin. The Soviet side was led by 'Major-General' Bogdanov, more like a diplomat than a professional soldier, impressive, low-key and bespectacled, much influenced by an obvious NKVD colonel. The Mongols were present under their shabby, ineffective, acting prime minister, Jamsarong, who resembled a country mayor and spoke foolishly. The Consul-General at Harbin led the Japanese delegation, the Kwantung Army was represented by Major Mishina, and the Manchukuoans by a Hsinking foreign affairs official. All were housed in the best, but heavily bugged, hotel in the quiet, snowy little town of Chita. The first Russo-Mongol presentation had placed the border further to the west than the Japanese had feared, but Tokio's instructions were correspondingly imprecise. At Harbin both sides became more intransigent, the Japanese insisting on the Halha as the border despite the Russian maps from 1734 and 1859.

Eight unsatisfactory meetings took place in Manchuria, the Japanese only conceding territory south of Arshaan. (Meanwhile, in Moscow, some agreement was reached on fishery, and the Japanese paid the last instalment on the Chinese Eastern Railway.) Mishina thought that the Russians, 'tied down in Finland and ejected from the League of Nations', were only probing their opponents. On 30 January negotiations ended with the unexplained departure of Bogdanov and Jamsarong from Harbin, allegedly because of threats from White Russians, working perhaps for Tsuji, against Bogdanov's life.

On 9 June 1940 in Moscow, Togo and Molotov had signed an agreement, possibly to free Moscow's hands in Europe after the Wehrmacht's victories there, covering the general shape of the Mongolian–Manchurian frontier. (Togo was then replaced as Ambassador by the General who had *started* the Manchurian incident!) The details were to be left to a boundary commission. This completed its work only in

May 1942, with the advantage to the Soviet side, when Stalin prettily observed that attackers would always 'receive a crushing repulse to teach them not to poke their pig snouts into our Soviet gardens', remarks directed as much to opinion in Ulan Bator as in Moscow. President Choibalsan in return expressed praise, gratitude and thanks, as well he might.

Huge quantities of medals – Hero of the Soviet Union, Order of Lenin, Orders of Red Banner and Red Star, Order of the Rising Sun, Order of the Golden Kite; Hero of the Mongolian People's Republic, Order of the Pole Star – were distributed by all three founts of honour, to units and to individuals. Mongolia and Manchuria are, nevertheless, places which people *leave*: as late as 1985, Coox tells us that only thirty-five thousand people were still living on the black soil of the unprepossessing Dornod district, devoted to unproductive State experimental collective undertakings. Togo became, as we have seen, Foreign Minister, once at the outbreak of Japan's 'Southern' war and once before it ended. Zhukov was later Chief of the General Staff, Commander before Leningrad, Western Front Commander, Deputy to Stalin as Supreme Commander, Marshal, after the war C in C Soviet Ground Forces, disgraced, then Defence Minister and final dismissal.

In October 1941, Generals Shtern and Smushkevich, both Jews, were executed on Stalin's orders, just before Barbarossa, the German invasion of the USSR.

# 24
# Zhukov on Victory

Zhukov, in his memoirs, remarked that the '[Soviet] units which had fought in Mongolia . . . when moved to the Moscow area in 1941 fought the German troops so well that no praise is too high for them'. MPR troops, particularly the armoured battalions (Panzer) at Bain Tsagaan in July, had also fought well in Mongolia, with the reservation about their cavalry previously mentioned.

He judged the Japanese objectives at Nomonhan to have been the seizure of territory claimed by the MPR west of the Halha river, and of land necessary to defend a railway line yet to be constructed. His own strategy had been to combine the air weapon with concerted armour, artillery and infantry in depth, both for offence and defence, operating in combat groups. Unfortunately, thereafter, the incompetent Voroshilov persuaded Stalin, until after Barbarossa had begun, to break up the existing mechanised corps. The production of aircraft and anti-tank armament was curtailed at about the same time in favour of heavy guns. Whereas Zhukov beat the Japanese in ten hectic days, it has been noted that the Russians took over three months to conquer Finland, a country with a population of less than four million.

As Coox observed, Nomonhan was the Russian 'first test of war with tanks, artillery and aircraft used on a large scale'. Zhukov found it possible to praise Japanese training, especially man-to-man, and the courage of junior officers. He was critical of their AFVs, artillery and aircraft, and of the lack of flexibility in the thinking of their senior officers. He assured Stalin that Tokio had been humbled by defeat and, of vital importance, had drawn correct conclusions about the Red Army and its power for the future.

His main emphases were on fire power in joint operations, and on securing *matériel* in overwhelming quantity and quality, particularly artillery, transport and AFVs. Planning, intelligence and reconnaissance had been deeply researched. Surprise was achieved most significantly between 20 and 31 August 1939, after which the Japanese had been driven out of the disputed frontier area without any further Soviet attempt to expand the war further into Manchuria.

The Soviet General Staff doctrines of superiority, mobilisation of the Home Front, political control, correlation of military, economic, scientific and moral–political forces had been satisfactorily co-ordinated. Concentration of the main strength, combat readiness, inexorability, large unit co-operation, maintenance of the reserve, simultaneity of attack in depth along the line, firm and continuous command and control had all been accomplished. Political aims, defence of the MPR and enforced reconsideration in Tokio of future military action against the USSR and the Soviet 'Family', were precisely secured, no more, no less. The mailed fist had been raised and brandished: Japan could not deny nor evade a reality which made wishful intentions yet more chimeric.

From the Japanese side, in excessive concentration on spiritual strength to the relative disadvantage of improved fire power, some Japanese commentators *did* try to evade that reality, although failures of mobility and artillery, severe enough to militate against the close combat in which the IJA excelled, were recognised. It was at least agreed that frontal assault should henceforth be eschewed, the artillery to dominate the enemy's guns while infantry and artillery went for the flanks . . . Too much blame was avoided: 23 Division had after all taken on four rifle divisions and five mechanised brigades for four consecutive days. Nevertheless, the degree of mechanisation had been crucial to the Russian 'victory' which most if not quite all Japanese admitted. A great error had been made in judging the Red Army on the basis of the IJA's experience with Chiang Kai Shek's armies, vastly inferior to the Soviets.

But not enough of a practical nature was done to strengthen the Japanese technological base in the arms factories. Even after the lessons of Nomonhan, the production of tanks and the mechanisation of artillery were neglected in favour of aircraft and horse-drawn guns. The Kwantung Army, at mobilisation in 1941, was allocated 350,000 more men and 370,000 horses. (There were, incidentally, only nine thousand non-official motor vehicles in all Manchukuo.) The ammunition supply also was so inadequate that 'guns were lined up without ammunition like inedible painted cakes'.

The brilliant Endo Saburo, Deputy Chief of Staff of the Kwantung Army, recommended that until the China Incident was concluded, military effort should be devoted exclusively to the China campaign, and to the avoidance of confrontation with the USSR. There should be no huge, provocative build-up on the frontiers. Russia was triumphant after Nomonhan, and her material strength could not be ignored. A defensive strategy to engage the Red Army *only on Manchurian soil* must be devised. The Japanese Army had worn itself out in China. It was incapable of destroying the Soviet armed forces in Siberia, let alone conquering the USSR itself. These arguments were superior to the panic warning of the operations section that the home islands themselves were vulnerable to bombing from Siberia. They were, however, unsuited to the mindless, continuing chauvinism and self-interest of the Kwantung Army, which successfully rejected them.

A British official opinion, more favourable, in this case, to Japan, judged that at Nomonhan the Red Army had shown itself to be definitely superior to the IJA in mechanised warfare. But although Soviet confidence and morale had been strengthened by the experience gained here and even in the Finnish War, it was thought that Russian advantages would diminish as the Japanese strove to end the China War and create a mechanised–motorised army. The British supposed that if there were to be war with Russia, the Japanese could afford to withdraw ten divisions immediately from China. Nor would she suffer the *matériel* surprise – eastern Manchukuo was not *tank* country – which the Kwantung Army had endured at Nomonhan.

But East Siberia had become *chasse gardée*. No words could describe the surprise, shame and humiliation suffered by the Imperial Japanese Army, even the whole nation of Japan, insofar as the facts reached it, at defeat by the principal and despised Russian enemy, and at the treason of Germany, the principal, most admired friend at least of some Army seniors.

The Strike North or fight Russia faction, the 'Imperial Way Group' which loosely included Foreign Ministers Araki and Matsuoka, Generals Mazaki and Hayashi, although it never ceased to flex its coils, was effectively smothered by the Strike South faction. The latter, if not without middle-rank Army support, was led by naval officers who sought to expand the fleet through the strategy of the Southern Advance, and to reach some accommodation with the USSR. But bitter discussion would follow before the executive decisions were reached, the carriers and battleships weighed anchor and, the fate of four empires determined, 'the expansionist urge shifted from North-East to South-East Asia' in Japan's search for autarchy.

# 25
# The End of Strike North

A door had shut. Japan's situation had not improved, over-populated and without land for industry and industrious people, without raw materials, a great nation in embryo without territory or resources, dragged down by the endless China War, economically unsatisfied by Taiwan, Korea and, above all, Manchukuo, *still desperate to expand abroad.* But where, other than the regions, barren enough anyway and now closed, of Russia and Mongolia?

In 1939, after Nomonhan, it was little remembered that, in November 1919, the United States had rejected a Japanese proposal to overthrow Admiral Kolchak and share the raw materials, markets and territory of Siberia. Popular revulsion in America against Intervention, and Japan's role therein, had triumphed.

As was shown in Chapter 2, between then and the spring of 1920, all Allied contingents other than the Japanese withdrew from Russia despite Japanese protest. So irritated had US relations with Tokio become that General Graves' Americans left Vladivostok harbour on 1 April 1920 to the strains from a Japanese band of 'Hard times come back no more'. Pleading chaotic conditions on 31 March Japan had reversed her own announcement of withdrawal, declaring that she would not abandon Russia until the lives and property of her nationals and the safe operation of the railways were secured.

On 14 April, as was earlier shown, in brutal, co-ordinated attacks, her army and the forces of her local puppets took control of all the Russian railway towns of the Primorski Krai, the Maritime provinces of East Siberia. (The Soviets, for their part, had established their own Far Eastern Republic under Krasnoshchekov at Verkhne Udinsk, a Leninist wolf in bourgeois democratic clothing, who drove the monster

Semënov out of Chita by October 1920.) A massacre by Soviet partisans of Japanese military and civilians at Nikolaevsk gave Tokio the excuse for occupation also of North Sakhalin, with its oil and raw materials, and the coastal areas. The Far Eastern Republic acted meanwhile as an 'anti-Communist' buffer state between, on the one hand, the USSR and Mongolia and, on the other, Japanese possessions in Manchuria and their Siberian commercial outlets, guarded initially by two hundred thousand armed men.

Japan sought to dominate, if not all Russia, then at least Siberia east of Lake Baikal chiefly through control of the Trans-Siberian Railway. This objective was made difficult by the Allied wish to achieve a settled, unified Russia, an aim quite opposed to Japanese dreams of hegemony. Japan sought iron ore, oil and other natural riches, with strategic control of continental territory as the key to trade with Western markets. It was not until October 1922, after the Washington Conference, that these objectives were temporarily discarded by the withdrawal from Siberia of the Imperial Japanese Army. North Sakhalin had to wait until the Soviet–Japanese Treaty of 1925 when, in exchange for aid and other concessions, it was rid of the IJA jackboot.

Japan had already taken advantage of Russian weakness in the Great War by demanding economic and territorial concessions. After the Tsar's fall, Tokio attempted to exploit the confusion by supporting rival successors to Imperial and, later, Provisional rule. Indeed, an article in the newspaper *Gaiko Jiho* referred as early as 1904 to Japanese military–political intentions: 'In the first war, it will be enough for us to reach Baikal. In the second war, we shall plant our flag in the Urals and water our horses on the Volga.' By the Russo-Japanese Treaty of 1916, Russia gave part of the Chinese Eastern Railway to Japan, a cession which was, in the event, not then implemented, and they agreed not to oppose Japan in China. At the same time, she was unsuccessfully urged to surrender North Sakhalin, *even all Siberia east of Baikal*, in exchange for the despatch of half a million Japanese soldiers to prop up the Eastern and Western fronts against Germany after the Tsarist Armies collapsed. In fact, as we have seen, the Japanese took North Sakhalin in 1920 in reprisal for massacres at Nikolaevsk, together with the Siberian coast.

Japanese participation in the Siberian intervention was therefore neither unexpected nor one which shared the objectives of the Allies, in particular of the United States, which sought precisely to *prevent* Japanese hegemony in eastern Siberia. Rule by terror through Kalmykov, and Semënov in his armoured train, was the preferred Japanese method, supplementing physical control of the railways and as much territory as was practical. (Semënov was described by Colonel Ward, commanding the Middlesex Regiment contingent, as 'an enormous head . . . with a flat Mongol face from which gleam two clear brilliant eyes that belong rather to an animal than a man'. He and Kalmykov tortured, robbed banks, murdered hundreds of unarmed prisoners at a time, whipped their victims with knout and chain; in battle, both behaved with great incompetence.) The Japanese objective in the Intervention was neither to make peace nor to unify a distraught and bleeding Russia, but to create as much disorder as was necessary to 'justify' armed Japanese presence in eastern Siberia, permitting the forcible exploitation of the region's oil, iron ore, lead, silver, zinc and the strategic use of the railways.

Japan's withdrawal in 1922 was, it will be recalled, followed by a retreat from North Sakhalin in 1925. Although that set-back was assuaged by oil, coal and timber concessions and a fisheries treaty, all negotiated between 1925 and 1928, the material and psychological damage inflicted on Japan by the ending of her dream of Russian conquest was considerable and unforgotten. Big business and the rising military expansionists, in the years leading up to 1939, certainly remembered.

'Big business', the *zaibatsu* such as Mitsubishi and Mitsui in shipping, manufacture, banking, trade and mining, provided the modern technology and increased capital formation that led from the 1920s to Japan's remarkable industrial development and attendant exports. These, further expanded after 1931 by the collapse of the yen, included cheap textiles, especially cotton, and non-textile consumer goods such as light electrical equipment, toys, canned goods and so forth, which eventually flooded British, European, African and Asian markets, admittedly balanced by raw material and other imports. According, however, to W. W. Lockwood's *The Economic Development of Japan*, by 1936 Japan was almost 100% dependent on foreign imports of petroleum, cotton, wool and rubber, 60–80% iron and steel, 95% superphosphates, 20% rice and beans and 35% fats and oils. This was dangerous dependence for an economy battered world-wide, as a consequence of the Depression, by tariffs and quotas against her exports.

This foreign protectionism, coupled with population pressure (an increase from 35 million in 1875 to 69 million in 1935) increasing at a rate of 700,000 per annum with an obvious threat to food supplies, bred, in the view of the British economist, Professor Penrose, 'social unrest, terrorism, the rise of the military and such events as the 18 September 1931 Manchurian Incident . . . the Army's increasing assumption of direct control over the State', which trade restrictions could only aggravate. Industrialisation at home, emigration and industrial expansion abroad against hostile trade boycotts, was the most advocated scenario, but one with obvious and depressing caveats, in particular the drain on Japan's few resources caused by the armaments programme and barriers abroad to trade, emigration, and Japanese capital.

In responding to the Manchukuo and China (1937) Incidents, neither the League of Nations nor the UK and US Governments favoured sanctions against a heavily armed Japan, nor was an economic boycott then approved. As we have seen, the export solution to the deteriorating standard of living was impeded by other countries' trade barriers and by 'insecure access to foreign natural resources'. In the meanwhile, banks failed, the great earthquake of 1923 shook the country's stability, scandals multiplied, agricultural prices plummeted, unemployment soared, Britain diminished the Anglo-Japanese Alliance under American pressure and to Tokio's justified resentment. In the 1930s, secret societies worked toward Fascism or the suppression of democracy, coup d'états were staged by soldiers *and* sailors, two prime ministers were assassinated, one after the London naval treaty had humiliated the navy. Rioting was frequent and widespread, a Korean attempted to take the Emperor's life. In 1936, an actual revolution was plotted by the 'Young Officers', even the attempted occupation of the Imperial Palace. In that year, the finance minister and the inspector of military education were murdered, the deaths of other ministers and the grand chamberlain narrowly avoided, the Lord Keeper of the Privy Seal killed over his wife's body, the overthrow of the entire system only just averted.

'Protection' by the British Empire, the United States and Europe, on the excuse of Japanese price undercutting through exploitative wages, had thus taken the usual form of preferences, quotas and tariffs, creating further unemployment, hunger, poverty and suffering in the islands. Xenophobia and violent nationalism driven by the military's despotic leadership followed inexorably, accelerating diversion of industrial production into rearmament. The conviction grew in both the army and the navy, descendants of the samurai now helping to dictate foreign policy, that in order to achieve economic goals while meeting the requirement for armaments, aggression abroad was the only practical course.

The government, after the Meiji Restoration, had gradually built huge enterprises to safeguard the realm, including steel and shipping which were then sold to business firms soon to expand into powerful financial combines, the *zaibatsu*, collaborating in the alliance of 'sword and yen' with the *samurai*. Victory in the Russo-Japanese War of 1905, successes in the Great War on the Allied side, in Shantung and through a naval presence assisting Mediterranean convoys, the acquisition for her industries of large Asian markets, had all confirmed the ascendancy of the military, weakening the claims of democracy and self-government. That ascendancy later became an unfortunate factor during a recession which deprived Japan of many markets for her manufactured goods in an economy which, because of her lack of raw materials, made self-sufficiency, let alone autarchy, impossible. Free trade was a dead letter worldwide, each national economy groping in a blind, panic-stricken rush to save itself, compounding all the problems.

Japan, although smaller than Texas, had by the 1930s reached a population of eighty million with a density of two thousand nine hundred people per square mile of arable land, the highest in the world, short of raw materials and import dependent. According to Lockwood, Government deficit financed by borrowing had risen from six hundred million to one thousand three hundred million yen in 1937, and then almost doubled again in 1941. Inflation rose, under pressure from the vast expenditure abroad on foreign armaments. Vexatious and distorting import controls were introduced and foreign exchange diverted to oil and steel rather than to consumer goods. Despite a general opinion in favour of peace, the incident contrived by the military in 1937 at the Marco Polo bridge ended in the draining, horrible war with China which ruined both countries and continued until Tokio's surrender to the Allies in 1945. As early as 1940, 17% of the GNP was devoted to war: the omens were clear and unpropitious for peace.

In 1939, there had been a massive crop failure in Korea, flooding in Taiwan, a slump in Manchukuo because of the diversion of resources from industrial construction to the prosecution of war in China. Demand fell for the Manchurian soya crop because of the growth of Japan's chemical industry and, perhaps, because of increased rice and sugar beet plantings. In Manchuria, supplies of cotton, wool and timber were inadequate for Japan's demanding economy and, in North China under Japanese occupation, cotton supplies shrank rather than grew. Manchurian and Chinese population growth, only 10% of the vital agricultural sector of Manchuria was filled by Japanese peasants, in relation to the development of new land, meant that by 1930 the area of unused but cultivable land had fallen considerably. Japanese *food* requirements were, however, roughly met by Taiwanese and Korean supplies, including 20% of Japan's grain consumption and, later, from Indochina and Thailand, although at heavy foreign exchange cost.

Less than 7% of Japan's petroleum consumption was met by the homeland and the colony of Taiwan. The remainder was imported from the United States, by far the principal supplier, and the Netherlands East India, plus some 100,000 tons annually from the Sakhalin concessionary reserve of three hundred million barrels. Military and aviation demands for iron ore could similarly not be met from Japanese or colonial sources, other than in smallish quantities from North Korea. In Manchuria the quality of iron ore, according to Christopher Howe in Doret and Sinha's *Japan and World Recession* was very variable, and few major oil sources, other than shale for coal liquefaction, were discovered. Coking coal was available in North China for the iron works at Anshan, but fluorspar, graphite, molybdenum, gold and silver, although available, were not exploited in quantity. Wood and timber supplies were also inadequate. Sugar-cane from Taiwan and potatoes were used to manufacture alcohol for combination with gasoline; gas and iron were produced from lignite and iron sand; aluminium was made in electrically powered factories; but none enough for long-run self-sufficiency after the China Incident began.

Japanese colonial attitudes, which theoretically emphasised racial and economic equality, in practical terms failed to engage the goodwill and whole-hearted co-operation of the colonial labour force. The colonies, therefore, provided no way out for planners, in particular military planners more protective of strategic security than of the needs of the common man. And as Howe ironically pointed out: 'Japanese attempts to control vital resources in China had been a major factor in drawing Japan to *war* with that country, but, on the other hand, the prosecution of the war was dependent on imports from the USA, Japan's ultimate enemy in a global Armageddon.'

Thus, the framework within which these factors operated was provided by the military's aim of harnessing the resources of the nation and, through autarchy, providing Japan's economic security in circumstances of total war. This ambition, implausible enough in the almost complete absence of home-grown resources, was further weakened by the apparently endless requirements of the China War, reducing slim chances of self-sufficiency while threatening ultimate confrontation with America.

In 1939, the military had at least partially understood. The General Staff's War Leadership Plan, 1938, emphasising the main objective of Preparation for War against the USSR, stressed the need to run down or at least compromise on the war with China, while strengthening Inner Mongolia and Manchukuo. Priority was given also to relations with the USA. But these moderate proposals were successfully opposed by others in the military. Another factor was the Chinese Nationalists' rare victory in 1938 at Taierchwang, which offended the 'face' of the Japanese North China Army and hardened attitudes accordingly.

Terms of trade deteriorated, imports of raw materials for manufactured exports were reduced, as was the export of goods hitherto earning foreign exchange but now pre-empted by the military. Inflation grew, the yen dropped, the balance of payments fell. By 1940, furthermore, the Americans had restricted exports to Japan, including iron, steel, nickel, copper, zinc, even high octane grades of petroleum. (It was not, however, until July 1941 that the fatal decision was taken by President Roosevelt to freeze all Japanese assets and embargo all exports of petroleum.)

In 1940, the planning board, which had already warned of the coming economic doom, reported that self-sufficiency in materials, despite all special measures, had not been achieved. Neither shipping nor foreign exchange were available to import the materials required for manufactured export in adequate quantity. Steel, and oil supplies whether imported or synthetic, were inadequate for civilian and military economies, as was shipping, particularly if war should lead to heavy losses. In such circumstances, said the board, production of most goods must fall, some dramatically. And, as late as October, the army was demanding that preparations for war against the USSR had to proceed in parallel with those for the Southern advance, including the occupation of Indochina. But even in 1937 the planning board had doubted whether 'even if Japan occupied all China and South-East Asia, and successfully developed North and Central China, she would still be able to wage a long war without relying on Anglo-American resources'.

Given the demand for autarchy, it is certainly the case that, apart from the ending of European supplies after Barbarossa and the navy's hectic demand for steel and other allocations, war was a consequence of Japan's 'terrible economic vulnerability and her decision in the light of the lessons of World War I, to do something about it'. In framing the *direction* for the decision, ancillary factors were the greater availability of raw materials, oil, rubber, tea etc, in South-East Asia than in Russia and the greater distance from her enemies by Japanese occupation of Batavia, Singapore, Saigon and Manila rather than Vladivostok, considerations additional to Tokio's conviction of superior naval air power against the USA.

But all together only provided superstructure to the real argument, the 'Nomonhan factor'. That battle, in John Pritchard's words from *Total War*, 'forced the Imperial Japanese Army to abandon any further serious design to mount a northern offensive to secure control over Eastern Siberia. Now the more bold and radical elements within the Army began to consider the merits of a Southern advance instead . . . a strategy [also] dear to certain middle-ranking cliques in the Japanese Navy with whom they were in contact.'

# 26

# The Comintern, Tripartite
# and Soviet - Japanese Neutrality Pacts

But first Japan must protect the rear.

The old Anglo-Japanese Alliance had been primarily a naval creation. The Anti-Comintern Pact between Japan and Germany, signed on 23 October 1936, was a document for which the Army and, to a lesser extent, the Gaimusho (Foreign Minister) were largely responsible. The project had, indeed, begun in conversations between Colonel Oshima Hiroshi, then Military Attaché but later Ambassador at Berlin, and Joachim von Ribbentrop, then merely the Nazi Party's foreign adviser, but to become the Reich's Foreign Minister, condemned to death at the Nuremberg War Crimes Tribunal. The pact was extended on 6 November 1937 by the accession of Italy under Mussolini, followed eventually by the bizarre trio of Spain, Hungary and Manchukuo. Efforts to secure the admission or 'understanding' of Britain and the Netherlands were unsuccessful. The USSR almost immediately postponed signature of a new Soviet–Japanese Fisheries Treaty, and attacked the pact.

The three main articles referred exclusively to the Comintern or Communist International, and did not specify the USSR. They dealt with exchanges of information and joint preventive measures, and invited 'third states . . . threatened by the Communist International' to adopt defensive measures also. A secret supplementary protocol, known to Moscow through Richard Sorge and other sources, required the signators, if one of the parties became 'the object of an unprovoked attack or threat of attack by the USSR, to consult immediately and take no measure that would tend to ease the situation of the USSR.'

Secret Article 2 undertook that the parties 'will conclude no political treaties with the USSR contrary to the spirit of this agreement without mutual consent'. But Germany, in signing the Nazi–Soviet Non-Aggression Treaty on 23 August

1939 *in the middle of the battle of Nomonhan* breached the letter and the spirit of that agreement, in a mode which shattered the confidence of Japanese smarting from severe defeat in war. Not only did the Tokio Government fall, but the wearisome negotiations for a tripartite defensive military alliance against the USSR (secondarily against Britain and France) were discarded.

That alliance had admittedly also not then been agreed by the navy, budgetarily dependent on the absence of war in the North for its own development and for mastery of the Southern Seas, and also opposed to war with the West. Specifically, Yonai Mitsumara, Minister for the Navy, who had earlier opposed force at Changkufeng, told a Five Ministers Conference in 1939 that Japan could not win a war against Britain, France, the USA *and* the Soviet Union. One source even had it that he had separately denied capacity to defeat the British Far East Fleet on its own.

And there were other obstacles within the system to those who sought to end Anglo-Japanese relations as the cornerstone of Japanese diplomacy in favour of alliance with Germany. 'The quiet question: the telegram drafted and redrafted until *no one* was really certain what it meant; the misplacement of key documents; messages that never reached their proper destinations...' But, increasingly, militaristic nationalism in the worldwide financial and economic crisis now led the nation towards totalitarianism and partnership with the Axis powers, ideologically hostile to the Soviet Union and to the democracies alike. The Shiratori 'faction' in the Gaimusho went so far as to demand the disarmament of Vladivostok, an end to Soviet subversion in Asia, and *the withdrawal of Soviet troops, not only from the MPR, but even from all Russia east of Lake Baikal.*

For the time being, however, the Nazi–Soviet Pact seemed in Tokio only to facilitate Soviet objectives in China, which had become a graveyard for Japanese blood and treasure and for Tokio's wider ambitions, as well as on the Russo-Manchukuoan borders. At the same time it had deprived

Germany of any reliability in Japanese eyes. British and American stock rose. Abe's new government sought an independent neutral foreign policy, but with particular emphasis on good relations with the United States. On the other hand, although nothing was done to advance Ribbentrop's latest proposal, for a *Soviet*–German–Japanese treaty, nor to antagonise London, the Anti-Comintern Pact was not disavowed.

Good relations with Washington, however, proved incompatible with Foreign Minister Arita's promotion of the 'New Order' powers' opposition to the 'Status Quo or Imperialist' countries, Britain, France, the Netherlands and the USA, whose removal from Asia, particularly from China, was Japan's principal concern. Washington did not renew the Treaty of Commerce with Japan and did grant further loans to Japan's enemy, Chiang Kai Shek, who stood most chiefly in the way of Japan's progress in Asia. The US Congress accepted (but did not pass), a bill to embargo all trade with Japan at a time when both prices and shortages of many commodities were increasing.

Already, therefore, under Foreign Minister Arita, Germany's military successes in the June 1940 Western European campaign and the potential benefits to Japan now glimpsed in Indochina and the Netherlands East Indies (NEI) had become significantly manifest. America's stubborn indifference and the British seizure of a Japanese vessel carrying German nationals, led to a revival of the Southern Advance concept and to a reduction in the cultivation of the West, on whom pressure was exerted to end supplies to China. The Army's attitude was expressed in a fiery document of July 1940 not excluding force against Indochina, the NEI, Hong Kong and Malaya, strengthening relations with Germany and Italy, improving relations with Moscow, and demanding preparation for war, except, if possible, against the USA, with Britain and the other colonial powers. But this war-like *military* policy, although Arita continued to advocate the New Order in East Asia and also closer ties with Germany, was not that of the Gaimusho, at least until Matsuoka Yosuke's appointment as Foreign

Minister on 23 July, when the Yonai Cabinet fell and Arita with it. Nor, subsequently, did it acquire the Navy's enthusiastic approval, fearing that a closer relationship with the Axis would actively provoke the USA. (Even in 1936, Admiral Nomura had told a German attaché that 'war with *Russia* would be a national disaster'.)

When in 1937, former diplomat Matsuoka was under consideration for the post of Foreign Minister, Baron Harada Kumao said in astonishment to Prince Konoye, then Prime Minister: 'You don't mean to appoint the likes of Matsuoka?' 'Volatile and unconventional' and a 'flamboyant brinksman', he had been President of the South Manchurian Railway Company during negotiations for the Anti-Comintern Pact and became, as we have seen, Foreign Minister in July 1940 during the second Konoye Cabinet. He was, in that capacity, responsible for the Tripartite Pact of 27 September 1940 and the Soviet–Japanese Neutrality Pact of 13 April 1941. He has been portrayed as driven by *sacro egoismo*, 'rather like the type of man who made the Meiji Restoration . . . abrupt, conceited and impatient of respect for old men . . . exaggeratedly west-ernised, but also exaggeratedly xenophobic, believing in an Anglo-American conspiracy to encircle Japan'.

His first move was to reject as too timid an existing Gaimusho draft on co-operation with Germany and Italy. 'Unless you go into the tiger's den,' he minuted, 'you cannot catch the tiger's cub.' Japan and Germany should not just co-operate 'short of involvement in war', but 'go into battle assisting and embracing one another . . . even if it means com-mitting double suicide'. (Matsuoka's draft on the Army's earlier paper had agreed to a military alliance against Britain, and even considered measures against the United States.) On 1 August, he sought transit facilities in Indochina for Japanese traffic to China through the French Ambassador at Tokio (Arsène-Henry) and, from Ambassador Ott, requested Berlin's views on the New Order in Asia, which resulted in the despatch to Tokio of an emissary from Ribbentrop, Heinrich Stahmer.

Hitler evidently feared a Japanese–US reconciliation, but feared also that the USA might enter the war. The Tripartite Pact was designed by Japan to present the 'appearance of a formidable German–Japanese military combination to dissuade the USA from pushing its opposition to Japan to a military show down', an aim also shared by Hitler, at least according to Stahmer on 9 September. Even the Navy was described by Prince Konoye on 14 September as having been half persuaded by Matsuoka's arguments: 'After we have completed [preparations], we will be able to defeat the USA provided we carry on "blitz warfare", if . . . the USA chooses, however, a protracted war, we shall be in great trouble . . . the USA is rapidly building more vessels . . . and Japan will never be able to catch up . . . now is the most advantageous time for Japan to start a war.'

Matsuoka was reported by Konoye as saying: 'To ally with Britain and the United States, we should have to settle the China Incident as the USA tells us, give up the New Order in East Asia and obey Anglo–American dictates for at least half a century . . . would our people accept this? The only way left is to ally with Germany and Italy.' A divided Navy, while agreeing to this last comment, did so with initial reluctance, partly in order to advance plans for the Southern advance and obtain an increase in the Navy Estimates through a Pact which might, at the same time, avoid war with the United States.

Matsuoka asserted to the Cabinet that Japan would obtain the German possessions in the Pacific and also receive supplies of oil in Germany's gift. Japan should be assured that Germany would help Japan to improve relations with Moscow and, specifically, work on the USSR to cede Moscow's oil rights in northern Sakhalin to Japan.

'Germany and Japan now have a common aim. They both wish to prevent armed confrontation with the USA.' Hara Yoshimidi, President of the Privy Council, feared that the Pact's immediate results could be a US iron and oil embargo, a boycott of Japanese goods 'so that Japan will not be able to continue the war', and an increase in aid to Chiang Kai Shek. Although the then Naval Chief of Staff, Prince Fushimi, continued to urge that every measure be taken to avoid war with the USA, the Emperor's agreement to the Tripartite Pact was obtained at an Imperial Conference on 19 September. On 27 September 1940, it was signed by all three Powers.

The main content was Japanese 'recognition and respect' for the leadership of Germany and Italy in the establishment of a new order in Europe with the same sentiments on the part of Germany and Italy for Japan's similar task in Greater East Asia. The three Powers now would mutually cooperate and assist 'by all political, economic and *military* means when one of the three Contracting Parties (is) attacked by a power at present not involved in the European War or in the Sino-Japanese conflict;' the United States of America, in other words.

Hosoya Chihiro, Professor of International Relations at the Law Faculty of Hitotsubashi University, concluded his commentary on the Tripartite Pact: 'Japan regarded it as a diplomatic prerequisite to the southern advance . . . government leaders decided to conclude the Pact to block American armed intervention in Japan's southward move.

'Matsuoka must have believed that only a brink-of-war policy . . . demonstrating Japan's readiness to go to war if need be, would deter the United States from such intervention.' Japan, he hoped, would thereby be able to complete its drive southward and at the same time avoid war with the USA. The outbreak of the Pacific War proved that his view had been wrong. His brink-of-war policy had failed; and it is said that when he was told of the outbreak of war, Matsuoka 'shed bitter tears' and said 'The conclusion of the Tripartite Pact was the greatest mistake of my life.'

He undoubtedly believed, at least on the signing in 1940, that the Pact would so alarm the USA as to cause the Americans to ease pressure on Japan and, at the same time, frighten the USSR into negotiating a Japanese–Soviet non-aggression treaty, if not into collaboration with the schemes of

Ribbentrop for a quadripartite alliance between Germany, Italy, Japan and the USSR. It had, in fact, exactly the opposite effect in Moscow and Washington, 'arousing Soviet suspicion and hardening American determination'.

On Ribbentrop's instructions, nevertheless, Ambassadors Shulenburg at Moscow and Ott at Tokio, pressed for negotiation of a Soviet–Japanese non-aggression treaty. (Ambassador Shiratori, in apparent contrast with earlier views, had sought, chiefly as one means of ending Soviet support for Chiang Kai Shek, a similar pact, to be followed by the four-power military agreement.) This would be achieved, *inter alia*, by recognition of Soviet administration in Shensi, Tibet, Sinkiang, Kansu, even Yunnan. Prime and Foreign Ministers Abe and Arita, Anglophiliac and anti-Communist, were opposed, but the Army now began to look for a settlement with China that was less than purely military and, thus, could include rapprochement with the USSR.

In pursuit of the policy of the Southern advance into South-East Asia, it had become essential to secure the northern seas, in other words the Navy's traditional slogan of 'Defend the North, Advance in the South'. On 2 July, the draft of a Neutrality, as opposed to a Non-Aggression, Pact was presented to Molotov by Ambassador Togo in Moscow. The Soviet Foreign Commissar expressed general agreement, but would not approve concessions in Sakhalin nor the end of aid to China, perhaps in deference to American susceptibilities. These and other preconditions were formally delivered to Togo on 14 August.

On 30 October, a new draft non-aggression treaty was submitted to Molotov, substantially the same as the German–Soviet non-aggression pact signed in August 1939. On 13 November, in a Berlin air-raid shelter under bombardment by British aircraft, Ribbentrop presented to the visiting Molotov a draft four-power entente. This contained a secret protocol which, apart from Europe, 'allocated' the Indian Ocean countries to the USSR, the South Seas to Japan, Central Africa to Germany, North and North-East Africa to Italy. He also advocated a non-aggression treaty between the USSR and Japan. The Soviet reply contained preconditions, including the evacuation of German troops from Finland and demands for renunciation of Japanese concessions in Sakhalin, which caused Hitler 'to reach his final determination for war against the Soviet Union', an objective spelled out as *Lebensraum* in *Mein Kampf* for anyone to read, as well as symbolising the final condition for victory over Britain. On 18 December, the operational order for Barbarossa ordered the armed forces to complete preparations by 15 May 1941 for the great assault.

Foreign Minister Matsuoka, hot for glory and ignorant of the decline in relations between his allies in Germany and the USSR, secured agreement from his peers to visit Europe and Russia in order to achieve a Japanese–Soviet diplomatic settlement. This would include the issues of Sakhalin, the respective Japanese and Soviet positions in North China and the Mongolias, a cessation of Soviet aid to Chiang Kai Shek, the 'division of the world' between the four powers, a Japanese military reduction in China, a fisheries agreement, frontier agreements with the USSR, MPR and Manchukuo. Matsuoka, rubbing his belly, 'the residence of the soul . . . in favour of soul-to-soul talks with responsible people', hoped to repeat his *coup* on the world stage when he led Japan out of the League of Nations in 1933.

In Moscow, under late snow, he denied to the American Ambassador that Japan intended to attack Singapore. To Molotov and Stalin, before leaving for Berlin on 24 March, he emphasised the importance of Soviet–Japanese relations. There, he was invited by Hitler to take Singapore before June, a request which he evaded without, of course, grasping its coincidence with the timing of Barbarossa, of which he seems to have known nothing. The Germans, nevertheless, were now so obviously hostile to the USSR that their new and surprising attitude made any plans for mediation by Berlin with Moscow over a non-aggression treaty, let alone a four-power pact, impossible. By the time Matsuoka returned to Moscow, the Balkans were on fire. Bulgaria had been forced to join the Axis, while the Wehrmacht had invaded Yugoslavia and Greece, a course which Matsuoka saw as favourable for his negotiations with the Soviets.

After stonewalling by Molotov and a quick visit to Leningrad by Matsuoka during which he was privileged to see Ulanova dance, a Soviet–Japanese neutrality treaty was signed on 13 April 1941, the main clause of which declared that 'in the event of military activity by any other power or powers against either of the contracting parties, the other contracting party shall maintain neutrality throughout the duration of the conflict'. An attached letter referred not to all of Matsuoka's conditions for a settlement, but only to a commercial treaty, a fisheries convention and to the concessions in Sakhalin. It ignored the issue of Soviet aid to China, and was accepted by the Japanese Navy only after assurance that it was a 'purely defensive arrangement'.

At the railway station on Matsuoka's departure, Stalin was personally present, embracing the foreign guest in a then unprecedented gesture under such circumstances, even admitting that the treaty could have been said to have saved his country from a two-front war. 'Now,' he said, 'the whole world can be settled.'

Matsuoka told the German Ambassador at Moscow that the neutrality treaty would impress Chiang Kai Shek and facilitate Japan's relations with his regime. Certainly, in its infringement of the Sino-Soviet non-aggression treaty of 1937, the treaty gravely weakened Chinese confidence in the USSR. His hopes, however, for a weakening of Washington's attitude were badly disappointed; the USA increased its defence preparations instead. The treaty therefore did little to 'sweep American influence' from the Far East or, substantively, to conclude the resolution of the China Incident on which all Japan's hopes for hegemony through the Greater East Asia Co-Prosperity Sphere depended.

There is no hard evidence for Soviet allegations that Matsuoka had been deliberately made conscious in Berlin of Barbarossa, and that the neutrality treaty was a deception to induce the Russians to move forces westwards out of Asia and thus enable Japan to take territory 'east of Baikal'. (It is, however, true that, at the Tokio Liaison Conference of Ministers and General Staff on 25 June 1941, after war had been declared between Germany and the USSR, Matsuoka recommended that Japan attack the Soviet Union. Earlier, even Tojo had done no more than advise 'the perfection of Japanese military preparations' in the admittedly improved conditions for 'tranquillity in the north'.) As for the Russians themselves, they ignored all warnings about Barbarossa, whether from Sorge, Churchill, Roosevelt, or other sources, seeking almost pitifully to lessen tension with their future invader. It is even possible that Moscow may have thought that, since Matsuoka, in April, had just come from Berlin, he would not have sought a neutrality treaty if Germany had really been planning imminent war.

Matsuoka said many things. In June 1941, he urged war in the north, i.e. against the USSR, as a means of keeping America out of the war, of avoiding encirclement, of achieving peace in China. ('He who would search for pearls, must dive deep. Let us act resolutely.') After the war, and under interrogation for his life, he claimed that he had only advocated war with the USSR because he knew that the Army and Navy were 'entirely against it', and he wanted them thus 'to abandon the advance South' or, indeed, in any direction, *as well*, a fairly obvious self-exculpation. In fact, although the Army might have considered a stab in the back at a Russia torn, bleeding and helpless through putative German success, at that time the Navy would not have considered *anything* against the USSR other than diplomacy. The lessons of Nomonhan were not forgotten and the Army could not, anyway, act on its own, even had it not absorbed its own lack of prowess against higher military technology.

Initially, a Japanese presence from July 1940 in Northern Indochina after the fall of France was symbolised only by Japanese military inspectors instructed to close the supply routes to Chiang Kai Shek via the Hanoi-Kunming railway. (The British closed the 'Burma Road' for three months from 17 July.) In June 1941, Matsuoka, under pressure from Ribbentrop to invade Russia, sought not only military action against the USSR, hopefully leading to the defeat of Britain and the firm establishment of the New Order in Asia, but also postponement of the advance into South Indochina. Although Hara supported both of Matsuoka's objectives, the General Staff had no intention in the North of adopting measures against the Soviet Union other than a preparatory 'bid for time', while confirming the original decision to act against South Indochina. The main conditions on which the Army would even contemplate war against Russia were a *halving* of Soviet ground forces in the Far East and a reduction of the Air Force by two-thirds! Neither was so much as imagined by a wary USSR.

Mobilisation of eight hundred and fifty thousand Japanese and their transportation to Manchuria for *kantokuen* (grand manoeuvres) were, however, ordered. But at this time of crisis in the Soviet war against Germany, the USSR still permitted itself in October 1941 to exploit Sorge's assurance of Japanese inaction and their own (Russian) post-victory confidence to detach between five and eight divisions to the Western Front (Kalinin), most from the Baikal region, not from the Amur–Ussuri.

An additional disincentive to Japanese military action against Siberia was, according to Professor John Erickson, 'the gigantic Soviet sabotage operation . . . on 2 August 1941 in Eastern Manchuria, when a number of Japanese fuel and ammunition dumps were blown up, devastating an area more than seven miles across'.

On 13 August 1941, the USSR acknowledged the assurance of Toyoda Teijiro, the new Foreign Minister *vice* Matsuoka, that Japan would observe the Japanese–Soviet neutrality pact. The Russians expressed total lack of conciliation over China, Sakhalin or any other Japanese proposal. *Sorge reported to Moscow on 14 September that Japan would not attack the USSR during 1941.* While it is the case that the *kantokuen* troops theoretically prevented the employment against Hitler of up to twenty-five Soviet infantry divisions and over two thousand aircraft, at least sixteen Japanese field divisions were tied up in Manchuria until 1 August 1945 without attempting hostile action against the USSR or otherwise helping Nazi Germany in the Tripartite Alliance. Most of them were then either slaughtered after surrender or imprisoned by Soviet armed forces bearing banners which they had first been seen to carry on the sands at Nomonhan. In the meanwhile, and most vitally, the USSR had not had to endure the two-front war which the planners had dreaded.

# 27

# Invasion of French Indochina, and the Franco - Thai War

As long ago as 1936, Nakahara Yoshimasa, a naval staff officer known as the king of the South Seas, had advocated an advance to the South, then directly involving only seizure of the Borneo oilfields. His presentation at the outbreak of war between Hitler and Britain in 1939 specifically condemned the Strike North concept: 'Finally the time has come. This maritime nation, Japan, should today commence its advance to the Bay of Bengal. *Moss-covered tundras, vast barren deserts – of what use are they?* Today, people should begin to follow the grand strategy of the Navy, altering their bad old habits. We should not hesitate even to fight the USA and Britain to attain that end.'

His proposal was for an advance 'east of the Netherlands East Indies to Malaya', and the acquisition of Australia and the British Pacific islands. Planning exercises directed against Hong Kong, Singapore and the South Pacific islands took place in May 1940. Staff conclusions thereafter were gloomy. Should US exports of oil be terminated, Japan could not continue to fight for more than four months unless it could acquire oil from the NEI and the capacity to transport it: even then, Japan could only fight for a year, beyond which time her chances of winning did not exist. Nevertheless, and despite the doubts of the Navy Minister, planning still continued, although some senior naval officers sought *first* to put an end to the war in China.

Fascinated by German victories in Europe, the Army, in order to free Japan from dependence on the USA and Britain, proposed in July 1940 what was to become the Greater East Asia Co-Prosperity Sphere, centred on Japan, China and Manchukuo, an end to ties with Britain. Their Plan included 'expulsion' of British and Dutch interests from the Far East, the capture of Malaya, the East Indies and Hong Kong. Little or no attention was paid to Japan's capacity in terms of raw materials to carry out the programme. It was not seriously opposed by the Navy apart from ambiguity over confrontation with the USA. Later, however, the Navy foresaw that a US embargo on oil and scrap metal must result from the projected attack on Southern French Indochina. It foresaw also the consequent, inevitable Japanese assault to secure oil from the NEI.

On 27 August, the Navy was further concerned. Military operations should take place only if a complete embargo were placed on Japan by the USA or if the USA and Britain co-operated to apply pressure on Japan or threaten Japan's existence. 'But if we undertake war, we must be prepared in the final analysis for a direct confrontation with the USA.' Yet, again, despite warnings from Admiral Namura, soon to become Ambassador at Washington and Japan's principal negotiator, about the danger of a long war, important sections of the Navy never asked whether potential resources would permit victory. They assumed rather that victory was so certain that the means thereto must be instantly supplied. 'The planners,' in other words, 'had forgotten the most important question – could Japan defeat America?' Admiral Yamamoto, the Commander in Chief, and Navy Minister Yonai were opposed to more junior figures in their personal certainty that it could not.

By September 1940, after the signing of the Tripartite Alliance, the then Navy Minister Yoshida believed that the Treaty might prevent the USA from declaring war within the year. If it did, he believed that Germany would have by then defeated Britain. The war would thus end without a US–Japanese confrontation. But when the absence of German landing craft and a less than total command of the air made an invasion of Britain impossible, Admiral Yamamoto said, fatalistically: 'To fight the United States is like fighting the whole world. Doubtless I will die on board the *Nagato* [his flagship] . . . Konoye and the others may be torn to pieces by the people.' In February 1941, at the time of a projected landing in French Indochina to take 'permanent bases near Saigon and Camranh Bay', the Admiral referred again to the dangerous possibility of a war between Japan and the United States and Great Britain.

In March 1941, the Navy believed that military operations in the south should only be mounted if the USA were to impose a complete embargo against Japan. The Army's aggressive policy for the south was nominally dropped in favour of economic negotiation with the Dutch East Indies, and of an end to 'unnecessary' provocation of the USA, Britain and Holland. (Meanwhile, in January, General Sugiyama had told Army Minister Tojo that the 'Greater East Asia Co-Prosperity Sphere included Japan, Manchuria, China, Thailand, French Indochina and, *if possible*, the Netherlands East Indies and Malaya'. Shipping, liquid fuels and munitions might all be inadequate for a war lasting more than two years, while Winston Churchill had already pointed out to Matsuoka another discrepancy: that Allied steel production ran at nearly ninety million tons per annum, and Japanese at seven million. The Foreign Minister thought the message 'extremely rude'.

On 27 March, in response to the Navy's reluctance to participate in an immediate military advance to the South, it was decided that military operations should only be undertaken if absolutely unavoidable 'for Japan's safe existence and defence', not just to exploit favourable opportunities. Thailand and French Indochina appear to have been exempted from this caveat.

It is, incidentally, curious to recall today that among the factors influencing Japanese caution over American potential was the fear of 'co-operation between Soviet and US bombers and submarines'. On the other hand, as Professor John Chapman has pointed out, the Japanese had drawn the conclusion from naval operations in Norway in 1940, when British naval superiority was negated by German air power, that the Japanese Navy might get the better of the US Pacific Fleet by increasing their land and carrier-borne aircraft.

As to Indochina, when France surrendered in June

1940, a small mission under Major-General Nishihara, which allegedly included one of the officers who had removed his trousers at Changkufeng, was sent to the pretty Tonkinese capital of Hanoi. His task was to negotiate with the Governor-General, General Georges Catroux, later to join de Gaulle, for the Japanese exploitation of Indochinese air and other bases against China, for the passage through Indochina of troops to China, and for an end to Allied supplies to China through the colony. Although the Southern advance was greatly on the minds of officers on the General Staff, this mission left before the advance itself had been formally adopted in Tokio: the Nishihara agreement was ostensibly reserved for the resolution alone of the China Incident.

Among the bougainvillaea and scarlet flamboyants, the dapper French *commerçants* and *fonctionnaires* in white duck or linen suits began to suffer the pain of the Metropolitan defeat. The soggy heat of summer descended on the tree-lined streets, on the lakes, bridges, pagodas and painted villas. No breath of air fanned the city's night-time. As the British had almost simultaneously closed their Burma Road and Hong Kong supply routes to China, the Japanese were soon surprised by Catroux's new demand for recognition of the integrity of French Indochina, in exchange for facilities to attack China. Catroux was then recalled, on succession by the little Fleet Commander, Admiral Decoux. The latter was confronted with a choice between invasion, and a Franco-Japanese alliance, French help in the settlement of the China Incident and in the establishment of the New Order.

The Japanese demands, apparently restricted to facilities for military operations in the Chinese provinces along the Indochina border, were accepted on 30 August 1940 in the Matsuoka–Arsène-Henry Pact. No mention was made therein of the evident intention of Matsuoka and the South China Army to use the agreement not only as a stage in the China Incident, but as a stepping stone to southern Indochina in the advance to the South. On 3 September, however, in the Palais du Gouvernement at Hanoi, Admiral Decoux was confronted by a seven-man delegation led by the arch fire-eater, Major-General Tominaga Kyoji, 'swords in their hands, their eyes flashing. We will meet you on the battlefield', they grunted. Next day in a note to the Japanese, he agreed, *inter alia*, to a maximum of twenty-five thousand troops in Tonkin, the stationing to begin on 5 September, a date later delayed until 22 September, to be executed 'by peaceful means'. The troop strength was reduced to between 5,000 and 6,000 men, with *passage rights* for 25,000 men through Indochina *en route* to the battlefields of China.

Administrative confusion and hot-headed, ambitious chicanery between the 22nd and South China Armies followed. The 5th Division under Nakamura crossed the border by force, against the Emperor's wish, at midnight on 23 September, to take Dong Dang and Lang Son, where more than ten years later Giap's People's Army of Vietnam also defeated a French Army. Later, on 26 September, the Nishimura Corps landed at Do Son. In a childish evasion of instructions, the Corps Commander and his chief of staff hid beforehand in a ship's store and under a lifeboat, so as to be 'unable' to receive expected orders from the Navy to halt the landings. That day also, a Japanese air squadron accidentally bombed Haiphong port, with casualties to local civilians.

Despite this administrative chaos and the distrust aroused by and between the armed forces, a bridgehead for the Southern advance had, nevertheless, been created, by ignorant, disunited but determined military officers. These, and their six thousand troops, requisitioned houses, seized foreign goods bound for China in local warehouses, and began public works, including barracks and the improvement of airfields. Some claimed to thirst for immediate action against Singapore. Others said they were tired and wanted to go home. Their occupation, nevertheless, bore the marks of permanence. The Japanese Press, throughout Asia, insisted that the Gaullists in Singapore were working with the British Army to infiltrate agents into Indochina, while simultaneously assuring their readers that the British forces in the area as a whole were of negligible quality and numbers.

The colonists, already demoralised by the fall of France, became much more so. The army and air force remained mildly 'pro-British,' but the historically Anglophobe Navy obeyed Decoux's injunction to refuse information to British consuls at Saigon and Haiphong. Their attitude was rooted in the feeble but not incomprehensible belief that resistance to Japanese power would lead to internment of all French forces, to the independence of 'Annam', and to an end to French sovereignty throughout Indochina.

Negotiations at Tokio in December 1940 resulted in French assurance of deliveries to Japan in 1941 of seven hundred thousand tons of Indochinese rice. In April 1941, the FIC (French Indochina) authorities agreed to provide fifteen thousand tons of rubber to Japan and twenty-five thousand jointly to Japan and Germany. A secret economic agreement was, however, negotiated on 4 January 1941 between the head of Decoux's military cabinet, Captain Jouan, and the British authorities at Singapore.

In January, Thailand, intoxicated by French weakness, was encouraged by the Japanese to lay claim to Indochinese territory including two islands in the Mekong and, later, Luang Prabang and Champassak in Laos, Battambang in Cambodia, and the 'Thalweg', in pursuit of the Thai dream of an antique 'Golden Land', Laos, Cambodia, Malaya, Singapore. After Japanese mediation, amid French charges that the British Ambassador at Bangkok had secretly supported the Thais, hostilities ended in the cession to Thailand of Paklay, of the region north of the boundary between Battambang and Pursat, partially of islands in the Mekong, of an area bounded by Stung Treng, Tonle Sap or Grand Lac, Battambang and Siem Reap, all as demilitarised zones, and a financial compensation to Bangkok of sixty-four million Indochina piastres. Fighting on land had gone Thailand's way, the Foreign Legion and Annamite troops driven back with some losses, the Legion allegedly suffering two hundred killed and wounded in a single

engagement; there is no doubt about Japanese Army participation.

The French cruiser *Lamotte-Picquet* and four sloops,
however, sank two Thai gunboats and three former Italian
torpedo boats at Koh Kung in a successful sea-fight in which
only eighty-two out of eight hundred and sixty Thai sailors
were saved. Later on in the 'war', the Thais, although equipped
and trained by the Japanese armed forces, were so nervous of
effective French air attack that they threatened, should the
French bomb their cities, to bomb Saigon, Hanoi and the main
seaports of French Indochina.

Decoux said subsequently that he had only concluded
the Thai–French Indochina Peace Treaty of 9 May 1941 under
Japanese pressure. There seems no reason to doubt him, cat-
egorised though he was by the British Consul-General at
Saigon as 'small physically as in mental outlook . . . irascible,
which deprives him of all charm, with an overbearing attitude which can add nothing to his popularity'. (The Admiral
spoke in comparably adverse terms about the British Consul-
General.) The defeat of French arms at Lang Son, the pathetic
land campaign against Thailand, the evident mastery of the
Japanese over the colony, and Decoux's inability to secure
substantial assistance from the UK and USA, all weakened his
already mediocre reputation among the colonists. Only local
resentment aroused by the British campaign against the French
in Syria saved his Government from even larger discontent.

On 20 July, the British Foreign Secretary, Anthony
Eden, declared that 'We had been consistently advised by the
Chiefs of Staff that we should not allow ourselves to become
involved in war with Japan over French Indochina.' He added
further: 'We must avoid war with Japan without a firm US
guarantee of active armed support if the NEI and ourselves
were attacked.'

On 22 July 1941, Admiral Leahy, the US Ambassador
at Vichy, reported that Admiral Darlan had told him that at
'the extremely strong insistence of the Japanese, he had been
forced to grant permission for the Japanese to occupy all of

Indochina'. (General Mordant, Decoux's C in C, an Anglo-phile, had wanted to resist.) Unless their ultimatum were accepted, Hanoi would be bombed and the Japanese Occu-pation initiated by force. The Japanese sought eight air and two naval bases and, by 30 July, were reported to be planning the disembarkation of at least forty thousand troops to 'guard against attacks from "Chungking soldiers", and from British bases in Burma and Malaya,' palpable Aunt Sallies. Fighter and bomber strength in Hanoi and Saigon was to be greatly increased. Fieldguns, tanks, lorries, 75 and 120 mm guns, armoured cars, were disembarked at Saigon and Haiphong in operations allegedly planned with the aid of trained attachés from the German Embassy at Tokio. Landings continued from July to 5 December, when a further twenty thousand men landed in Haiphong. The occupiers took over public services in Saigon, at least temporarily, as infrastructure in that tropical Aix-en-Provence for what one French official estimated as an eventual one hundred thousand Japanese troops and five hundred aircraft en route for the Southern advance.

The US State Department, as early as 24 July, con-demned the Japanese 'objective of expansion by force or threat of force' . . . Japan's actions 'bear directly upon the vital problem of our national security'. President Roosevelt, the British and Dutch Governments followed one another between 25 and 27 July in freezing Japanese assets in their respective countries. Serious US, British and Dutch restrictions, if not yet total embargoes, were introduced on shipments of oil, steel and a range of raw and manufactured materials. By the second half of 1941, Japan had only enough oil for twenty-four months, without hope of further commercial supply from either US or Dutch sources.

The French Army was, mostly, sent north to 'guard the border and the Mekong', while in the main towns the Japanese set about the subversion of French rule and public order through Annamite and Tonkinese supporters. This was a cause in which they soon met competition from the Com-munist Party of Indochina, an offshoot of the Soviet barbarians who had defeated them two years before at Nomonhan in, it might be said, the First Turn of the Wheel. That Party's leader, Nguyen Ai Quoc alias Ho Chi Minh had already, by 1941, made plain his intention to integrate an independent Annam into the USSR.

# 28
# Netherlands East Indies Under Threat

The Japanese bases in Indochina had been originally required in the context of her China campaign. Because of the more general demands of the Greater East Asia Co-Prosperity Sphere, they were equally essential for the acquisition of those raw materials whose import to Japan had been gradually reduced by US and other Western restrictions, such as that on aircraft, and by the abrogation of the commercial treaty. Indochina thus had led to Thailand. The advance on the South would then require the resources of the Netherlands East Indies which could not be forcefully secured without the simultaneous occupation of the Malayan peninsula and Singapore, a concept envisaged by Nakahara as early as 1936. He had then also employed the phrase: 'Naturally, Australia will come under our control.'

Part of the fleet, as we have seen, deployed against a 'potential Western invasion of the NEI by British forces' was sent in May 1940 for exercises off the Palau islands in part preparation for the occupation of Borneo and the seizure of the Celebes nickel.

As long ago as October 1939, the Gaimusho had expressed fears about a British or even US occupation of the Indonesian Archipelago. Nomura, then Foreign Minister, had ordered economic negotiations with the Dutch Government to include a Japanese guarantee of the security of the islands rejected by The Hague in January 1940. On 15 May, both Japan and the Western powers had declared their support for the *status quo* of the NEI but, on 29 June, Foreign Minister Arita expressed Japan's intention to form an Eastern Bloc, implicitly including the Netherlands East Indies.

On 20 May, after the German assault on the Netherlands, the Japanese Ambassador, saying later that he felt as if he had gone 'to dun a dying man for a debt', sought annual sales by Holland to Japan of thirteen commodities, including one million tons of petroleum. Under pressure, the Dutch Government and the Governor-General of the NEI agreed. On 26 June, the USA put aviation fuel, No. 1 heavy melting steel and scrap iron on 'licensing requirement'. President Roosevelt was advised that a *total* embargo on oil and scrap iron would 'goad the berserk Japanese Army into an attack upon an already crippled Britain and an almost helpless Netherlands', and could thus lead to American involvement in war. But in July, US Ambassador Grew at Tokio, in response to representations to the United States, reported to the Japanese Government that his country had no intention of abandoning Chiang Kai Shek; that peace could only be promoted by peaceful means and by worldwide free trade and independence; and that settlement of fundamental differences must precede normalisation of commercial relations between the United States and Japan.

Kobayashi Ichizo, Japanese Minister for Commerce and Industry, was sent to Batavia in August to negotiate on economic issues alone, i.e. specifically without mentioning Japan's intention to make the Indies part of the Greater East Asia Co-Prosperity Sphere, to support self-determination for the 'Indonesian people', and to conclude defence agreements within the Sphere. The Dutch rejected Japanese demands for 3.75 million tons of oil annually against the current level of 600 K tons, eventually granting two million tons, although no high-grade petroleum, less than half their requirement. But the amount of oil licensed by the USA over the past year 'represented more than twice the normal annual pre-war import of Japan from all sources', without counting the NEI supplies or orders not yet licensed. These would bring the total to *three* times the pre-war import and in a quality of, or convertible to, aviation use. Japan was therefore *not* short of oil, at least in 1940.

A new delegation under former Foreign Minister Yoshizawa took the reins in January 1941. In that month, the new Foreign Minister, Matsuoka, in formal debate in the Diet, included the Netherlands East Indies within the Greater East Asia Co-Prosperity Sphere. To 'prolong negotiations as long as possible in order to give Great Britain enough time to bring about a change in Europe', the Dutch protested against that statement and against Japan's refusal to recognise the Dutch Government exiled in London. Yoshizawa told Tokio that military action might now be necessary.

Between 26 September 1940 and 4 February 1941, the USA embargoed scrap iron, copper, zinc, bronze, nickel, brass, iron ore, pig iron, ferro-alloy and several other commodities. Batavia, on the grounds that Japan would re-export them to Germany, refused to increase exports of castor oil, rubber, copra, tin and palm oil. Matsuoka told Sir Robert Craigie, British Ambassador at Tokio, that 'for Japan, a major power, to accept the demands of a minor power that we promise not to re-export materials to Germany, would be a humiliation'. On 14 July, Yoshizawa's delegation was withdrawn, further negotiations to be conducted by the Japanese Consul-General at Batavia. The most important Japanese demands had not been met, but Japan had acquired future rights in certain categories.

# 29
# The Southern Advance Confirmed

After Barbarossa, Matsuoka and some officers of the General Staff were almost alone in advocating a jackal rush against the Soviet rear in Siberia.

But by 1 July, even these views had lost credence. Rather, in mid-1941, Japan now hoped that Hitler's Germany, despite apparent contempt for Tokio's interests, would deal with Russia easily and rapidly, in almost a 'police operation'. In any event, neither the Kwantung Army nor the Imperial Japanese Army as a whole were ready or, perhaps, would ever be ready for a winter war. Nor could the China Incident with its mortal drag on the Empire's resources be ended by victory in Russia. And South-East Asia, some thought South-East *and* South Asia, not Russia, held the treasure chest for dominion, the keys of the corn-bin. There remained, above all, the recognition of the final argument that Japan had been irrevocably thrashed at Nomonhan and that, subsequently, no technological or other improvements had occurred to make possible the defeat of Russia and the conquest of Siberia.

A majority in the Japanese Navy, while opposed to striking North, i.e. the seizure and occupation of Siberia, had always supported an advance to the South while preferring that the war in China be first of all brought to a successful conclusion. The army itself did not seek to end its involvement in China but, other than that very small minority still advocating war against the USSR, wished simultaneously to advance South. The Prime Minister, Prince Konoye, – so thought Emperor Hirohito – agreed to the Greater East Asia Co-Prosperity Sphere in all its consequences, provided that Japanese forces in China were *not* reduced: in the end, the Government did not insist upon that condition. The Japanese High Establishment was far from monolithic.

The 'people', as a whole, truly believed in Japanese

leadership of Asia, even hegemony, under, if necessary, forcible circumstances, without the least conception of the risks and perils in other than the shortest engagement against Western enemies. (Thought control had reproduced an almost xenophobic race.) Among the many things they did not know was their masters' new conviction that they could not win in China, a conviction which, combined with new US and other economic sanctions, led the Japanese Government to explore negotiations with Washington. Such a programme, even were it to fail, would at least provide a space for Admiral Yamamoto to complete his preparations for Singapore, Manila, Batavia, Rangoon and, at Kagoshima, for Pearl Harbour itself.

The new Japanese Ambassador to the United States had arrived at Washington in February 1941, Admiral Nomura Kichisaburo, a former Foreign Minister, aged sixty-four, and very tall, at six foot, for a Japanese. He had been personally acquainted with Franklin D. Roosevelt, the President, on a previous posting during the Great War at a time when FDR had been Assistant Secretary of the Navy.

His views on US–Japanese relations were at hopeless variance with those of Matsuoka, Konoye, Tojo, and even Matsuoka's successor, Admiral Toyoda. It was the latter who had earlier, at Matsuoka's insistence, dishonestly induced Nomura against his will to take up the appointment. Nomura believed that any improvement of relations with America was incompatible with the Tripartite Pact; that the USA and Britain were 'inseparable'; that war with the USA, in particular because of its effect on the China Incident, should be rejected; that a forceful advance on the South must not give the USA an excuse for war; and that Italy and Germany should not become Japan's main prop and stay. Tokio or, at all events, the Navy, feared that the invasion of Indochina would set off a chain of explosions, from Allied embargoes to the invasion of the Netherlands East Indies, to war against the British as well in Borneo and Malaya, and so to the final deadly confrontation with the USA whether at sea, in Hawaii or Manila.

Admiral Nomura, warned the great Yamamoto, had

been strung along by Toyoda. 'He has no illusions about his chances for success and it is really too much to ask him to straighten out relations . . .'

Before the Admiral's arrival in the United States, two persons more easily recognisable in the columns of Beachcomber or Peter Simple, Bishop James Walsh and Father James Drought, the infamous 'Maryknoll Fathers', had inserted themselves into the Peace Process as it might be termed today. Maryknoll is a Catholic College or Seminary, strongly Irish, 'liberal' and anti-British, whose graduates have interfered in many enterprises of which they chose to disapprove, including in our times a series of illiterate and unhelpful interventions in Latin America and in the conduct of the Vietnam War. Walsh, incidentally, was imprisoned in China by Mao's Government and only released in 1970.

These two prodnoses conveyed a proposal, falsely presented as supported by the Japanese *Government*, to Robert Walker, the Catholic Postmaster General, guaranteeing to nullify the Tripartite Pact and to withdraw all troops from China, in return for a Trade Treaty with the United States 'allowing free entry of certain commodities', oil, rubber, tin and nickel. Full withdrawal and the Tripartite Pact were not concretely mentioned in the later Draft understanding. Subsequent amendments referred to (a) the resumption of the Open Door and (b) a coalition between Chiang Kai Shek and Wang Ching Wei whose 'regime' in China was supported by Japan. The misunderstandings, lies and oversimplifications, even before they eventually emerged in the Draft Japanese–American Understanding, had already been described by the Far Eastern Division of State as failing to 'take account of Japan's present policies and current practices . . . The procedure is not adapted to the facts . . .'

On the other hand, when the Draft Understanding was received in Tokio on 18 April, it was the first indication that the Foreign Ministry had received that private talks, let alone discussions, with the President, Secretary Hull, or Harry Hopkins, were in progress at all. And it was not until 8 May that Ambassador Nomura glancingly referred to Cordell Hull's Four Principles, 'respect for territorial integrity and sovereignty, non-interference in internal affairs, equality of opportunity, maintenance of the status quo in the Pacific', which were exactly those attributes meant by Hornbeck 'as in conflict with "Japan's current policies and practices"'.

The United States, nevertheless, did not discontinue negotiation. Since their cryptographers had broken all the cyphers operating between the Gaimusho in Tokio and the Embassy at Washington (MAGIC), State and other Departments or rather, their masters, could read their opponent's mind in a fashion equalled only by ULTRA at Bletchley. Human error, alas, spoiled the achievement at the very last minute. Because an official was asleep in bed, the bombs fell almost unopposed, the great ships went down, the sailors died.

Matsuoka, on his return from Berlin and Moscow in April, had violently opposed the 'Understanding', demanding rather that the USA wash its hands of China; that any US–Japanese agreement not contravene the Tripartite Pact, but prevent US entry into the European War; that the USA advise Chiang Kai Shek to negotiate direct with Japan; that the Japanese armed forces attack Singapore. On 16 July he resigned under overriding opposition and distrust, but *his* draft, not the Maryknoll draft, was preferred by Konoye and the military. Matsuoka himself disappeared from history, and so did the usurping clerics . . . Toyoda, on succession, temporised over policy towards the USA and the USSR until Japan could tell what was happening in the German–Soviet struggle. He maintained the conquest of French Indochina and the preparations for the Southward advance. On 9 August 1941, the Army, for the reasons shown in Chapters 24–28, again confirmed their decision not to use military force against the Soviet Union, a decision earlier given by the new Foreign Minister.

On 4 August, after Japanese assets had been frozen and the oil embargo imposed, Japan offered to guarantee Philippine neutrality, and to withdraw troops from French Indochina after 'a settlement of the China Incident'. Concurrently, however, Toyoda asked the USA to cease military measures against Japan in the Pacific, to agree to Japan's acquisition of natural resources in the NEI, to restore US–Japan commercial relations, to mediate between Japan and China, and to recognise Japan's position in French Indochina.

Washington did not respond favourably to this unbalanced programme. In Tokio, Admiral Nagano told the Emperor that 'there was no chance of victory in a war with Britain and the USA'. (Indeed, it was the case that no calculations had been made over *how* such a war was to be won.) The Emperor warned that 'this means embarking on a war of desperation . . . truly dangerous'. On 5 August, when General Sugiyama assured Hirohito that victory in the South Seas could be secured in 'three months', the Emperor reminded him that he had once promised to settle in *one* month a China Incident which had now been in progress for four years. 'If the hinterland of China is vast, isn't the Pacific Ocean even more vast?' At the Imperial Conference next day, the Emperor took the extraordinary step of advocating diplomacy, not war, by reading aloud one of the Emperor Meiji's poems:

> Across the four seas
> All are brothers.
> In such a world
> Why do the waves rage,
> The winds roar?

Sugiyama and even Minister of War Lieutenant-General Tojo were deeply moved, but a proposal for Prince Konoye to visit Roosevelt in Honolulu was to come to nothing. 'We can begin consultations,' said Cordell Hull to Nomura, 'only when Japan stops using force.' Grew's recommendations for this summit as alternative to an 'all-out-do-or-die' military operation was fiercely countered by Hornbeck's view of a powerless Japan requiring surgery: 'The US Government should sit tight' on the three issues of – an end to the China Incident, the

Greater East Asia Co-Prosperity Sphere, and the Tripartite Pact.

In the same fortnight in which Sorge had reported to Moscow that Japan 'contemplated no attack on the USSR until the spring of 1942', American decryption of Japanese radio telegrams revealed that Japan would in August 1941 begin to rearm against Britain and the USA and to prepare for the advance to the South. Tsuji Masanobu, remembered from Nomonhan, now a Lieutenant-Colonel commanding Planning Unit 82, forecast in late July that Japan would take Manila by 1 January 1942, Singapore by 11 February, the Netherlands East Indies by 10 March, and Rangoon by 19 April. Reinforcements were sent to the Kwantung Army, not in preparation for a strike-North assault, but in replacement for troops sent to join 'Tiger' Yamashita's strike-South. But, still, Yamashita and Count Terauchi, his Supreme Commander, both agreed with Yamamoto that war should be the last resort.

At the Imperial Conference of 6 September, however, it was agreed that the 'Empire shall complete preparations for war by the approximate deadline of 10 October . . .', changed on 25 September to 15 October. In Washington, 'the State Department's policy remained completely inflexible'. Roosevelt rejected the proposed meeting with Prince Konoye. Cordell Hull told Nomura on 2 October that nothing would serve except 'explicit agreement' on the Four Principles and, effectively, both a Japanese withdrawal from China and an end to the Tripartite Pact. These conditions, even in the confusion among Japanese politicians and military, were not those to reverse Japan's stumble into war behind uncertain leaders enslaved by doctrine, *faits accomplis*, and 'face'.

Yet, in October, the Chief of the Naval Affairs Bureau questioned policy: 'Can't we think of ways to proceed without taking the Philippines?', e.g. without war with the United States? Fukudomo, Chief of Naval Operations complained: 'I have no confidence in South Seas operations . . . 1.4 million tons will be sunk in the first year . . . there will be no ships for civilian requirements in the third year'. Oikawa, the Navy

Minister, wanted to leave to indecisive Prime Minister Konoye the decision to reverse the Imperial Conference vote for war in favour of negotiation. But, on 18 October, the Emperor appointed General Tojo as Prime Minister, Minister of War and Home Minister, removing Konoye and his vacillation.

On 23 October, however, when considering the doubts of the Navy and the wish of the Emperor 'not to have a war with the United States under any circumstances', even Tojo confided: 'The two hundred thousand souls who died in the China Incident would never forgive me if I were to turn back now.' (He said nothing of Chinese forgiveness for those massacred by the Imperial Army.) 'And yet, if it comes to war . . . great numbers of men will have to be sacrificed. I am truly in the dark about what to do.' (Admiral Yamamoto, after war began, said that he had known that, 'there could be no final victory against the United States'.) The Liaison Conference of 1 November, after satisfying the Navy's demand for steel and urged by Generals Sugiyama and Tsukada, decided to 'continue with diplomatic measures in an effort to reach a compromise agreement, while completing preparations for military operations'. Admiral Nagano had just warned that, 'if there were to be a protracted war', the outcome could not be predicted. Perhaps there might yet be a little hope for sanity.

The deadline for an end to diplomacy and the initiation of war was to be 1 December 1941, a date to meet the sailing schedules of 26 November and 4 December when the fleets left for Hawaii and Malaya respectively.

During November, initiatives begun included 'masterly inactivity', a *modus vivendi* which excluded the China question, interventions of a sort by the British and the Australians, discussion about the Tripartite Pact. Others were, The Hull Note, (return to the status quo before the occupation of South Indochina and the US freezing of assets), and Japan's Plan B, each one an ultimatum, drafted to be unacceptable to its recipient and forwarded only for posterity. The Liaison Conference thereafter, between 27 and 29 November, was unanimous for war, and decided on that course, but a war excluding the Soviet Union.

On 1 December 1941, the Imperial Conference confirmed the decision: 'Negotiations with the United States based on the "Essentials for Carrying Out the Empire's Policies" approved on 5 November, have finally proved unsuccessful. The Empire will go to war against the United States, Britain and Holland.'

The tragedy had been inevitable, even determined, born of ignorance, frustration and arrogance on either side. In attacking the American prosecutor at the International Military Tribunal in 1946, the historian General Ishiwara Kanji, said: 'Haven't you ever heard of Perry? Don't you know anything about your country's history? . . . Tokugawa Japan believed in isolation; it didn't want to have anything to do with other countries and had its doors locked tightly. Then along came Perry from your country [in 1853] in his black ships to open those doors; he aimed his big guns at Japan and warned, "If you don't deal with us, look out for these; open your doors, and negotiate with other countries too." And then when Japan did open its doors and tried dealing with other countries, it learned that all those countries were a fearfully aggressive lot. And so for its own defence it took your country as its teacher and set about learning how to be aggressive. You might say we became your disciples. Why don't you subpoena Perry from the other world and try *him* as a war criminal?'

Our fathers forgot Japan's contribution to the Allied cause in the Great War, just as our grandfathers forgot that country's 'admission to Great Power status' after defeating Tsarist Russia in 1905. Japan did *not* forget. In 1946, Emperor Hirohito said: 'When we look for the causes of the Greater East Asia War, they lie in the past, in the Peace Treaty after World War I. The proposal on racial equality put forth by Japan was not something the Allies would accept. Discrimination between yellow and white continued as before . . . With such popular resentment in the background *it was no easy task to bring the military to heel once it came to the fore.'*

'Japan was the first nation of colour to become a Great Power, but its people were denied racial equality,' according to Professor David Titus. 'Its accomplishments drew special attention, even murmurs of admiration, but they did not bring genuine respect.'

The Meiji restoration involved, as Ishiwara claimed, expansion overseas in collaboration, it was hoped, with Britain and the USA. This was a great nation, without raw materials or great territory, reforming itself internally in order to become part of the great world and 'the community of advanced powers'. But after Manchukuo in 1931 and the retreat of the 'moderate liberals' in the face of the shocked and hostile West, power fell into the hands of jingoist soldiers and, in foreign policy particularly, the navy, hastened by that body's desertion by its British friend in favour of the United States' requirements. There was little hope for peace after that, but while the West may be blamed for the deformation of Japan from 1868 to 1931, blame for the Pacific War lies with the militarists in Tokio, especially with their failure at the Khalkh river.

In 1941, war, even defeat in war, thus became preferable to concession, loss of honour and submission.

# 30
# The Western Empires Fall

President Roosevelt sent on 6 December, mainly for posterity, a personal message to the Emperor of Japan which concluded that both had 'a sacred duty to restore traditional amity and to prevent further death and destruction in the world'. But his concern was now rather for the British in Malaya, not for Pearl Harbour the *imminent* danger to which had not been grasped, who had just learned that two Japanese convoys were in the Gulf of Siam proceeding to the east coast of the Kra Isthmus. On 7 December, however, the Emperor declared war, his Rescript ending: 'The source of evil will be speedily eradicated and an enduring peace immutably established in East Asia, preserving thereby the glory of our Empire.'

Owing to gross incompetence in the Japanese Embassy in Washington, the fourteen-part cypher telegram from Tokio breaking off relations with the USA was read and delivered to the President by US code-breakers before Nomura could present his copy to Cordell Hull. (No one cleared for high classification in the Embassy could type properly.) The latter, after ten staged minutes, excoriated the ambassador and ordered him to leave.

But because of the Malayan fallacy, no US base, including Pearl Harbour, was then ordered to battle stations. Radio operators, however, in a US liner picked up traffic indicating Japanese fleet movements in the area and so informed Honolulu. Nothing was done. Traffic from Admiral Nagumo's carrier, incorrectly identified as a fishing fleet, north-west of Hawaii, was intercepted by an American naval officer in San Francisco who reported it to his superior. 'The superior knew Roosevelt personally.' Nothing was done here either. A notation on a map in Naval Intelligence in Washington itself, showing Japanese carriers 'half-way to Hawaii', was seen in early December by a Dutch Naval Attaché. The

Dutch in Java later intercepted a Japanese message suggesting an imminent attack on Hawaii and citing the code sign 'East Wind, Rain' for that eventuality. That message *and* the later 'winds' signal itself were ignored in Washington. A US naval patrol vessel, subsequently known to have been in the direct line of the Japanese Fleet's advance on Hawaii, simply disappeared. On 6 December, the British AOC Middle East warned the Americans in Cairo of an imminent Japanese attack on the USA itself. In response, Catalina aircraft patrols from Hawaii were almost simultaneously reduced; US radar on Oahu, an hour or so before the actual air attack on Pearl Harbour, picked up, firstly, Japanese spotter aircraft and, then, their bomber fleet. The operator was told by Command that they were US reconnaissance aircraft or a flight of US bombers.

That morning a Japanese submarine, which had penetrated the harbour itself, was engaged and sunk by US naval forces without any consequent increase in the base's alert status. On 7 December, a despatch rider *on a bicycle*, carrying detailed telegraphed warnings from General Marshall, the US Army Chief of Staff in Washington to General Short, GOC Hawaii, had had to jump into a ditch before he could deliver the message, *after* the carriers had begun to let loose their bombs and torpedoes all round him.

All the warnings failed to raise the alarm at Pearl Harbour. Ill-intentioned observers have suggested an attempt, proof against hostile US critics, to slide America into war in undemocratic mode. Bad administration, slack records and negligible inter-Service co-operation may be more probable explanations.

For many years, Admiral Yamamoto had been the chief promoter of naval air power, becoming Vice-Minister of the Navy and, in 1939, Commander in Chief of the Combined Fleet. Before him, existing doctrine had been to await a westward advance by the US Fleet and then to destroy it in the latitudes of the Western Pacific, in the Marshalls or Carolines. He, however, decided to follow Admiral Togo, who in 1904 had destroyed the Russian Fleet at Port Arthur, where

Yamamoto had himself fought, and destroy the US Fleet from the air, in harbour, at Pearl Harbour. (Togo, incidentally, was trained in HMS *Worcester*, *Victory* (Portsmouth Command) and at the Royal Naval College, Greenwich.)

In this present endeavour, he had taken careful note of the devastating attack in November 1940 by ancient British Swordfish biplanes on the Italian Fleet at Taranto, minor though that was in comparison with the forces opposed in December 1941. His Force now consisted of six carriers, two battleships, six cruisers, eleven destroyers, three submarines and a Fleet Train under the direct command of Admiral Nagumo, Yamamoto himself ashore at Hiroshima on Shikoku island.

Secrecy, as we have seen, was splendidly achieved, surprise total. In the blackness, a heavy swell running, one hundred and eighty bombers and fighters took off at 06.00 and over the next fifteen minutes. Their commander came in 'above the white line of the surf, the green mountains beyond, through a pink-stained morning mist. Before me lay the whole US Fleet in a formation I would not dared to dream of . . . I have seen the German ships assembled at Kiel . . . the French battleships in Brest . . . our warships assembled for Review before the Emperor, but I have never seen ships, even in the deepest deep, anchored five hundred to a thousand yards from one another. Had these Americans never heard of Port Arthur?'

A second wave was as successful as the first, the two strikes destroying or severely damaging at least eighteen vessels, including five battleships. (Two, *Arizona* and *Utah*, remain sunk today, now national shrines.) When Admiral Halsey, in the carrier *Enterprise* returned to the 'huge ruin, its flaming ships, decimated garrison and monumental disorganisation . . . chaos enveloped in smoke,' he said, 'Before we're through with them, the Japanese language will be spoken only in hell.' But whatever he said then, on *that* day their 'entire fleet sailed back in safety to Japan'.

Meanwhile, the Japanese fleet in the Gulf of Siam, two battleships, eight cruisers, fourteen destroyers and nineteen transports, started landing troops at Kota Bharu. North and south, up and down the Thai and Malayan coasts, in the little *kampongs* buried in the palm and rubber, their red-roofed wood and rattan houses on stilts, the *rayat* (peasantry) nervously watched the unprepossessing enemy, on foot, on bicycles, even in tanks, thrusting through rubber and jungle which the British had thought impenetrable, and had therefore never bothered to defend. When the British soldiers resisted, the Japanese outflanked them and, in bloody, howling hand-to-hand conflict, reached the Johore Causeway to Singapore.

With Malaya once conquered, the 'impregnable sea-fortress' Singapore fell from landward within two weeks, victim of British long-term incompetence, strategic neglect and complacency, often remarked at the beginning of our wars. In this case, only a little will would have been needed to reverse the pitiable defeat. The Japanese were only half as strong as the British and Australians together who, if properly led and inspired, could have forced a *renversement*. But they were *not* properly led and inspired and, in the great gale of the world that followed, decency was not enough. Neither Malays nor Chinese 'went over', as it were, to the enemy, although some Chinese went over to the subsequent Communist enemy. Very many,, indeed, co-operated most gallantly against the occupier. But after Japan's defeat, it was fairly soon plain to Britain's subjects that *Britain's* defeat had invalidated her absolute right to govern. (This was not a conclusion which the US citizens of Hawaii, Wake and Guam were encouraged to reach about their own rulers.) The British Empire in South-East Asia, like the Dutch and French, had lost its credibility.

The capture of Borneo – Sarawak, Brunei with its water-village, and British North Borneo – followed, easy enough after the sinking off Malaya of *Repulse* and *Prince of Wales*. (Those sleepy enclaves of Dayaks, Malays and Chinese traders were to retain their Somerset Maugham attributes into the 1980s.) All fell, but the British and the Dutch in the oil companies had first fired the wells and blown up the derricks at Miri and the oilfield at Seria which burned underground for months. The Dutch Navy destroyed two Japanese destroyers and sank or damaged five transports, but Balikpapan in Dutch territory to the south was taken, again after 'firing', on 23 January. Today, the Sulu pirates continue to run in and out of Tarakan, medieval and savage.

That same day, the Japanese took Rabaul in New Britain, commanding, potentially with Port Moresby in Papua New Guinea, the sea lanes to Australia.

The Royal Netherlands East Indies forces, although deposited in packets over the many islands of the archipelago, numbered nearly a hundred thousand men. Their far-flung distribution, and the inability of the Commander in Chief, General Hein Ter Poorten, to rely on all his Javanese and Sumatran, as opposed to Ambonese, native levies, caused the High Command to regard combat as wasteful. At sea, meanwhile, five Dutch cruisers and the few British light cruisers still at sea in these waters, were sent to the bottom in the hopeless Battle of the Java Sea.

Most Dutch were selfish, exigent, sometimes brutal colonists, whose civic and rural virtues were outweighed by their wounding disregard for the susceptibilities of the majority of their native subjects. Shattered by the collapse of Malaya, their almost *passive* military conduct in the field, and rapid surrender in Bandung on 12 March, after initial Japanese landings on 6 January, confirmed an *almost* Pan-Indonesian determination to confine them to Holland in any circumstances. (This the Japanese ingeniously exploited in their cultivation of native politicians.) There was no demand at all for a return of Dutch Government, at the time or after the Japanese gave up and went home. That Empire too was already doomed.

Before Admiral Nagumo's failure to take Port Moresby at the Battle of the Coral Sea, it had been the Army's intention to invade Australia where, until General MacArthur's escape from the Philippines, defence had been in the hands of only seven thousand regular troops, the rest being in the Middle East and the UK. Until then, all the Australians could hope for was to hold their continent south of Brisbane, ceding the north where, in February 1942, Darwin had already been ominously and effectively struck by the Japanese Air Force.

Victory in the Battle of Midway on 5 June 1942, and the gallantry of the Australian 7th Division in the hell of Papua New Guinea marked, however, 'the end of the Japanese offensive', perhaps the turning point of the entire Pacific War, although not then remarked by the victorious Allies.

Elsewhere, having secured their rear in Thailand with little or no opposition from Bangkok, 55 Division of the Imperial Japanese Army under Lieutenant-General Takauchi, the first contingent of Mutaguchi's 15th Army, crossed the Thai–Burmese border at Mae Sot on 18 January 1942. By May 1942, 'the battered scarecrow units' of the shattered British and Indian Burcorps (17th Indian Division, 7th Armoured and other Indian and British units) had retreated under Major-General Slim into India, with thirteen thousand killed and wounded. Here, in fevered valleys and razor mountains, they licked their wounds, trained incessantly, and set about protecting India and retaking Burma. The Army's failure to protect the Burmese had been as feeble as their efforts to put matters right were now massive, under their Great Captain, most magnificent commander of the Second World War, Field Marshal Lord Slim.

But, allegiance, even respect for British rule, except among the unfortunate Kachin, Chin, Karen and other minorities, had been lost there beyond recovery, a gap filled by Japanese Intelligence to install a successor regime, inherited by Ne Win's vile, authoritarian Government. Colonel Suzuki Keiji, an army officer drafted out of China for an unknown excess, posing as a newspaper man, raised the Burma Independence Army, led by 'thirty Thakins' or 'master gentlemen'. The army, with a strength of about five thousand, was hijacked by the high proportion of local criminals or *dacoits* and was, in the end, dropped by the Japanese in favour of an orthodox administration and armed force. But that had no love for the returning British Administration, whose predecessors were chiefly remembered as idle and incompetent.

Hong Kong, with its limited and vulnerable water supply, held out for an improbable two weeks under continuous shelling against twenty thousand men from four divisions. A mixed bag of British, Indian, Canadian and almost untrained civilian businessmen truly fought on 'the hills, beaches and landing grounds' against overwhelming force pouring down through the New Territories in China proper. The first Japanese target was the reservoir, which they surrounded in a five-day battle against General Maltby's men on the ridges, ending in the seizure of the pumping station. Now there was water only in the town storage tanks. The power station, defended to the death by civilians mostly armed only with rifles, was the next objective to go. On Christmas Day, Maltby persuaded the stalwart Governor, Mark Young, to surrender. But troops and civilians at Stanley refused to believe the report until the Japanese began the rape and dismemberment, limb by limb, of patients and staff in the Stanley hospital. 'In the morning British prisoners were brought in to clean up: they literally waded in blood as they gathered corpses for burial from the execution room . . . carried away a hysterical lieutenant, the husband of one of the prettiest nurses abused and bayoneted.'

The Japanese in the Stanley gaol beat up, and noisily, as well as slowly and inefficiently, killed Chinese prisoners. They carried out a mock execution on Two-Gun Cohen, adviser to Sun Yat Sen, smuggler, arms dealer, soldier, spy, Far Eastern legend. As he knelt, he murmured: 'Hark, Israel, the Lord is our God, the Lord is one' and, aloud, 'Get on with it, you lousy bastard', until the guard kicked him over.

Here at least, between the Scylla of an occupied China heading for Civil War, and the Charybdis of a militant Japan, many among the indigenous population sought the return of legitimate and lucrative foreign sovereignty.

The Philippines is an island chain, part of the series which includes both Japan and Taiwan, *and* Sulawesi and New Guinea. Conquered by Spain in search of gold, silver and spices in the sixteenth century, it was ruled for three hundred years thereafter by the Catholic Church through half-Chinese and half-native *mestizos, ilustrados* or enlightened ones. A revolutionary movement under José Rizal, Bonifacio and General Emilio Aguinaldo, led to Philippine Independence under US 'protection' in 1898 after the Spanish-American War. In that year, Spain ceded the country to the USA for $20M but resistance, brutally suppressed, continued against a US colonial Government run by the *ilustrados*. Americanisation, through an English language public schools system, eventually emerged in a quasi American culture, diminishing to some degree indigenous nationalism.

One US economic faction supported colonial agricultural exploitation, another sought to protect US agricultural and other economic interests from Philippine competition. The confrontation eventually resulted in an economy attractive to US traders and investors, and a colony providing cheap raw materials and a market for US-manufactured goods. Local political power lay in the hands of Filipino landed élites who still, however, sought to placate the peasantry with a measure of independence. In 1934, the US Congress established a Philippine Commonwealth under Quezon and Osmena with independence to follow in ten years. At the outbreak of war in December 1941, the Philippines, nevertheless, contained a substantial united left-wing front including a merged Socialist Party and the Communist Party of the Philippines.

On 8 December, as the Japanese were attacking Pearl Harbour, they also destroyed some hundred US Air Force planes on the ground at Clark Field on Luzon, north-west of Manila. General MacArthur, son of a military Governor, an officer with a distinguished staff and battle record, had been loaned to the Commonwealth by Washington for ten years, of which he had already spent six, to organise the future Philippine Army. After this air assault and subsequent Japanese landings, he withdrew his fifty thousand Filipinos and Americans to the ancient fortress of Corregidor on Manila Bay and to Bataan, the peninsula on the northwest of the Bay. Here, disbelieving that even the disaster of Pearl Harbour would prohibit a relief expedition, he and his army faced two hundred thousand Japanese.

On 22 February, he was ordered by President Roosevelt to leave the Philippines and assume supreme command of the Pacific War in Australia, 'shared' with the Navy under Admiral Chester Nimitz in the Central Pacific. Handing the conduct of the present battle to General Jonathan Wainwright with the famous pledge 'I shall return', he broke the Japanese seaward blockade in an MTB at great risk. Wainwright, a brave and able officer, conscious of his force's hopeless position, beset by disease and hunger, without any chance of relief, surrendered Bataan on 9 April and Corregidor on 9 May. The murderous 'Death March' followed, those surviving left to the mercy of the Kempei (secret police) and of the most brutal troops in a brutal army.

The Filipino troops in Wainwright's and MacArthur's Army had stood and died by their 'colonial masters'. It may be that Japanese soldiers would, in Wainwright's situation, have held. The Filipinos had fought well but, by the end of March, a thousand of them, on half rations and afflicted with malaria, were falling out of the line each month.

After the surrender, although a small part of the colonial leadership was more or less involuntarily integrated into the Greater East Asia Co-Prosperity Sphere, most of the leaders and nearly all the people 'resigned themselves to a period of enemy occupation, confident that it was to be temporary. They regarded America's war as their own', an attitude unique among the subject peoples of South-East Asia. But America's Empire had suffered a severe blow.

Earlier, the American island of Guam in the Marianas, later to become the scene of a remarkable mass Japanese suicide imitating the actions of the lemming, surrendered on 10 December to a force of Japanese Marines. The first Japanese assault on the coral atoll of Wake was repelled by Major Devereux's 5-inch guns and six Wildcat fighters, the invaders losing a destroyer and five hundred men for the loss of one US marine. The second attack, incorporating two aircraft carriers, six cruisers, fifty aircraft and a thousand men, led to eight hundred Japanese casualties and, alas, to the loss of the island.

Nomonhan, a battle in the wastes of Central Asia three years before had caused the Stars and Stripes to be lowered over the islands, and the Union Jack, too, over Burma, Malaya, Singapore, Borneo and Hong Kong in 1942. France in Indochina and the Dutch in the Netherlands East Indies, both yielding their honour almost without a struggle, endured yet sharper humiliation and, their own *homelands* also defeated, became the more determined on vengeful return. For that, all the parties had to wait, in varying states of pain and sadness, for over three more years.

For now, the Empire of the Rising Sun had taken their place. But, far away in Western Europe, Japan's eventual nemesis was secured by Russian freedom to move Far Eastern forces westwards to the defeat of Germany.

# 31
# Independence

The overwhelming Allied victory of 1945 and the consequent confinement of Japan within its home islands instantly obliterated that Empire's presence and governing role in Asia. Quite soon, by one means or another, the rest had gone too.

'We will never be able to hold up our heads again in Burma,' said a British colonial servant after his country's defeat there in 1942. 'A military victory could not absolve the British in their civil capacity,' said another after the final Japanese collapse throughout Asia and surrender in 1945. 'Had there been victory in the first instance and the Japanese been defeated on the frontiers, the Burmese and the British would have been brought close together. The Empire would have been proved a working proposition. The Burmese might have been content to remain in it at least as a working partner. But the other would not do. A ruling power through whose neglect they had been subjected to two invasions, two devastations, had not a shred of credit left.' Burma became independent outside the Commonwealth on 4 January 1948.

French and Dutch colonialists would not acknowledge these truths for themselves in their own territories. The former, as is well known, fought until 1954 with gallantry but without much credibility against a nationalist movement hijacked by a Stalinist Communist party. Thereafter, the Americans, just as unsuccessfully, took over the struggle. The Dutch, for their part, opposed loyalist distrust and increasing guerilla movements, initially with British and even Japanese military support, until the Netherlands East Indies (less Irian Jaya and East Timor) became independent Indonesia in December 1949.

Similar considerations to those in Burma led Britain, after the uprising of the largely Chinese Malayan Communist Party (MCP) in 1948, to promise a rapid move to the independence of Malaya institutionalised on 31 August 1957 in a Malay–Chinese–Indian Alliance, the MCP at last comprehensively beaten. Independence for Singapore, Sarawak and British North Borneo (Sabah) followed, these joining the Federation of Malaysia in 1963, although Singapore was removed in 1965. Hong Kong, despite US attempts to have it returned to China, remained a British colony until June 1997 when the lease on the New Territories expired, perhaps one of the two colonised possessions in Asia whose future *might* have been the same even had Japan chosen to attack the USSR and not 'go South'.

The other was, of course, the Philippines, in 1934 already promised Independence for 1944 by a generous or embarrassed United States. The Americans' or MacArthur's return in 1945 was widely applauded, except by the large number of Filipino collaborators with the former occupiers. These split the nation and drew the new government's attention away from reconstruction. But on 4 July 1946, Manual Roxas became the first President of an independent Philippine Republic.

India, over whose territory decisive battles – Kohima, Imphal – had been waged, but which had not really been *invaded* in the same way as had the others, nor indeed passed under Japanese sovereignty, achieved Independence on 15 August 1947. It is impossible that so early a date would have been selected if Russia, not South-East Asia, had been the object of the *furor japonicus*, if Britain's authority, in other words, had not been so damagingly compromised by defeat nearby. London's exhaustion made it a botched job.

Four Empires had thus gone with the wind that raged out of Nomonhan. The fifth and largest begetter of these triumphs and disasters, the Empire of Japan, now lay stripped of all her newest conquests as well as of Korea, Taiwan and North China. After the terrible Russo–Mongol assault of 1945, it had also lost Manchukuo, where Japanese military hubris in 1939 had begun the violent history which ended in the cauldrons of Hiroshima and Nagasaki. Japan's peaceful skills thereafter, however, led popular opinion to suppose that that country might not have lost the second war, but have emerged as the real winner. Today, in the Asian markets of 1997, it seems improbable.

In the meanwhile, the two *world* Empires left, Soviet and American, have been reduced to one, with only a putative Chinese imperium coming up on the rails. 'And thus the whirligig of time brings in his revenges.'

# Selected Bibliography

Admiralty (NID) *Indochina*, BR 510 (NID) 1943
—— *Netherlands East Indies*, Vols I and II (NID) 1944
Austin, Hangin, Onon *Mongol Reader*, Indiana University, 1963
Babel, Isaak *Red Cavalry*, Knopf (UK), 1929
Barnett, Corelli *Hitler's Generals*, Weidenfeld, 1989
Barnhart, Michael *Japan Prepares for Total War*, Cornell, 1987
Bawden, Charles *Modern History of Mongolia*, Weidenfeld, 1968
Bergamini, David *Japanese Imperial Conspiracy*, Heinemann, 1971
Best, Anthony *Britain, Japan and Pearl Harbour*, Routledge/ISE 1995
Bradley, J. F. N. *Allied Intervention in Russia*, University Press of America, 1968
Brement, Marshall 'B of kh–Gol' *Military History*, Houghton Mifflin, NY, 1998
Bruce Lockhart, R. H. *Retreat from Glory*, Putnam, 1934
Burk, J. D. 'Red Sun/Red Star', *Strategy and Tactics*, Issue 158, 1993
Calvocoressi P., Wint G., Pritchard J. *Total War*, Viking, 1989
Carver, Field Marshal Lord *The War Lords*, Weidenfeld, 1976
Chamberlain, W. H. *Japan over Asia*, Duckworth, 1938
Chapman, Professor John *The Imperial Japanese Navy and the North-South Dilemma*, Edinburgh University Press, 1994
—— *Anglo-Japanese Relations*, LSE 1985/3
—— *Price of Admiralty*, Private, Saltire House, Ripe, 1982
Chaney, O. P. *Zhukov*, David and Charles, Newton Abbot, 1972
Chiyoku, Sasaki *Der Nomonhan Konflikt* (Inaugural Dissertation at Reimschen, Frederick Wilhelms Universität Zu Bonn, 1968)
Colvin, Admiral Sir Ragnor *Memoirs*, P. E. Balfour, Wintershill Publications, 1994

Cooper, Donald S *Thailand*, Minerva, 1995

Coox, Alvin D. *Nomonhan* 2 Vols, Stanford University, 1985

Craigie, Sir Robert *Behind the Japanese Mask*, Hutchinson, 1945

Cruikshank, Charles *SOE in the Far East*, OUP, 1983

Deakin, F. W. D. & Storry, G. R. *Case of Richard Sorge*, Chatto and Windus, 1966

Djamsrandjav, Sh. *The Mongol Army's Role in the Battle of Khalkin Gol*, MPR Army Publishing House, 1965

Dobson, Christopher *The Day We almost Bombed Moscow (1918–20)*, Hodder and Stoughton, 1986

Dodd, Martra *Through Embassy Eyes*, Harcourt Brace, NY

Doret and Sinha *Japan and World Recession*, Macmillan, 1987

Drea, E. J. *Nomonhan: Japanese-Soviet Tactical Conflict*, Leavenworth Papers 2, 1981

Duncker and Humblot *Neue Deutsche Biographie*, Bavarian Academy of Sciences, 1944

Dupuy, R. E. and T.-N. *Encyclopedia of World History*, Janes, 1986

Duus, Myers and Beattie *Japanese Informal Empire, 1895–1937*, Princeton University Press, 1989

—— *Japanese Wartime Empire, 1931–1945*, Princeton University Press, 1996

Erickson, John *The Soviet High Command*, Macmillan, 1962, Westview Reprint, 1984

—— *The Road to Stalingrad*, Harper and Row, 1975

—— *Barbarossa, The Axis and the Allies*, Edinburgh University Press, 1984

Euchtwangler, E. J. *From Weimar to Hitler*, Macmillan, 1993

Fleming, Peter *The Fate of Admiral Kolchak*, Hart-Davis, 1963

Footman, David St Anthony's Papers, No. 12 (Ed), Chatto and Windus, 1982

Fraser, General Sir David *Knights Cross*, Collins, 1993

Gabriel, R. A. *The New Red Legions*, Greenwood Press, 1986

Gilchrist, Sir Andrew *Bangkok Top Secret*, Hutchinson, 1976

Glantz, Lt.-Col. D. M. *Soviet Air Borne Experience*, Fort Leavenworth Combat Studies Institute, Research Survey, No. 4, 1984

—— *In Pursuit of Deep Battle*, Frank Cass, 1991

Harries, M. and S. *Soldiers of the Sun*, Random House, 1991

Jackson, Robert *At War with the Bolsheviks*, Tom Stacey, 1972

Johnson, Paul *Modern Times*, Harper and Row, 1983

Kaze, Toshikazu *Eclipse of the Rising Sun*, Cape, 1951

Keay, John *Last Post*, John Murray, 1997

Kennedy, M. D. *Military Side of Japanese Life*, Constable, 1924

Kutakov, L. N. *Japanese Foreign Policy*, Diplomatic Press, Florida, 1972

Lancaster, Donald *Emancipation of French Indochina*, Octagon NY, 1961

Lockwood W. W. *The Economic Development of Japan*, Princeton University Press, 1954

Lory, Hillis *Japan's Military Masters*, Westport, Greenwood Press, 1973

Mackintosh, Malcolm *Juggernaut*, Secker and Warburg, 1967

Manning, Clarence A., *Siberian Fiasco*, Library Pubs, NY, 1957

McClure, S. G. *Anglo-Japanese Relations* (Siberia), Thesis, University of London, 1960

Milsom, J. 'Russian Tanks, 1900–1970', *Arms & Armour*, 1970

Morley, J. W. (ed.) *Deterrent Diplomacy*, Columbia University Press, 1976

—— *Fateful Choice*, Columbia University Press, 1980

—— *China Quagmire*, Columbia University Press, 1983

—— *Final Confrontation*, Columbia University Press, 1994

Moses, L. W. 'Soviet Japanese Confrontation in Outer Mongolia', *Journal of Asian History*, No. 1, 1967

Myers, Lt.-Cdr. A. O. 'Khalkin Gol', *Military Review 43*, No. 4, April 1983

Nish, Ian (ed.) *Some Foreign Attitudes to Republican China*, LSE

—— 'Conflicting Japanese Loyalties in Manchuria', *Japan Forum*, Vol. 6(2), 1994

Nobutaka, Ike *Japan's Decision for War*, Stanford University Press, 1962

O'Neill, Robert *German Army and Nazi Party*, Cassell, 1966

Pratt, Sir John *Before Pearl Harbour*, Caxton, 1944

Pritchard, John 'The Chankufeng Battle', British Association for Japanese Studies, *Journal of Asian History* 1, 1967
—— *Total War*, Viking, 1989

Quarrie, B. *Tank Battles in Miniature*, PSL, 1975

Sabattier *Le Destin de l'Indochine*, Plon, 1952

Sanders, Alan 'Wings over the Steppes', *Air Enthusiast*, Nov-Dec 1996, Jan-April 1997

Sekigawa, E. 'The undeclared Air War', *Air Enthusiast*, May-July 1973

Sella, A. 'Khalkin Gol: the forgotten war', *Journal of Contemporary History*, 1983

Shishkin, Colonel S. N. *The Soviet Army Version of Nomonhan*, US Refs: JSM 11 Part 3/6

Simonov, Konstantin *Daleko na Vostoke*
—— *Tovarischii po Oruzhiyu*, Young Guard, Moscow, 1954

Smiley, Col. David *Irregular Regular*, Michael Russell, 1995

Snow, Philip 'Nomonhan, The Unknown Victory', *History Today*, July 1, 1990

Stephan, John J. 'Russian Soldiers in Japanese Service: The Asano Brigade', *Waseda University, History Journal*, 1977

Storry, G. R. *Double Patriot; A study of Japanese Nationalism*, Chatto & Windus, 1957

Thompson, Virginia *French Indochina*, Norton, NY, 1944

Thorne, Christopher *The Issue of War*, Hamish Hamilton, 1985

Washington, Booker T. *The Siberian Intervention*, Greenwood Press, 1969

Wheeler Bennett, Sir John *The Nemesis of Power: the German Army in Politics*, Macmillan, 1953

White, J. A. *The Siberian Intervention*, Princeton University Press, 1950

Whiting A., and General Shiang Shik Tsa *Sinkiang: Pawn or Pivot*, Michigan State University 1958

Whymant, Robert *Stalin's Spy, Richard Sorge*, I.B.Taurus, 1997

Willoughby, Charles *A Shanghai Conspiracy*

Yergin, Daniel *The Prize*, Simon and Schuster, 1991

Young, K. H. Mrs 'Nomonhan Incident – Imperial Japan & USSR', *Monumenta Nipponica*, Vol. 22, 1–2, 1967

—— *The Japanese Army & the Soviet Union*, PhD University of Washington, 1965

Zhukov, Marshal G. *Memoirs*, Cape, 1971

# Other Sources

VOENNYE MEMUARY (including 'Istrebiteli' by VORO-ZHEIKIN and NA VOSTOKE by FEDYUNINSKIE); VORONOV's NA VOENNOI SLUZHBE; VOENNO ISTORICHESKI ZHURNAL; AVIATSIYA I KOS-MONAVTIKA.

'HOW THE SOVIET-MONGOLIAN ARMIES SMASHED THE JAPANESE AGGRESSORS' BY T. S. SAMOANG-ELEG IN MONGOL, State Publishing House, Ulan Bator, 1981

JAPANESE STUDIES on Manchuria contained in *War in Asia and Pacific, 1937–1949*, Vols. 10–11: Garland Publishing Co., United States

'Small Wars and Border Problems: Nomonhan and Changku-feng Incidents' in J. R. D. J. S. M. 11, Part 3, Books ABC (US Armed Forces, Far East 8th Army: Chief of Military History, US Army)

Handbook on Japanese Military Forces, US War Department, October 1944, republished by Greenhill Books, USA, 1991

Encyclopedia Britannica (Russo-Japanese War, 1904–1905; Manchuria)

Palmer's index to *The Times*, April–September 1937

Keesing's Contemporary Archives, 1937–1946

*Far East and Australia*, Europa Publishing, 1980 *et seq.*

## Public Record Office, Kew

WO 287/35 Notes on the Soviet Army, WO 1940
WO 287/89 Notes on the Soviet Army, WO 1939
FO 371/23558 to 23562, 23494, 23497, 22145–6, 24710
F 9469/87/10, 8502/6457/10, FS 133/193/61, 800/298 & 299; Mukden (CG) Despatch to Tokio 125 of 20.viii.38 (Changkufeng); Saigon (CG) Despatch FO 371/27767 (1941)

# Index